Strategic Intelligence
Century

Strategic Intelligence for the 21st Century

The Mosaic Method

Alfred Rolington

OXFORD
UNIVERSITY PRESS

OXFORD

UNIVERSITY PRESS

Great Clarendon Street, Oxford OX2 6DP
United Kingdom

Oxford University Press is a department of the University of Oxford.
It furthers the University's objective of excellence in research, scholarship,
and education by publishing worldwide. Oxford is a registered trade mark of
Oxford University Press in the UK and in certain other countries

First Edition published in 2013
Reprinted 2014

Published in the United States of America by Oxford University Press
198 Madison Avenue, New York, NY 10016, United States of America

British Library Cataloguing in Publication Data
Data available

Library of Congress Cataloging in Publication Data
Data available

ISBN 978-0-19-965432-1

Foreword

by R. James Woolsey

For the last 20 years the fading of the conventional and nuclear Cold War threats has made Western society generally more secure from traditional geopolitical conflicts. But the coming of a new, electronically networked age has seismically altered our world and its security dynamics. Networked globalization and easy access to communications and electronic information systems have made borders far more open to exploitation than during the Cold War and have allowed terrorists, especially, an extraordinary range of options. This electronic and largely borderless world has both helped create new players and helped them and their state sponsors mask their intentions.

In early December 1992, several weeks before I was asked to serve as Director of Central Intelligence (DCI), I said in a speech that we had been fighting a large dragon for some 45 years and now, after having slain him, found ourselves in a jungle full of poisonous snakes—and the snakes were much harder to keep track of.

During my time as DCI these snakes—proliferation, terrorism, cyber threats and the rest—began to affect many aspects of intelligence collection and analysis. Those effects have deepened and broadened over the last two decades.

The established strategic vision of governments and intelligence agencies has been severely challenged by the need to track and understand the movements of many poisonous snakes instead of just one dragon. Traditional geopolitical issues are of course still highly relevant. China, for example, behaves to some extent the way Imperial Germany did at the dawn of the twentieth century. But terrorism, insurgency, cyber threats, biological, chemical and nuclear weapons, international crime, the social effects of climate change, and tensions over access to oil, water, and some minerals have had complex and interacting effects, creating new roles and challenges for analysts, intelligence collectors, and policymakers. The snakes will not stay quiet.

Consequently, today the amount being spent on intelligence by the US government (and many others) has significantly increased. Since 9/11 the US government has expanded the intelligence focus by including a broad range of threats and the subsequent conflicts in Iraq and Afghanistan. Recently we have seen added the effects of the Arab Spring on the Middle East and Africa.

Because of this growth, seismic changes in issues and the new flows of information—take the internet as only one example—the requirement to introduce new intelligence models and new collection and analytical technologies has been exploding.

Recent developments in information technology, for instance, have introduced significant capabilities to analyse data, even very unstructured data, in a far more focused and perceptive way. Today, at least 80 per cent of all the data available to governments and corporations is unstructured and the percentage growth of this type of data and information is still increasing. The new reality is an increasingly connected and globally networked world and this has huge consequences for the way information and data need to be analysed. These changes are especially relevant to intelligence agencies since the agencies are always trying to understand present reality in order to provide actionable intelligence to policymakers in a timely fashion.

These issues affecting the intelligence process are fundamental and there have been many government reviews of the structure and organization of the agencies. These have often been driven by what have been termed intelligence failures and have produced organizational reform. However, the challenges of the last two decades require methodological as well as structural changes to the intelligence process. This latter set of issues is the focus of this volume.

I met Alfred Rolington, the author, when I was DCI and he was CEO of Jane's Information Group. Over the years we have stayed in touch and regularly met. He brings his wide experience, and the perceptions of many others, into these chapters. Rolington and his colleagues review the traditional intelligence cycle and mission-based approaches and then bring new methods and perspectives to the new snake-filled environment which both intelligence analysts and policymakers will find interesting and useful. Their ideas about new models, structures, and methods should help us all gain a deeper understanding of how to deal with the changing reality we face.

Preface

My reasons for writing this book are ingrained in my professional and personal life. I have been involved in different aspects of information and intelligence for the last 30 years. My engagement has been mainly from an open-source publishing point of view and during that time I have witnessed first-hand the radical changes that have taken place in publishing, international strategy, and intelligence.

When I was part of the senior management team at Jane's Information Group, I came to learn that the information that is published and offered as true is sometimes manipulated to meet a publishing, political, or management requirement. One example of this problem, which was not unique, occurred when we at Jane's were considering using a photograph that had appeared on the front cover of a prominent magazine. The picture had been taken on the streets of a particular war zone, or so it appeared. A senior Jane's editor came to me and said that the team wanted to use the photograph as part of a piece of analysis they were doing but that two of the analysts had questioned the photograph's validity. One of them had pointed out that two of the guns shown in the picture were not used in that area and another had said that some of the clothes were not right. We checked with the magazine's publisher and after some discussion it was admitted that the picture was similar to real pictures taken in the war zone but that this particular photograph was a mock-up and had been shot in a studio.

Such manipulations, and the shifting perceptions of truth that we have to negotiate on a daily basis, are increasingly complicating the information picture. As a number of analysts have said to me, the black humour of the film *Wag the Dog*,[1] in which a spin doctor and a Hollywood producer join forces to fabricate a war in order to cover up a Presidential sex scandal, can be viewed as a marker of what some governments and media will do to change or get a news story. *Wag the Dog* was released in 1997. Since then, today's globally linked digital culture has caused the plot, in many senses, to thicken.

This book will argue that it is not only the traditional geopolitical and macroeconomic models that have been ruptured by the electric shockwaves of the last two decades, but so has the traditional intelligence cycle. The electronic revolution has transformed intelligence and security operations, and large parts of the corporate competitive landscape, to the point at which other models need to be created and used to give policymakers a clearer view of the current situation and possible futures. In order to look forward, the book will also look back. It will

---

[1] Directed by Barry Levinson and starring Dustin Hoffman and Robert de Niro.

analyse the history of current information sources, along with past intelligence practices, before reviewing the current expectations of strategic planning and intelligence processes. It will then analyse the issues and possibilities for future planning methods. The new methodologies will be used to outline and analyse the strategic intelligence perspectives going forward in the digital age—towards an e-networked, but still fractured, post-modern Cold War configuration.

Acknowledgements

The book is dedicated to dearest Ingrid and Emily, and to Peter, Alyson, and Leianne with love.

Thanks to R. James Woolsey, Sir David Phillips, Dr John Phillips, Sam Wilkins, Ian Kay, Chris Stagg, and Ingrid Holden for directly contributing to the book, and Sarah Edmonds, Krystyna Plater, Emma Hawes, Sally Pelling-Deeves, and John Firth for helping with aspects of the editing and review of material.

I would also like to thank the people who have contributed through their comments, conversations, discussions, and reading over the years, in particular Lucy Alexander, Lawrence Ampofo, Christopher Andrew, Andrew Backhouse, Jack Barclay, Gary Barker, Jamie Bartlett, Geoff Beattie, Alex Boden, Paul Burton, Anthony Campbell, Marina Cheal, Shelby Coffey, Richard Collier, Alan Condron, Rik Coolsaet, James Copeman, Simon Craven, David Croom, David Crosswell, Peter Daniell, Michael Dell, Carol Dumaine, Colin Dyer, David Gautrey, Rick Gekoski, Anna Gilmour, David Gloe, Al Gore, Giles Grant, James Green, Gavin Greenwood, Kevin Hand, David Hartwell, Charlie Hobson, Richard Hooke, Mark Houghton, Graham Hutchins, Robert Hutchinson, Hal Jackman, Erik Jackson, Zina Kaye, Scott Key, Dr Joanna Kidd, Peter Lake, Paul Langlois, Richard Lloyd, Robert Mackenzie, Ewen McAlpine, Sir Colin McColl, Ron Marks, Stephen Marrin, Tim Marsh, Peter Martland, Mia Marzouk, Carl Miller, Ilan Mizrahi, Linda Moore, Ron Murphy, Gerry Murray, Joe Murray, Patrick Murray, Victoria Powell, Julian Richards, David Robson, Katie Rothman, Mark Salisbury, Anette Savastano, Ian Simms, Mike Staton, Robert David Steele, Lord David Thomson, Ken Thomson, Peter Thomson, Patrick Tilbury, Tom Wales, Karin Wentworth Ping, Roger Woods, David Worlock, and David Young.

Contents

Part Three An Intelligence Review

Introduction: The Current Landscape

Open your memory and travel back into the past—now go forward into an electronic future that engulfs every aspect of the present.

The medium has been radically altered, new networks have been built, and innovative infrastructures are being created. Communication's reach and information's speed, compounded by the expanding globalization of delivery, have all been radically changing our strategic perspective. The quantity of messages and gossip we all receive has dramatically increased and has altered our cultural understanding and our interconnectivity, and this has radically increased within the expanding social networks.

Today's communication landscape offers a radically different picture to that of 30 years ago. Since the advent of the internet and its popularization in the 1990s, most traditional media have been redefined and remodelled, new communication networks have been created, and infrastructures built. The new technology has been incorporated into almost every aspect of modern life, changing the spaces and timescales in which we work and think, affecting our everyday engagement with others, and inundating us with an abundance of information. The global reach of the internet and the speed at which it delivers information have combined to bring about an unprecedented interconnectivity that has impacted not only on our cultural understandings and our personal relationships, but on our strategic perspectives. Marshall McLuhan's theories of media message and dynamic,[1] first expounded in the 1960s, have taken on new life in the face of network proliferation and electronic dependence. From an intelligence point of view, the communication revolution has significantly challenged the traditional aspects of the intelligence cycle. While the overarching objective of securing useful, timely intelligence upon which decisions can be based remains the same, the roles

---

[1] Herbert Marshall McLuhan, Canadian educator, philosopher, and scholar, 1911–80. Known for coining phrases such as 'the medium is the message' and 'the global village'. It is claimed he predicted the World Wide Web almost 30 years before it was invented.

of policymaker and analyst are changing, not only in terms of their relationship with each other, but also the way in which they are required to assimilate information and make connections. The mass of information now available has dramatically challenged the analyst's ability to encompass it, while the speed at which the policymaker can make decisions and public relations agencies can respond necessitates working within far shorter timeframes.

Let us look at some of these changes and their impact in more detail, starting with human intellectual operation, habit, and behaviour. The way in which we gather and process information has changed dramatically in recent years. For example, fewer people read books from cover to cover—or, as is increasingly the case, from electronic beginning to electronic end. The tendency is to scan and flick through large areas of information online, both related and unrelated, often making new connections, with 'surfing' entering common vocabulary as a description of this rapid and multidirectional movement through the sea of knowledge. It is estimated that 28 per cent of the world's rapidly expanding population (or just over 2 billion people) now has direct access to the World Wide Web, while nearly 5 billion people have mobile phone access. On average 247 billion emails are sent each day (an estimated 81 per cent of which is spam), a figure which is increasing by roughly 24 per cent each year. While this allows us to engage with many millions of times more information than has been the case for any previous generation, our ability to separate the good-quality, pertinent, and useful data from inaccuracies, gossip, propaganda, or mere marketing material has been greatly reduced by the volumes involved.

The rapidity of delivery has now led many people to expect data on demand, as well as the ability to be in contact with each other as and when desired. Having information readily available at our fingertips changes the way in which we think about the world and how we view others and ourselves. It impacts on the structure of the organizations we work for and the manner in which we work. Laptops and hand-held smart devices now enable us to remain connected while on the move and, for many, the home has become an alternative work environment to the office, changing the shape and length of the working day. The insistent ping of electronic messaging can sound at any time of night or day. These changes have been supported by the sheer pace of transformation in the technology arena where, since Moore's law was first posited in 1965,[2] there has been an increase in computer capacity, and a significant reduction in cost, every 24 months. This

---

[2] Gordon Moore, Intel co-founder, stated that the number of transistors on a chip doubles every 24 months. This has been the guiding principle of the high-tech industry ever since, explaining why the computer industry has consistently been able to deliver products that are smaller, more powerful, and less costly than their predecessors. The often-quoted period of 18 months is attributable to another Intel executive, David House.

exponential improvement in the channels of delivery has been a force driving change behind the electronic revolution, radically expanding the internet's capability, and networking us ever more closely together, while muddying traditional demarcations and boundaries in the process; and all this in a world in which the global population has doubled its size from 3.5 to 7 billion in just over 25 years.

Socially, electronic networking websites have connected hundreds of millions of users in an unprecedented manner, making reality the notion of the world as a global village. Perhaps the best-known service is Facebook, conceived and launched in 2004 by Harvard undergraduate, Mark Zuckerberg. When it was floated in May 2012, Facebook had 900 million followers and was valued at over $100bn (£63bn). Despite disgruntled shareholders subsequently bringing court action for nondisclosure of information, Zuckerberg remains one of the richest men on the planet. The concept of Facebook is simple. Users, once registered, may create a personal profile on its website, add other users as friends, then exchange messages and information with them. What distinguishes Facebook, and what has turned it into such a phenomenal success story, is its worldwide reach, made possible by the internet.

Other websites have followed suit, notably Twitter, created in 2006 by Jack Dorsey. Twitter in essence acts as an internet forum or message board, on which people can hold conversations in the form of posted messages. Its users can send and read text-based posts of up to 140 characters, known as 'tweets'. Twitter.com positions itself with the slogan 'instantly connect to what's most important to you. Follow your friends, experts, favorite celebrities, and breaking news.' It is this interconnectivity, facilitating the exchange of ideas, news, and gossip, that has helped to change the world politically. The recent restructuring in the Middle East, for example, was a consequence of the Arab Spring, the term given to the revolutionary wave of demonstrations and protests that took place from the end of 2010. The protests crossed national borders and deployed techniques of civil resistance such as strikes, demonstrations, and rallies to bring about change. It was through web and mobile phone-based social media, such as Facebook and Twitter, that awareness was raised and actions organized in the face of state attempts at censorship and repression. By February 2012, the governments in four countries—Tunisia, Egypt, Libya, and Yemen—had either been overthrown or forced to change.

The dramatic events in the Middle East have drawn attention to other potential shifts in parts of China, the Far East, South America, and Africa, as well as Europe and America. Indeed, if the globalizing world is prepared to reinvent government and social understanding, the question arises as to whether the old colonial and traditional ways of describing parts of the world—names such as the West, the Middle East, or the Far East—still make sense. And as the changes start to affect language, its meaning, and use, including accepted name tags, they also affect attitudes towards traditional authorities such as governments, the church, or academic teachers and we now are more sceptical of these institutions' status as truth and authority providers. There is awareness on the part of individuals that these new channels of delivery can allow governments to track, monitor, and change the tone of information, altering its bias and nudging it into the realm of propaganda. Where people were once offered facts and beliefs as a series of unchallenged verbal or printed texts, official versions of the truth have begun to be questioned and resisted. Instead of simply accepting what is presented to us, we are more likely to make comparisons between different sources of information and draw our own, independent conclusions. Interactivity has become a key feature of today's information environment and where awe and respect were previously demanded, independent thought has taken over. The changing relationship with traditional authority has also altered the relationship between analysts, senior management, and policymakers, a realignment this book will examine at greater length in Chapter Nine. The process is happening within government, the security services, the military, law enforcement agencies, and corporations. The new environment is also altering the way outsiders engage and respond to the policymakers and politicians and the way they may in turn act on, react to, and even sometimes ignore, the analysis and intelligence being offered.

The Current Crisis

Just as the world has been changing technologically, intellectually, and socially for individuals and commercial organizations, likewise it has been changing for governments, the military, and law enforcement agencies. In recent times they have experienced a series of information and technological crises, often described as intelligence failures. These crises have arisen from tumultuous global events, ranging from the destruction of the Twin Towers in New York in September 2001, otherwise known as 9/11, to the waging of war in Iraq based on incorrect intelligence about Iraq's weapons capability from a rogue source. Other crisis events include the 7/7 bombings of July 2005 in London; the global economic recession that took a particularly sharp downturn in September 2008; the events of the Arab Spring from December 2010; and the London riots of August 2011. They also embrace smaller-scale shocks caused by the actions of individuals, such as Mohamed Merah who killed seven people in three gun attacks in Toulouse and Montauban in March 2012. Clues missed by the French intelligence service, the Central Directorate of Intelligence (DCRI), included the fact that Merah was on both their own watch list, and a no-fly list in Washington DC. While this book was being written, the threat of potential attack on the British Olympics was raised to high-level, necessitating an even more extensive set of security measures to be put in place than originally planned. The chances of an attack were considered high due to the wide range of potential targets and numerous entry points at the venues. In May 2012, the UK government changed the law and allowed greater intelligence access to media such as email. This allows Government Communication Headquarters (GCHQ), the British intelligence agency responsible for signals intelligence, and other agencies to monitor communications more broadly. But even after being given permission to collect and connect the plethora of data, the concern remained that this might not be enough to stop a dedicated group or independent rogue attacker from striking.

Significant change, paradigm shifts, and even information revolutions have caused major transformation in commercial organizations, military units, and governments throughout history. Changes to intelligence organizations, however, often come to current attention when there has been a failure of detection or to effectively connect the dots. Such descriptions are too simplistic, though, and do not treat the analytical efforts and collection complications that often happen in real time, with the subtlety and understanding required to analyse the currently changing situation. Of course, as some in the intelligence community will say, intelligence successes are rarely publicized since secrecy continues to be required.

Some notable intelligence successes have been very openly publicized, however. The Cuban Missile Crisis of 1962, the 13-day confrontation between the Soviet Union and the United States over the siting of nuclear missiles in Cuba, was brought to a head and resolved after a US reconnaissance plane captured intelligence photographs of the missiles. The Crisis is regarded as one of the major confrontations of the Cold War and the moment when tensions came closest to turning into a nuclear conflict.[3] More recently, the killing in May 2011 of Osama bin Laden, founder of al-Qaeda and the orchestrator of the events of 9/11, was hailed as an intelligence success, as was the October 2011 change of government in Libya, with the ousting and killing of the dictator Colonel Gaddafi.

My research suggests that intelligence organizations, law enforcement services, and commercial organizations should now break their traditional intelligence cycle and strategic planning models and build new information and intelligence models that are far more responsive to the current electronic environment. All organizations should become more deeply and continuously interlinked, while retaining and improving their specifically required operational independence. This rethink and reorganization requires changing the traditional pyramid organizational structures and becoming more collaborative, networked, and interconnected.

To illustrate this requirement, let us consider one example—that of the United States of America, where the intelligence community comprises 17 agencies and organizations and costs nearly $100bn a year to operate.[4] In many analysts' view

---

[3] The Cold War spanned the period from 2 September 1945 (the date the Japanese formally surrendered at the end of the Second World War) to 26 December 1991 (marking the official dissolution of the Soviet Union). It never featured direct military action between the major parties, as both sides possessed nuclear weapons, the use of which would probably have brought about mutual assured destruction.

[4] The member agencies in the intelligence community are Air Force Intelligence; Army Intelligence; the Central Intelligence Agency; Coast Guard Intelligence; the Defense Intelligence Agency; the Departments of Energy, of Homeland Security, of State, and of the Treasury; the Drug Enforcement Administration; the Federal Bureau of Investigation; Marine Corps Intelligence; the National

it should be completely reorganized and a number of aspects merged and networked. In addition, there is a feeling that it would benefit from an internal, domestic intelligence agency, similar in operation to some of the internal agencies in parts of Europe. Such a body should focus on, monitor, and analyse international criminal and terrorist activity within the United States and should be linked to international and cross-border law enforcement. The new model should reorganize the Federal Bureau of Investigation (FBI) and the range of intelligence services to enable connected pictures to be drawn of international threats, terrorism, insurgency, illegal activity, and threat intentions, and, in turn, give intelligence employees on the ground continuous, focused flows of data and intelligence so that they can question and feed back information from their investigations as these take place.

The United States is far from unique in its need to review its underlying model to enhance strategic operation and connectivity. In the United Kingdom, a reorganization of police and law enforcement structure along more thoroughly networked lines has been mooted. Instead of the 47 separate bodies and county services, a single integrated structure is envisaged with different county or regional sections reporting to the centre. Some of the immediate intelligence effects of such a restructuring would be profound. Crime in one region could easily be analysed, computer-checked, and compared with that in other areas. It would improve the organization and make the management structure more effective, focused, and efficient. It would also require a smaller, more networked, and less hierarchical management team. On a financial note, the economic savings through police buying from fewer suppliers would be substantial, and this would make swaps and exchanges between counties and police regions more straightforward. A part of this connecting process has already begun, with the creation of the National Policing Improvement Agency, which is developing a Police National Database (PND). The first step to this end is Project Athena, which is bringing together nine separate IT systems—eight from forces in the south-east of England, and that of the British Transport Police. There has also been a paradigm shift towards Intelligence-Led Policing (ILP), a specialized police practice involving the identification and targeting of high-rate, chronic offenders, to be followed by strategic interventions based on that intelligence. Sir David Philips, former Chief Constable of Kent Police, introduced ILP as a concept to the UK police force. Together with Dr John Philips, Sir David has written an analysis of the shift towards ILP that forms Chapter Eleven of this book.

The whole of this broader intelligence review process has potentially significant ramifications for the longer-term structure of how information and intelligence are searched, analysed, stored, and used effectively. It generates specific efficiency changes in organization structures, relevant to all large organizations from the CIA to Shell, Microsoft, and Unilever, to governments, police organiza-

---

Geospatial-Intelligence Agency; the National Reconnaissance Office; the National Security Agency; and the Navy Intelligence Office of the Director of National Intelligence.

tions, and the military. These organizations should no longer have pyramidal architecture as their primary structure but they should consist of a series of analysis and action teams that are flatter in construction. They should be more fluid and networked in their operating methods, incorporating into their methods of analysis sources of information and data that are far more open, along with tailored information, and separate, classified data and intelligence. To put this into perspective the book will review aspects of information history in Chapter Two. Communications and strategic intelligence methods and a new, tiered model of strategic planning and intelligence analysis is proposed as a clearer way out of the current media fog. Analysis should use and create new metadata, taxonomies, and data visualization practices to significantly improve current tactical, scenario, and strategic understandings and assist potential future actions.

In the broader picture the review process for the book has analysed data from international war zones, terrorism activities, cross-border crime, and local crime. The book discusses how nations and commercial organizations are much more globally interconnected than ever before and how this has significantly changed their outlook and their macro-economic, legal, political, and ethical positions. With its range of networks globalization has affected everything from conflicts (international and internal) to terrorism to cross-border and local crime rates. It also highlights the merging of, and conflicts between, what were quite separate territorial cultures and belief systems. Putting these current changes into a new global context is part of this book's purpose and is explained in Chapter Four.

On a political level, some aspects of the Arab Spring must have been experienced as shockwaves by the people affected by them, yet those people have emerged able to discuss their feelings about government control with a freedom that was not possible before. Some governments have responded by calling the uprisings 'electronic insurgency', but however the process is termed, the multi-language messages and semantic capabilities of our current technology are altering the attitudes of unrelated social groups to themselves, their employers, and their governments. Also, it is changing organizations and governments' attitudes to cyber networks and mobile communications. All of this, in a very short time, has radically challenged our ideas of information, knowledge, truth, and particularly intelligence. In an effort to control the flow of information some governments have begun to counter, alter, and even shut down electronic communications, including the web itself. Cyberspace is the new threat arena and it can now be considered in a similar category to land, sea, air, and space, the more traditional areas of warfare and defence. There were cyber attacks on Estonia in 2007 and on Georgia in 2008, which are assumed to have been attacks by Russia; and now criminal as well as government attacks on computer systems are considered real threats. In April 2009 US Air Force General Kevin Chilton said that the Pentagon had spent more than $100m in the previous six months responding to cyber attacks. In Iran, for example, as I write, millions of users are being cut off from popular social networking sites as the government rolls out its plans to establish a national intranet. Services like Google, Hotmail, and Yahoo! are being blocked and replaced with government services such as Iran Mail and Iran Search Engine. At this stage, however, other areas of the World Wide Web remain accessible. Where books were once burned, plugs might now be pulled but, as in previous ages, the revolutionary technologies are proving resilient and their sheer scope difficult to contain and manage, while the democratizing power of the internet is producing some of the broadest protest against regulated authority in history.

It is estimated that between 15 billion and almost 1 trillion pages have been indexed by the popular search engines like Google, Yahoo!, and Bing. However, these pages account for only 2–3 per cent of the total number of pages on the whole web. There is a wealth of additional information that goes well beyond that retrieved by the popular search engines and is in a sense buried in what is known as the Deep Web. The Deep Web represents between approximately 97 and 98 per cent of the total information on the web. This and the Dark or Criminal Web will be discussed in more detail in Chapter Five. Moreover, even the whole web only forms part of the open and closed information sources that are potentially available (in whole or in part) to many individuals and organizations and are certainly required for the intelligence process to work effectively. These include everything from closed databases, written reports, letters, libraries, telephone calls, emails, social networks, newspapers, radio, television, mobile communication, computer data, diplomatic contacts, spies, and discussions, to anti-information in the form of propaganda and counter-intelligence. And the huge volumes of open information and closed sources are set to increase in many parts of the world as the web's influence and connectivity improve. However, the likelihood is that the control and conditioning of systems, data, imagery, and information by governments and corporations will increase in turn.

This book analyses the intelligence strategies, methods, data analysis techniques, management structures, and new technologies that can be used to help clarify this shadowy and very dense information fog. It reviews past and current tensions, conflicts, and technologies and the 'black economics' that have given rise to our globally connected, but locally fractured world. My research suggests that intelligence agencies within government, law enforcement, and commercial organizations should now break with their traditional models and become more deeply and continuously interlinked, whilst retaining and improving their strategic and operational focus. As Nietzsche said, 'every discipline is constrained by what it forbids its practitioners to do',[5] and every organization should consider how it functions within the new environment and whether it has adequately changed to act effectively in the revised reality.

Future historians will rue the days of the email and social internet, as they did those of the telephone, since now even fewer records are kept of what is read, written, or said. New ways of finding information, talking with others, and

---

[5] Friedrich Wilhelm Nietzsche, 1844–1900, was a German philosopher whose questioning of the value and objectivity of truth has attracted much subsequent interpretation.

working together have put a use-by date on our shared reality. Cyberspace is here defined as the range covered by the internet, social networking, data collection, software operations, and cloud computing—the latter is described as access to storage and computing software as a gathered service, like a cloud, for many users to access. This is collected in a networked system similar to utilities like electricity grids. Cloud computing will radically alter our collection, analysis, and processing of intelligence. It has allowed and encouraged new ideas and threats into our social and commercial life and changed the traditional concepts of what we perceive reality to be.

The concept of cybernetics, the study of systems and processes, has taken on a new perspective, offering a series of alternative realities. These have made some people feel unable to control their current activities in a way they are comfortable with, affecting their sense of self as individual and social beings. As with many seismic shifts in understanding, usually brought about by radical changes to technology, there are many individuals and organizations that have not seriously considered the changes going on around them and consequently failed to step into the present reality. They continue to rely on their memory, experience, and past understanding and stay in the place where they were most comfortable, both intellectually and socially, despite the fact that this world is rapidly disintegrating and reforming around them. As the more traditional, underlying, strategic processes are altered by technology and changes in thinking, so there is a requirement to shift our working relationships to stay active and effective as individuals. Cyberspace, its messages, and its technology, are the new reality. Although it is open to attack, criminality, fabrication, and propagandist deception, it also offers radical new opportunities to clarify understanding and build new relationships and new business as it offers a real gain in knowledge and positive remodelling of politics and commercial economics.

This is the story of how the twenty-first century's global information revolution is impacting and affecting intelligence actions, methods, processes, and planning, especially from a strategic perspective. In the broader context, these electric communication and information shocks are affecting all aspects of society for individuals, their conceptions of art, religion, and science, and their relationships with others. There may now be more people regularly using Facebook and Twitter than the combined 2012 populations of Europe and the United States. The population of Europe is roughly 738 million and the United States is 312 million; during 2012 Facebook's subscribers reached almost 1 billion, or 14 per cent of the world's population. These electronic shocks will not only radically alter the tactics, planning, strategy, and organizational structures of nations but they should be making policymakers seriously consider the reality in which they operate and the methods they use to gather and analyse information and how they then create more focused, useful intelligence about the environment and competition within which they engage.

The internet and new mobile and social communications technology have breathed new life into networked activity and have broadened the potential communications impact of all organizations. They have also given individuals, criminals, political extremists, and small groups a new platform. This is encouraging everything from networked relationships, organizational coordination, and global marketing to cyber crime as well as government electronic interference. It allows even small groups to attempt to shut down large areas of electronic networks. These opportunities and threats pose serious questions about the way in which the current reality is pictured by policymakers and by analysts and this has affected the way in which intelligence is collected, analysed, distributed, and used.

This book offers historic, current, and future perspectives on the use of information and intelligence. It discusses the growing, 'post-modern' data swamp and the need for new theories of intelligence analysis, effective implementation methods, and changes to organizational structures to make them more networked and operationally effective. I have spoken to and met many people involved in different aspects of information and intelligence across the globe, from North America to China. I have seen the need for organizational and operational change and have been involved in the change process in a few organizations. Some of these necessary changes are about reinventing corporate strategy and organization structure, and remaking aspects of the role of technology and data analysis. In organizational terms these strategic shifts change the roles of policymakers and analysts as well as corporate executives, police officers, and journalists.

Currently, many management structures and functions, analytical methods and practices, have not kept up with the technological and global social change that the information revolution is helping to create. This book is an attempt to give some strategic perspective and practical understanding to this new reality. It has been written to engage and actively challenge some of the current perspectives of policymakers, analysts, and corporate executives in intelligence and strategic planning operations. The analysis and argument in the text is particularly aimed at those who have a professional requirement to engage with strategic, operational, and competitive intelligence and are trying to plan for change or surprise. Its purpose is to offer a new strategic perspective—perhaps even a post-modern alternative—to traditional intelligence strategies and operational methodologies.

The book's conclusion will suggest a post-modern strategic intelligence model, together with other, more detailed, and broader aspects. The past, current, and potential future intelligence models have been analysed from different vantage points and the book offers a series of analytical perspectives that organizations might consider in this new, electronic, globalized environment. These new operational methods include continuous news and reporting from an intelligence operations viewpoint, a new intelligence cycle that recognizes and reviews the difficulties with the traditional models, a new strategic analysis, changes to scenario forecasting models, and a mosaic method that actively breaks with 'groupthink' and cultural bias and present to the policymaker a new, personally tailored

Strategic Intelligence – post-modern method

1. Mission and Vision – created by policy makers

2. Daily briefing and discussion by analysts and policymakers

3. News and analysis – continuously updates mobile data, information, and intelligence

4. Intelligence Cycle – intelligence request by policymaker

5. Strategic planning – longer term view of the planned future

6. Scenario planning – potential future outcomes

7. Mosaic Method – historic, current, future, and strategic perspective of the different views of the different players

8. Planning meeting – discussion every four to six weeks of the results, problems, and processes

Figure I.1 Strategic intelligence—post-modern method

view of the traditional and current social-competitive landscape that they are currently engaged with. This book has used an eight-tiered approach to intelligence and has incorporated aspects of the process into its construction, as shown in Figure I.1.

At the outset the policymaker should set a vision and mission statement which will drive the purpose and strategy going forward. These statements are incredibly important and give the organization or government its purpose and intentions. Setting them is not a small task and requires a lot of work and consideration; they can be quite different, depending on the organization or government. Once in place the day-to-day work begins, using intelligence methodology. The process starts with the analysts reviewing the work from the previous day and then creating the elements that will be presented and discussed with the policymaker that morning. For the policymaker, the process therefore starts with the second step, a daily briefing discussion between himself and the analysts. The briefing is short and focuses on the issues of the day before as well as those being considered that day. These briefings should be face-to-face or electronically connected and should allow points to be raised, along with questions and explanations. This interchange should take on average between 15 and 20 minutes.

The third element of this new approach is to give the intelligence agents, law enforcement officers, and commercial employees on the ground a 24/7 mobile information, intelligence, and question-and-answer service that is continuously updated, allowing them access to relevant, focused, and current data at all times. Fourth, the intelligence cycle and linear intelligence analysis should be used to allow policymakers some scope for questioning to drive some of the information gathering and intelligence creation. This should be viewed as a process to build improved responses and it should be integrated with other methods and techniques in the eight-point system.

At the fifth stage there should be a strategic planning process that attempts to offer a longer-term understanding and plan for the operation's intended future, purpose, and goals. This review should include the traditional, longer-term, strategic approach to planning and also offer ways of reducing bias and fixed-vision focus by incorporating scenario and aspects of the mosaic network method. This process should be seen as continuous and not something that is created and then put to one side until the next round of planning takes place, as is often the case. Sixth, there should be scenario planning for potential future outcomes—this process begins with a debate about the current situation and outcomes for the perceived reality. It will break the group into separate teams whose task is to play out different scenarios. The teams should contain both generalists and specialists and there would be three or four separate teams that would each arrive at different outcomes based on different scenarios. The object is to produce a series of three or four possible pictures of the future and have the group openly debate different outcomes. The teams should look at both gradual change and radical rethinks of what is considered the given reality. The purpose is to break up groupthink and to offer some seriously considered, possible outcomes from the current reality. Seventh is the Mosaic Method, which is used to put the intelligence process into a jigsaw of historic, current, and strategic perspectives and to give the analyst and the client a clearer understanding of the current reality as perceived by different players based on their cultural background and bias. In a conflict it is important to understand what the enemy perceives the reasons for the conflict to be, the purpose of its engagement and its desired outcome, and how and why these differ from your perspective.

The eighth and final aspect of the process is the requirement for planning meetings to take place every four to six weeks. These should discuss all six different intelligence methods, the results and problems that have occurred, and how the process might be improved going forward.

This whole process should include both electronic and regular face-to-face meetings between the people involved. It is vital that the relationships between different players are regularly reviewed and consideration given to the different issues that arise from the process of intelligence, the workings of their jobs, and the requirements put upon them. This process, its problems, and its successes, will be reviewed in greater depth in Chapter Twelve.

As I said at the outset, the current, globalized, electronic age has not just given the medium a new message; it has created a paradigm shift in communication. This has created a new medium with radical electric messages that are changing our beliefs, offering enormous amounts of information and propaganda, and offering new ways of analysing data, thus creating, potentially, more accurate and broader intelligence perspectives. This book is my contribution to the new, post-modern, strategic intelligence story in the twenty-first century.

PART ONE

The Changing Definitions of Information and Intelligence

This section reviews intelligence through history and how the definitions of intelligence often reflect what are considered the current threat issues of the time. It looks at the more recent changes to intelligence practices that a new geo-political perspective has created since the end of the Cold War and discusses the West's perspective after the fall of the Berlin Wall as it moves away from its main external enemy, the Soviet Union. Although Russia remains an important intelligence focus today, the West's focus has moved on to include issues with Japan's increasing importance and also the rising power of China. Recently, a change to globalization has brought new terrorist and cyber threats and has again changed the way in which friends and enemies are seen and analysed. Aspects of the traditional methods and theories of intelligence have been altered by changes in the creation of information, its circulation, exchange, interaction, and use.

The history of information forms part of this section, which discusses both the quantities of information and the way in which information delivery has changed over the centuries. It reviews the ways in which some of these changes affect individuals and society's understanding of reality, the way they communicate, and how, politically and commercially, they operate. Briefly, information from cave-painted records to the electronic media and its effects on decisions and intelligence are discussed.

Finally, Chapter Three considers some of the leading and still prominent intelligence literature of the past from China through Greek and Roman methods to the modern period.

1

Intelligence for Asymmetric Threats

This chapter reviews the concepts and definitions of intelligence and the way in which threats to the West and the rest of the globe have changed since the end of the Cold War. The Western perspective has moved from a two-dimensional, regional standoff to a partially connected series of global, asymmetric actions and threats affecting many countries in different ways. A series of analytical methods and structural changes to organizations are discussed as the new way forward.

Intelligence Definitions

Like philosophers, as a group intelligence theorists rarely agree on clear definitions of their work. Nevertheless theories about intelligence generally explain that information is gathered and analysed, sometimes secretly, and then used to understand a particular situation and act with advantage in it. This process offers prescriptive information and possibly prescient knowledge, usually to a policy-maker, and is described as intelligence. In an operation and function almost as old as systematic records it is perhaps surprising to find little agreement on a precise definition of intelligence. Sometimes the problems with statements and theories of intelligence have been the assumptions built into the proposed theory, process, and practical methods. And these assumptions have affected not only what is being collected, but also how the analysis will be undertaken. Also, in a broader sense these assumptions can affect the structure of the organization, what underlying purpose the intelligence will be used to achieve, and by whom. One of the effects of the recent Information Revolution and its web access has been to highlight, often with an ever-increasing array of conspiracy theories, the operations of the intelligence services. Public responses by some of the West's intelligence services have been to authorize and commission academic reports and papers concerning recent operations, sometimes through to the creation of open-source, publicly accessible websites. This process has become part of the West's democratic approach and has again altered the understanding and discussion of a definition of the intelligence process and purpose.

There tends to be agreement by all types of intelligence agencies that intelligence can be created by analysts using a myriad of different collection methods and sources of information. Everything from current communication and data records to diplomats, spies, and photographs is used, and the results and subsequent discussions deployed to assist the policymaker in making decisions. Traditionally, and still today, this information and intelligence is used as part of the intelligence cycle when commanders and policymakers make tactical decisions and put them into action. In a broader time sequence intelligence is used as part of an operational and strategic process of planning for the future, which may include forecasts and scenario predictions. Therefore intelligence can include an understanding of the current reality, often incorporating some current and past knowledge or validated beliefs about a particular individual or organization's intentions, their actions, and the potential threats they represent. The concept and methods of intelligence contain the implication that the opposition will not know that you have this specific information about their actions and or intentions, and for that reason this aspect of your knowledge is termed intelligence and is often classified as secret. The inherent belief is that the side that receives or creates an intelligence understanding from important information about the opposition, the environment within which it is operating, and its probable intentions, without the other side being aware that this information is known, has potentially an important advantage. Often wars, conflicts, and market dealings have been won and lost on the basis of the intelligence used and actions taken. Over the centuries many methods have been developed for the collection and analysis of the data that is used to form intelligence offering one side an advantage. Also (Robert Clark says in his book *Intelligence Analysis: A Target-Centric Approach*), as a process, 'the goal is to construct a shared picture of the target from which all participants can extract the elements they need to do their job'.[1]

Generally these understandings are what traditionally distinguish intelligence from general information but a number of different definitions of specific intelligence have been strongly argued about and adjusted with the times. Some of these disputes and definitions will be discussed here. However, I first want to add to the argument and lay out what I believe the intelligence process should be today. I will begin with what I perceive to be the definition and purpose of intelligence, and then talk later about the methods and processes I have outlined in the Introduction.

Intelligence is one part of a nation's, or a commercial organization's, thinking about the current situation and the actions they might take to achieve their

---

[1] Washington DC: CQ Press, 2004, p. 17.

specific, advantageous goals, or defeat or deflect the enemy or competition in their actions against you. Therefore, prior to the immediate need for intelligence, there should already be an agreed strategy and a list of issues and intrinsic understandings of the current situation, the opportunities, problems, or areas of argument or conflict. The most obvious of these are what your side's strategic intentions and planned outcomes are, what the problems and advantages are, who the enemy or the competition are, and perhaps what is it that they are intending. It is important that these assumptions are clear to your own side, are regularly reviewed, and form part of your longer-term strategy. Having done this, it begins to become apparent where your knowledge is lacking, and where are the gaps, uncertain assumptions, and areas in which it would be useful to have more understanding. All of this and more forms the basis of information's collection. Intelligence is then created from the information collected by using focused research, which has been targeted and based on the strategic understandings and beliefs, in order to give policymakers more clarity, knowledge, and understanding during the decisions they are making.

Status of Open-source Information

One point that recurs in discussion is whether open-source information can ever be described as intelligence. Different types of open-source information have been available, sometimes in more limited ways, for hundreds of years. Nonetheless analysts have tended to prefer restricted information, as they then know that fewer people have access to it. Often therefore, because open sources are not classified, the intelligence agencies have downgraded their status and this of course reflects different aspects of the secrecy an agency embodies in its internal bias and culture. This lack of engagement is partly because, traditionally, intelligence and information organizations, like strategy and corporate planning departments, are often created as a reaction to particular, past circumstances, when the myriad of open-source information sources did not report or have useful information on the particular crisis the agency was created to detect, monitor, and assess. By its organizational practice intelligence activity is usually very restrictive and few have access to it, its information sources, and the subsequent intelligence produced. To give the process protection and, sometimes, political credence, it is often classified by the creators or their bosses, and often remains secret within the organization that has access to it. Can open sources be real intelligence when potentially so many people have access to the same information, it is often asked? Often therefore, information is only considered intelligence if it is secret. Internally, intelligence agencies would frequently maintain that they could not see how, if it were widely available, open-source information, could be of any real use as intelligence. Accordingly, open sources are often downgraded or ignored inside some intelligence agencies and this has influenced the psychology of secrecy and the way these organizations are structured. Sometimes this means that the organization is prone to internal secrecy levels, with layers of access being part of the security structure within the organization's construction.

However the debate often misses the point about the analysis process and what part open-source information can play. Open sources have at least three purposes: first, they might tell you something new or add to something you already have some knowledge of. Second, they tell you what the opposition probably knows or has been trying to alter for their advantage. Third, and much more importantly, they might add to information or intelligence that you already have or will receive from another source, so that when added to the classified data the open source material can be re-analysed or used in ways that make the original intelligence far more effective. This process therefore creates new intelligence.

Traditional theory suggests, and it is generally thought, that initiation of the intelligence process comes from the policymaker driving the intelligence cycle. However the analyst can begin the process, as can some of the people and technologies that the analyst and policymaker have contact with and use to gain insight, information, and intelligence. My research suggests that both policymakers and analysts can instigate the creation of new intelligence, each at different times believing they started the process. This process ranges from short-term and tactical, action-based intelligence to operational planning and longer-term strategic perspectives concerning the broad geopolitical and macro-economic situation, and the intended objectives of the enemy or competition. The overall aim is still to give those in charge an advantage and a clearer understanding of the changing reality they are facing. This whole process should be seen as a structured construct that gives different timeframes to information and intelligence ranging from the immediate tactical situation through to a longer, strategic perspective. The analysts should give intelligence briefings capable of prompting action, which should include views and understandings, not just from their own side's viewpoint, but from the view of friends, competition, and the enemies. This process should use scenarios, in order to give a small series of perceived outcomes that will not predict the future, but should offer both analysts and policymakers a better understanding of the present situation and where it might lead. To achieve this goal the intelligence process must collect information about states of affairs that have created the current reality, and where it is that the different parties might be going, from different points of view. What are some of the intentions of the opposition and how might the climate, marketplace, size of the opposition, and their technology all change or be adapted depending on your own side's perception, bias, and intentions?

Overall, the information that is collected in this process should be data-based, sourced, and dated, as should the analysis of the sources and beliefs. The resulting information should be regularly reviewed in order to ensure it is up-to-date and can be used when needed. Much of this can be done in real time for tactical advantage and be given an on-going broader perspective for operational and longer-term, strategic planning. Intelligence is therefore knowledge that offers specific advantage in the short, operational term, contributes to the longer-term, strategic planning process, and should include the different sides' changing viewpoints.

Strategic Threats and Intelligence Focus

Formulating a clear strategy is not as straightforward as it may seem. What should be included and how far forward should the picture look? And on a broad strategic level it is clear that, as the threats alter, so the process must change to suit the new reality. Today, because of our globalized, interconnected world, nations and large organizations have to take everything from direct threats to underlying threats into the strategic picture. These can range from the environment, international legislation, international and national economics, international criminality, viruses, and pandemics to the 'known' threats from other nations, insurgents, and terrorist operators. However, on all levels of intelligence there is a requirement to be as clear about strategy as possible and recognize that this will frequently need adjustment and change. It is therefore important to learn from failure and also to understand why success works. All of these aspects affect the way in which information, data, and intelligence are collected, analysed, and created. According to academic writer, Sydney Finkelstein: 'Learning from failure is a hallmark of innovative companies but…is more common in exhortation than in practice. Most organizations do a poor job of learning from failures.'[2] However, this is also true of learning from success: few organizations do that. They perceive a failure as something to move on from and a success as something to celebrate; they cherish the luck but do not evaluate and understand it. To spend time understanding the current situation, its problems, and capabilities, and then to look forward and to impose the current on the potential future, and to see where the advantages and problems lie is not often done systematically. To take one pertinent example, before 9/11 criticism was posed about the then-current US intelligence process. In 1997 Russ Travers, an intelligence community insider, predicted that 'the year is 2001…analysis has become dangerously fragmented…collection was not the issue. The data were there, but we had failed to recognize fully their significance and put them in context…despite our best intentions, the system is sufficiently dysfunctional that intelligence failure is guaranteed.'[3] George Tenet himself had spoken of and reported his concerns about Bin Laden and al-Qaeda. A lot of information, as is often the case, had been collected but its linking or analysis, its interpretation or the underlying bias in the culture, or the political belief, or the perceived immediacy of short-term requirements, meant that the longer term was not sufficiently understood and acted upon. Viewed with hindsight after the awful events of 9/11 or 7/7, criticism

---

[2] S. Finkelstein, *Why Smart Executives Fail and What You Can Learn from Their Mistakes* (New York: Portfolio, 2003).

[3] R. Travers, *A Blueprint for Survival, The Coming Intelligence Failure* (Studies In Intelligence—Vol.1, No.1, 1997).

can easily be made of the analysts and has been directed at the intelligence community but policymakers must take some of the blame, and suggestions that the problems can be 'fixed' by organizational changes, centralizing the overview, better technology, and more resources do not address the root of the problems. Within the intelligence community this problem is deepened by the emphasis on secrecy and the lack of information sharing and collaboration. As Russ Travers, again in 1997, explained: 'By operating under the premise that we can divide intelligence analysis into military, economic and political sub-components and then parcel out discrete responsibilities to various agencies, we are sowing the seeds for inevitable mistakes...From the vantage point of 2001, intelligence failure is inevitable.'[4] He was hardly alone in this assessment.

However, before we review the structural changes we must discuss the theory and conception of what intelligence and the overarching strategic process are attempting to achieve. Sherman Kent said that 'intelligence is knowledge which our highly placed civilians and military men must have to guard the national welfare'.[5] Anthony Campbell, the former head of Intelligence in Canadian Prime Minister Chrétien's Cabinet Office, believes that 'the confusion of what intelligence is there to do and what definitions and weight we should give to each aspect of it run very deep, and yet even these issues still do not get to the real heart of the problem', which also requires, '...a change in management and training for analysts and users'.[6]

And so in essence what is first required is clear understanding of what are the strategic and tactical issues facing the nation or organization, and what current structural advantages and faults have been built into the system. This itself should give specific, tactical, or strategic advantage capable of being put into action, and it should begin to give the policymaker new, specific, knowledge to act on, which should have been built up through a series of independent, and as far as possible unbiased, information collection and analysis methods, and this should be an on-going process as laid out in the Introduction and Chapter Twelve's Mosaic Method. This process will improve strategic understanding and a targeted, specialized focus will give the policymaker a broader, focused perspective on the wider situation and the different views held by your own side and the opposition.

Now I want to take you back in time and then gradually move more up to date, looking at different aspects of the geopolitical, macro-economic, and related intelligence perspectives, but let us begin the intelligence process itself with information's collection.

---

[4] *A Blueprint for Survival, The Coming Intelligence Failure.*

[5] *Sherman Kent and the Profession of Intelligence Analysis* (Occasional Papers—Vol. 1, No. 5, November 2002), available at <http://www.cia.gov>.

[6] Anthony Campbell—Executive Director of the Intelligence Assessment Secretariat of Canada. See 'Bedmates or Sparring Partners' in *Spinning Intelligence: Why Intelligence Needs the Media, Why the Media Needs Intelligence* (New York: Columbia University Press, 2009), pp. 165–183.

Information Collection

The process of information collection can involve anything from visual surveillance of people and activities, delving into databases, listening to phone calls, breaking into offices and copying files, to satellite surveillance and photography. At the outset there should be a broader, background view to help the analyst decide what information is needed that will give the analyst a broader perspective across the wider situation on which to base the information collection process, which might include where to find specific sources that may have particular viewpoints or distinct knowledge. Once collected, this information must be checked for gaps and verified by cross-reference to other sources as it is analysed and gradually becomes intelligence ready to pass on to the policymaker. A myriad of methods are available which must be chosen and focused for specific projects in order to collect what appears to be relevant information before a second and often interconnected analysis process will attempt to turn the information into useful intelligence. This formulated intelligence is then delivered and explained to the policymaker or commander in good time for it to be advantageous and ready for action.

The range of systems and activities that might be used to collect information, and require monitoring, has grown significantly from the diplomatic and spying, to the myriad of open sources from television, radio, and newspapers to the internet and mobile devices. The use of mobiles has also changed the way in which street demonstrations and riots have been organized and fuelled as they happen. This communication activity should become part of the intelligence process used by analysts and policymakers on the move. As Holly Jones reported, 'the (London, UK) riots started on Friday (5 August 2011) following a peaceful protest over the death of Mark Duggan, who was shot dead by police officers during an arrest attempt…The rioters are believed to be using the Blackberry Messenger (BBM) network to organize their activities.'[7] All of these changes mean that ongoing intelligence that is action-ready is required for the police and intelligence services. Use of information from messaging and texts in a focused, networked, and interactive way can give them instant information and intelligence about a current event.

Shifting Views on Intelligence

The practice of modern intelligence was discussed and laid out by the historian-turned-analyst Sherman Kent in 1949 and much of current thinking on intelligence remains in the shadow of his book, *Strategic Intelligence for American World Policy*. Perhaps partly because of his continued influence, the theory and practice

---

[7] Holly Jones, '*London Riots Destroy Homes and Businesses*' <http://www.inspiresme.co.uk>, 9 August 2011.

of most intelligence operations remain at least partially locked in Cold War operations structure and psychology. Kent begins by defining intelligence as knowledge and he goes on to describe strategic intelligence and the methods and processes necessary for it to function effectively. The purpose of intelligence, Kent explains, is to get firm understanding from a variety of diffuse and often unconnected data, conversations, and information.

> Intelligence activity consists basically of two sorts of operation...the surveillance operation, by which I mean the many ways by which the contemporary world is put under close and systematic observation, and the research operation. By the latter I mean the attempts to establish meaningful patterns out of what was observed in the past and attempts to get meaning out of what appears to be going on now. The two operations are virtually inseparable...[8]

Going back 60 years to Sherman Kent's views on intelligence is certainly important as his definitions and functions are relevant, widely quoted, and still actively used. For Sherman Kent 'intelligence is not knowledge for knowledge sake alone, but...intelligence is knowledge for the practical matter of taking action'.[9] Kent focuses the knowledge on use in action as a major function of intelligence but there are other aspects, which he considered very important, and these are the organizational structure that collects and analyses intelligence, and the methods, processes, and activities employed to create intelligence. The structure of the organization is important to ensure that it effectively produces the right kinds of trained individual and that the right kinds of collection and process are employed and improved on to produce timely intelligence. While knowledge is still the most quoted aspect of Kent's intelligence definition, given the history and different processes to get to this specific type of knowledge there is dispute about the kinds of information and process that complete the intelligence process. Also importantly, for Sherman Kent intelligence and strategy were linked and had a broader context. He used both words in the title and first chapter of his book, and regarded strategic intelligence as separated from other types of intelligence. He saw strategic intelligence as specifically about areas of foreign or overseas focus where the information and analysis related to non-American countries, properties, and borders. Strategic intelligence, required by policymakers, aims to give them knowledge and thereby potential advantage concerning foreign threats and possibilities. For Kent, the CIA's foreign focus defined the type of intelligence they produced, and this he called strategic intelligence. Although I believe his reasoning and discussion are still very relevant, in the current, broader global context this definition is considered too narrow as a definition. In this book's context strategic intelligence is intelligence that gives an organization's planning cycle relevant understanding and advantage. This need not just be over foreign powers but can be focused on different targets and their background over longer periods. Every element, from localized criminals, insurgency,

---

[8] *Strategic Intelligence for American World Policy*, (Princeton, NJ: Princeton University Press, 1949).
[9] *Strategic Intelligence for American World Policy*, p. 3.

and terrorism, via commercial markets and competition, to the global environment, can be included in strategic intelligence that is needed to give perspective to the specific operation in which an organization is involved. Strategy is concerned with the real and intellectual horizons, and is not about just today and tomorrow but looks one to three years ahead. Strategic intelligence in this definition is specifically seen from the coordinating organization's perspective. However, in order to achieve this perspective that organization requires a review of its position, structure, and bias, and this should be undertaken at least annually as part of the strategic review and planning process.

Intelligence practice, like many human endeavours, is often preset by the organizational structure and the intellectual time period it acts within. Yet its strategic outlook and the engagement of the practitioners continue to adjust and shift its capabilities and they often try to extend the confines of current policy thinking. However the organization's culture will also try to resist suggestions and more radical policy suggesting larger structural change. All organizations resist changing their underlying make-up as, even though individuals might privately criticize aspects of it, the current structure is what the organization is comfortable with. This will often mean that new perspectives and methods that might be more effective are also resisted within the organization. In the particular case of an intelligence service the organization's underlying purpose is still traditionally seen as serving requests from the commanders or policymakers for an intelligence advantage. The objective is seen as giving them tactical or strategic insight into a situation and/or the opposition, and although this is of course still very relevant (as we have said) this process needs to be reviewed when the opposition radically changes and the information to track and monitor the new opposition has also changed. In this situation not only does the intelligence organization need to be altered to be really effective but the policymakers also need to be made fully aware of the new enemy and this needs to take place outside the traditional intelligence cycle.

Intelligence is often described as data or imagery that the opposition certainly would not want our policymakers to know about and this of course remains relevant in a new threat environment. However intelligence is a unique process and what characterizes the process and outcomes are briefings, discussions, and occasionally disputes about not just the process but of course also the results. Often the reasons for these debates are seen in the kinds of answer and outcome that the different intelligence processes are attempting to provide, and the shifting perspectives that the process starts from. Intelligence can range from being very specific—describing the psychology of an individual or the actions of a small group—to the broader fields of macro-economics or geopolitics. Intelligence has had many different definitions, roles, and purposes over the thousands of years since its first purpose, concepts, and practices were invented. However, the fundamental point still often remains unchanged—intelligence is useful knowledge that changes the response to the current reality. It is about knowing something important, probably secret and functional, that you do not want others to know that you know, at least until after you have effectively used the information. Intelligence can at best be seen as a predictive warning process used to clarify and understand, or alter proposed and current actions. And so the basic aspect of traditional intelligence theory is still about helping the policymaker's understanding of the current situation and improving their decisions and actions without the opposition's knowledge that crucial information is now in your hands. Traditionally, within these uses we have at least two connected but different ways of defining intelligence. The first is defensive and is intended to counter surprise. The second offers insight into the opposition's position and operations and is potentially offensive. These two can and often are refined, merged, and shifted by the changing realities. And of course, over the course of generations, the intelligence process changes and adjusts as new and different methods of monitoring, collection, and analysis are employed. The process of how you get the information to make focused analysis and create usable intelligence has been a continuously changing reality. In some places this process, which used to be a relatively small aspect of the military, has dramatically grown in size and has altered its focus and broadened the range of individuals, techniques, equipment, and technologies that are employed in its production.

The processes and communities that create intelligence from the data, information, and imagery often define the process. By its nature it is very restrictive; few have access to it; and (as has been said) it is often classified as secret within the organization that has access to it. In particular the target of the intelligence, the groups and individuals that are being monitored, obviously should not know that the collectors and creators of the intelligence have particular information about them and their intended actions. Probably these groups and individuals would also define this information as secret. Trying to tie down the precise purpose of intelligence at the time of process and use is vital but trying to define intelligence too narrowly in the academic sense perhaps misses the subtlety and some of its purpose. In Wittgenstein's terms, intelligence could be defined by its particular and intended use and the belief systems of the analyst and policymakers involved. The meaning of intelligence cannot be divorced from the process, the intentions, and bias of the intelligence creators and users.

To return to Sherman Kent's classic definition of intelligence: 'Intelligence, as I am writing of it, is the knowledge, which our highly placed civilians and military men must have to safeguard the national welfare.' Kent is aware of the differing views on the concept of intelligence, since he says 'as I am writing of it', with the full knowledge that the definition would change with time and circumstance. In 2002, Andrew Rathmell wrote 'the central concept is that the business of the intelligence community is the production of knowledge. Not just any knowledge, but targeted, actionable and predictive knowledge for specific consumers. Secret sources and methods will contribute to this process but only as part of the whole.'[10]

---

[10] Andrew Rathmell, 'Towards Postmodern Intelligence', (Autumn 2002) 17(3) *Intelligence and National Security*, pp. 87–104.

However until quite recently the more closed and secretly connected view of intelligence was the one shared by the general public as it is portrayed in spy fiction. This is understandable as intelligence was often seen only as a proactive arm or weapon of government. There are however deeper academic discussions concerning its ontology, and the different cultural perspectives surrounding what makes this aspect of targeted information about a particular subject different and unique. There is at least a second argument about the nature and scope of the activities, their epistemology, and the extent of the social monitoring that should be allowed to make it happen. This arises from the different perspectives that different individuals and organizations bring to the different realities that they believe they face and the ways in which they might obtain information to help them plan and act in the future.

Recently, according to Western monitors the range of threats has altered and now includes the environment, financial markets, economic structures, drugs, weapons, prostitution, child trafficking and trading, the spreading of virus and disease, water shortages, and agricultural activities as well as organized, local and international crime, insurgency, national conflict, and terrorism. The list of potential intelligence requests has multiplied and the resource and methodologies for dealing with these 'new' threats has been stretched. There has been a revolution and rethinking of the intelligence landscape to include far more than the protecting of local land and skies that was fundamentally the focus of American, European, and Soviet intelligence during and after the Cold War, even if this meant acting on and monitoring more than the immediate activity that might threaten the national borders.

In this new globalized environment, controlling and/or positively influencing the media message is also now actively seen as one of the important aspects of modern government. Propaganda has risen up the list for many governments and organizations. Intelligence is still seen as the tool, the lever, to add focus and tactical dimensions to their plans but the more objective process of its construction has occasionally been shifted by policymakers. Their plans—their overall strategy—are the governmental driving force and the control or influencing of the media and the use of intelligence and counter-intelligence are seen as important tools within this process. Because of the wealth of state publicity today, the quantity of information available, electronic gossip, conspiracies, and known government manipulation of news and information have all altered the public's belief in and relationship with information and intelligence. On many national news channels it is now sometimes stated that governments have purposely released information, or manipulated or altered open-source messages, to help them to put their ideas and plans across to their public and their international friends and foes. And occasionally the intelligence process has been used to assist in this process, along with its traditional areas of influence.

In democracies and in other more controlled environments, intelligence is often very controversial, particularly as the intelligence operation will sometimes spy on what is considered the country's own citizens. Also, the process is often seen as intrusive as it is not focused just on action that has taken place but also on potential actions that might or might not materialize. Therefore through this process some innocent civilians will undoubtedly be spied upon without their knowledge or agreement. This will happen particularly during times of war or potential international conflict in which agents or double agents that are thought to be working for the enemy will be monitored. Regardless, throughout history insurgency, terrorism, or organized crime have also been monitored and some innocent people have mistakenly been targeted. In non-democracies varying degrees of intelligence surveillance of the general public have also taken place over the centuries and of course this practice still widely occurs. However, other, far more controversial actions that have been taken in the name of intelligence, even in the West, have come to light that offer at least a little substance to some conspiracy theories. One was uncovered in 1975 in the United States investigation by the Church Committee into government covert activity, known as Project Shamrock. The Committee discovered that, for more than 30 years after the Second World War, the National Security Agency (NSA) intercepted all in-bound and out-bound communications from three US telegraph companies. At Project Shamrock's peak over 150,000 communications were analysed each month. The Committee discovered that the Nixon administration had been using this information against its domestic political enemies and this same process was suspected in the Watergate scandal. It became apparent that the CIA had been internally spying on the USA since the early 1970s, if not earlier.

Another example of controversial government action became public early in September 2011 when the Human Rights Watch group were shown documents that appeared to make it clear that the CIA, MI6 (SIS), and French intelligence had been working closely with Colonel Gaddafi's intelligence operation. They had apparently used buildings in Tripoli to torture and interrogate suspected al-Qaeda operatives and all three organizations seemed to have close relations with what soon became a government that they would go to war with under the UN banner. These conflicting qualities do not augur well for an unbiased and independent, or particularly precise, definition of intelligence and its usage. Some analysts will say that to be intelligence information must be independent and unbiased, and this must be a hallmark of intelligence production.

And so the tactics, broader issues, and definitions of intelligence should be seen as an on-going argument and discussion within an organization, which should be seen through as a continuous process. Philosophy, religion, and current post-modern theories have raised many arguments and suggested definitions of purpose but disagreements still remain. We continue this discussion with a focus on the United States strategic review just after the Second World War.

Before and after the Cold War

The creation of the CIA in 1947 in part reflected the growing potential threat America felt from the USSR and communism. It also reflected discussions and arguments within different aspects of the US government surrounding President Truman's wish to have a central intelligence collection and assessment process controlled by the President. Different elements of established government, particularly the FBI and (G2) Military Intelligence, argued and tried to counter the proposal put forward by William J. Donovan, wartime head of the Office of Strategic Services (OSS), of the need for a Central Intelligence Group. Donovan argued his case both before and after the dissolution of the OSS. Even though the process went through the ups and downs of internal argument, with Truman appearing not to get on with Donovan, the President still wanted a more coordinated, structured, and analytical process, believing that, had this existed previously, it might have brought more clarity and focus prior to the attack on Pearl Harbor. It was therefore not without internal conflict and compromise that the National Security Act of 1947 created the Central Intelligence Group that became the CIA, realizing Donovan's hopes for a centralized, peacetime intelligence agency.

Yet today, nearly seven decades later, the CIA's underlying structure and perceived purpose retains this creationist physiology. There have of course been many government reports recommending changes and many of the organizational changes have been implemented in part but still many of the underlying organizational, information, and intelligence data problems continue to exist. The requirement to change in the wake of perceived failures or changes in technology, economics or the accessibility of information, is often recognized in state organizations from education to health care, from the military intelligence and the police and prison services to commercial organizations of all types. However, fundamental changes to structural and methodological processes are seen to be difficult to achieve and are often actively resisted. Given the way in which civil service departments function and are administered, this is understandable. Any new government that has forced its way in or recently been elected in a democracy will change many aspects of the current structure but the civil servants' underlying purpose will be to retain their jobs, their current structure, and their activities, and this is true of all organizations, government or commercial. Primarily, it is not in the interests of the personnel or management of any established organization to review and overhaul their purpose even if, on the face of it, they seem to partially agree with initiatives recommending organizational change. Their culture reflects past realities and more importantly their methodologies; processes, structure, and outputs reflect the reasons for their initial creation and this is often supported by the way in which employees were employed, the specific tasks they feel confident about, and the way the organization is funded and managed. As an example, in the political design of Western democracy this concept of changing times is locked into the election process, and government evolution happens every four to eight years when new pressures may be put upon the internal organization structure. Commercial organizations are put under different, non-cyclical pressures to change. These come from the working of markets, competition, share price, growth, deficits, shareholder opinion, and profitability. Within the civil service the pressures to change are more diffuse and this is far harder to achieve. This applies to organizational structure but even more so to internal process methodologies. Therefore, in many governments, cultures, and local societies worldwide departments, groups, and gatherings can fall between the cracks, remaining almost dormant for years. Often because of secrecy within the intelligence agencies the lack of change has remained part of the institutional make-up over decades and, to a large degree, they remain unreconstructed. As has been said it is not in the interest of their structural organization, management, or economy to change either their structure or the methods and processes they use when operating.

The Man who was Thursday and the Public's Understanding of Intelligence

This is not, of course, a new problem. G.K. Chesterton parodied two intelligence techniques in his novel *The Man Who Was Thursday*, first published in 1908. It was published at a time when there had been terror attacks in London and Europe and, in the novel, Chesterton creates 'Philosophical Policemen' who are separated from the average beat bobby patrolling the streets. One of the Philosophical Policemen explains their methods and some of the outcomes. 'The ordinary policeman tries to discover from a ledger that a crime was committed. We discover from a book of sonnets that a crime will be committed...We say that the most dangerous criminal at large is the entirely lawless modern philosopher. Compared to him burglars and bigamists are essentially moral men.'[11]

However darkly amusing Chesterton's view, we need a more current example of changing intelligence needs and will start in the grey daylight of the world after 9/11, 7/7, and the Arab Spring, in which there is a real requirement to have a broader and deeper understanding of current, strategic, linear intelligence and analysis that may be put into action. These analytical methods and considerations will echo Chesterton's suggestion of philosophical policemen, which can be seen in a modern context as a requirement for more subject-matter expertise to obtain far more focused and deeper analysis. All forms of intelligence, from the military to intelligence agencies, law enforcement, and corporate, require a network of academic and specialized experts on specific subjects that can be called upon to give their views and analysis. Chesterton's model suggests the need for future scenarios and also suggests our underlying mosaic theory. This model's aim is to offer a deeper understanding of the current situation with the intention of clarifying future actions.

Putting this into a more recent, American context, in the 1940s Sherman Kent argued that social sciences and intelligence analysis needed systematic methods 'much like the method of physical sciences'. However, the records also show that Kent found individuality, eccentricity, and 'odd ball' thinking valuable for units

---

[11] G.K. Chesterton, *The Man Who Was Thursday* (London: J.W. Arrowsmith, 1908).

facing tough challenges. He understood the need for complete loyalty from his analysts but when McCarthyism threatened to force an unreasonable standard of conformity on the bureaucracy in the early 1950s, he said: 'when an intelligence staff has been screened through too fine a mesh its members will be as alike as tiles on a bathroom floor—and about as capable of meaningful and original thought'.[12] However, for all his creativity, scientific analysis, and hard work Kent's method failed to anticipate that in 1962 the USSR would base nuclear weapons in Cuba. Kent believed the best analytical standards had been applied but in his subsequent opinion they had not been applied rigorously enough. It seems that, perhaps intuitively, he did not want to argue with the limitations of traditional, linear methods of intelligence and he had not introduced other, contrasting methods. In part, therefore, Kent's methods have subsequently been contrasted critically with a range of writers from David Riesman to Jan Jacobs and Jacques Derrida. Their methods of social patterning and post-modern predictive analysis seemed sometimes to succeed almost against the odds. These apparently opposite ways of looking at intelligence, parodied by Chesterton, go to the centre of some of the issues currently surrounding strategy and intelligence, and they range from an empiricist view to a perspective that could be described as post-modern, in the sense that the very process and the current, underlying, cultural bias and reading of reality have to be brought into question.

Reflections after the Cold War

There are some commentators who believe that the Cold War gave a form of stability to the geopolitical strategic outlook and gave consistency and structure to threat planning. John J. Mearsheimer, Professor of Political Science at the University of Chicago, has written 'the Cold War, with two superpowers, served to anchor rival alliances of clearly inferior powers'.[13] This position would not be shared with the likes of Robert McNamara who, in the film documentary *Fog of War*,[14] complains that people who consider the Cold War as predictive and stable should have understood what he experienced. As far as he was concerned as US Secretary of Defense, it was a hot war that too often came close to nuclear conflict. However, McNamara is also accused of creating part of the Cold War tragedy in Vietnam and not being clear in his linking of systems strategy with social considerations. 'In Vietnam, he [Robert McNamara] was the architect of one of America's greatest tragedies... He will always be associated with the futile effort to apply "systems analyses" to human behavior.'[15] The Cold War lasted for

---

[12] *Sherman Kent and the Profession of Intelligence Analysis,* above n 5.

[13] John J Mearsheimer, *'Why we will soon miss The Cold War'* (1990) 266(2) *Atlantic Monthly,* pp. 35–50.

[14] *Fog of War,* directed by Errol Morris, Sony Pictures, 2003.

[15] Richard Immerman, a historian at Temple University in Philadelphia and a former intelligence official in the George W. Bush administration. The comment was made on the Temple University website in July 2009.

nearly 50 years and elements of its perspective and influence remain in places like Cuba and parts of South America, Africa, and the countries that emerged from the Soviet Union. Nevertheless, when the Berlin Wall came down in 1989, and the macro-economics of Soviet Russia changed, the perceived threats to Western culture altered. The military and aspects of the intelligence process always need to define a new enemy. Some opponent, or opponents, they can focus upon are needed and after the fall of the Soviet Union the focus fell first on Japan as the new challenge, and then later moved towards China, which is to some extent now considered the focus of the new Cold War.

After the fall of the Berlin Wall the world perspective became more intercon-nected. Trade barriers changed and opened, travel, communications, and trans-port started to become more networked. The new world of news, conjecture, and analysis had never been so accessible. From any national perspective, this is the new, global, post-modern age in action and it requires a new set of strategies and intelligence to construct an effective response. This is in part because the new information world responds far more immediately and has given confidence to new actors in an environment in which technologies of connectivity have encouraged discussion, blogs, and social organization and promoted some rela-tively small-scale but profound violence. The new media, like many aspects of the new electronic environment, have dramatically expanded the quantity of content available. They have apparently encouraged users to retain less memory and even less analysis, since the web apparently offers these aspects, delivering instant information at the tap of a keyboard. It has altered the public's response to events and their perceived global reality. Certainly, it is more short-term and based on momentary news and electronic gossip. And so over the last two dec-ades a series of crises has thrown government and some commercial strategic planning and traditional intelligence methods into review and critical relief. However, these paradigm shifts (revolutions, perhaps) are not as unusual as some of these current media suggest, since throughout history different, but similar, types of change have occurred to different commercial organizations, military units, and governments. In government and the intelligence arena, these shocks of change are often preceded by what was considered an intelligence failure. That the use of information and intelligence for strategic and tactical planning and for action has failed is often said to be because the intelligence dots were not ade-quately joined up. As an example of this terminology, on 5 January 2010 Presi-dent Obama explained that the US intelligence agencies had had enough information and intelligence to disrupt the Christmas Day bombing threat to a US airliner, but 'failed to connect the dots'. However the term 'joining up the dots' originated from pictorial games. In the intelligence field the term is rather simplistic and hardly suggests the difficulties, that the sheer quantities of data and often the time pressures involved, create. Intelligence is not obvious and it is rarely easy to make the really relevant connections. Intelligence tends to come to the public's attention through these types of failure statement. Of course the public also learns some of the techniques through fictional spy stories and films, or when failures to stop a destructive action have created misjudgements or inaccurate views of the intentions or capabilities of the people and groups involved. As many in the intelligence community will say, intelligence is often a very detailed and unglamorous activity and the successes are rarely publicized, since policymakers or politicians will claim the success as their own and will not refer to the intelligence process because of the often-understandable need for secrecy.

9/11 and the Contemporary Threat

It is now over a decade since the 9/11 attacks on New York and Washington DC yet this turning point in interconnected communication has yet to be fully understood. This was Osama bin Laden's major message: 'it is obvious that the media war in this century is one of the strongest methods; in fact; it may reach 90 per cent of the total preparation, for the battles to come'.[16] Bin Laden recognized that shock and terror were his strongest messages and that the more public his attacks, the more press and public attention his organization would receive, especially from the people he wanted to recruit. The insurgency and terror groups realized that, even if they claimed a radical dislike of Western culture, they could use the new Western technologies to communicate their message and propaganda in order to promote their brand. They now look to shocking events and what they describe as martyred death to project and market themselves across the global media.

One particular view from the Center for Security Policy in 2011 suggests that some of the complexities and some of the problems of defining the new threat to the USA and the West stem from a misunderstanding.

> Today, the United States faces what is, if anything, an even more insidious ideological threat: the totalitarian socio-political doctrine that Islam calls *shariah.* Translated as 'the path,' *shariah* is a comprehensive legal and political framework. Though it certainly has spiritual elements, it would be a mistake to think of *shariah* as a 'religious' code in the western sense because it seeks to regulate all manner of behavior in the secular sphere—economic, social, military, legal and political.[17]

The Center are not alone in this type of analysis. They believe that the West and other parts of the developed world face a totalitarian ideological threat that aims to enforce a restrictive behavioural policy over all elements of social, political, and personal life. They describe these 'Islamists' as supremacists who are out to defeat the West by whatever means they believe will succeed. Like many so-called radical organizations, insurgents and terrorism groups—from the IRA to Aum Shinrikyo to ETA to November 17—they often attempt to communicate their views with fear and propaganda included.

---

[16] *Letter from Osama bin Laden to Mullah Omar*, 2003.

[17] *Introduction to Shariah The Threat to America An Exercise in Competitive Analysis* (Report of Team B11, Copyright © 2010 Center for Security Policy October 2010 Edition).

Recent Threats and Failures

In a broader perspective Western governments have recently had to deal with a range of threats and actions. The more current crises, and what have been described as intelligence failures, that have had a lasting impact include the 2001 terrorist attack on the Twin Towers in New York and the Pentagon in Washington DC and the attacks on 7th July 2005 that resulted in the successful detonation of three suicide bombs in the London Underground and one on a bus by locally based activists. This attack changed the parameters of UK policing, putting emphasis on the need for new, intelligence-led and problem-oriented policing methods. In addition, besides terrorism and insurgency, there was the 2008 economic crash and the subsequent global recessions, both of which had been largely predicted by different parts of commerce and academia but unpredicted by governments; the oil explosion in the Gulf of Mexico, a crisis that has repositioned America's view of oil exploration and of the corporate intelligence that failed to recognize the significance of these potential disasters; and the 2011 'Arab Spring' that has resulted in new and reforming political landscapes in the Middle East. Again, the far smaller, city riots in England in August 2011 were actively prompted by the use of electronic communications within the groups and individuals involved and these were given prominence by the lack of early police counter-activity: initially none took place. The uses of the web are one of the effects that the Arab Spring is having on other parts of the Middle and Far East with their large and growing younger populations and older, narrow political regimes. All of this is now being reviewed and considered by all governments before, during, and after such issues arise but generally they have only partly been taken account of as the new, globalized, generation gaps widen. In part, aspects of the Arab Spring and the London riots might have been predicted by monitoring social networks, yet prior to the broader social unrest governments and their intelligence agencies undertook minimal amounts of this.

The television coverage of the August 2011 riots in England, which began in London and quickly spread to other cities and towns, initially showed the London disturbances not being directly dealt with by the police. Television began and social media and the web quickly spread the news, gossip, and rumour that the police were not countering the looting of shops. Later, police in Norfolk in the UK criticized *Facebook* pages and *Twitter* messages for spreading 'fictitious and malicious rumours'. Police forces quickly began to arrest online posters for inciting greed and criminality. However the effects of the recession, banking greed, and the MPs' expenses scandals in the UK had altered the political and civil landscape. There are many who, even though they would not join riots, felt that politicians and senior business people were breaking the rules and causing social unrest and civil disobedience. These occurrences and others have altered the political and strategic planning perspective and put traditional models of predictive intelligence into the spotlight.

Broader Threats and the Changing Strategic Perspective

Rightly, the Western world is concerned at insurgency and radical terror attacks, but according to a growing number of authorities there are also well-documented, underlying threats to humanity that get little broad analysis or wider media attention:

> In terms of real threats to humankind, terrorism does not make the A list. It is in a different league to climate change, pandemic disease, the scourge of chronic underdevelopment and, for that matter, such problems as transport safety and the explosive growth of tobacco use in underdeveloped countries.[18]

Perhaps this highlights our deeper underlying problem, which is our lack of broad perspective and our lack of forward scenario-planning and counter-action. This is suggested by our lack of '...capacities for managing new realities. From Madrid to London, Bali to Mumbai, from Katrina-ravaged New Orleans to the tsunami's devastation all around the Indian Ocean, to the most recent financial crisis, the alarms went unheeded until after disaster had struck'.[19]

During the Cold War there was a focus on the two global powers, the Soviet Union and the USA. All others were considered connections or jigsaw pieces and were secondary to and moveable by the main players. These secondary pieces were the tools and options used by the superpowers as pawns in their deadly game. This process of pressured threat and conflict was the Cold War landscape. During this conflict intelligence theories from Sum Tzu to Sherman Kent were employed. These had primarily been about the security of a country and the way in which information may become active, 'secret' knowledge that can help secure an understanding of the enemy's capabilities and intentions so that effective and positive outcomes are achieved. These methods have been used in the last 50 years by corporations to produce strategies, and to an extent in the last 10 to 20 years by police forces to create Intelligence-Led Policing methods. However, all of these traditional methods assume that the enemy is easy to identify, comes from and resides in, a specific, recognizable place that can be monitored and if necessary attacked, and that we understand the enemy's motives and techniques. Yet the enemy has radically altered, depending upon cultural perspective, and no longer includes just nations and superpowers. If your perspective is American or European, then China has some of the elements that might give it the potential to become a key player in the next Cold War. From a more local outlook there are threats that each nation needs to consider, including globally active, international criminal groups, insurgents and fragmented terrorist cells, environmental

---

[18] Daryl Copeland, Professor at the Munk School of Global Affairs, University of Toronto, Canada in a conversation with the author.

[19] Carol Dumaine, Deputy Director at the Office of Intelligence and Counter Intelligence, US Department of Energy in a conversation with the author.

and macro-economic issues. In the commercial world newly networked markets and international operations have changed the understanding of potential opportunities and competition, creating a new version of the global economy. To analyse and strategically plan these issues and threats, this new, global, strategic perspective requires new methods and an organizational rethink. The first Cold War created intelligence-reporting models (part of which included the *US Presidential Daily Brief*, which did not recognize the internal economic landscape as a significant part of its security mandate and therefore did not analyse or report the financial crisis to the President). And George Bush, when President, complained about the lack of advance warning of the economic crisis, which sounded quite out of step with a modern, connected, information experience. Other broader, longer-term issues such as global warming, water shortages, and farming reductions and disruptions have meant that the current strategic planning and intelligence methods have been heavily criticized for their weak analysis and lack of predictive response to these various crises.

The traditional intelligence cycle has been ruptured and a new strategic perspective now seems necessary. These and similar issues are also challenging corporate scenario-planning methods, as governments and organizations respond to the ragged ends of the Cold War. In addition, a new phase of digital, semantic globalization, sometimes called Web 3.0, is revolutionizing the commercial and political strategic-planning processes. We now have access to millions of times more information than any of our forebears, yet the issues of validation, interpretation, planning, and scenario forecasting have not reduced, they have multiplied. There is currently more open intelligence in the form of Wikileaks and other once-classified sources within the tens of billions of pages on the web. Yet our ability to separate the good-quality, pertinent information from the oceans of gossip, propaganda, and biased data has not increased in turn.

New Intelligence Cycle

There is now a real need to alter the methods and practices of intelligence, the relationships with the policymakers, and the organization structures that have been created to monitor, analyse, assess, and distribute intelligence. The concept of relying on the intelligence cycle (IC), even though some of its practices have changed, is out of tune with current events and the technologies being used. The IC was created for a tactical and immediate response and is based on a master–servant relationship. The master asks for information on a specific subject and the civil servant duly goes off, collects, analyses, and brings it back to the policymaker for understanding and action. This process has little theoretical appreciation of the current technologies that provide the policymaker with on-going media information and opinion, and takes no direct account of what is already known of the history of the situation being analysed, and the feelings and bias of the analysts and the policymaker *vis-à-vis* the subject being assessed. Also, it does not offer alternatives based on possible outcomes.

Intelligence Services

The Open Government Plan on the CIA's open-source website begins by explaining what it sees as the intelligence requirement:

> The need for a secret intelligence service as a first line of defense to protect a free society is well understood, and has been a part of the fabric of our country since George Washington utilized a spy network to help win the Revolutionary War. Nevertheless, there has always been a concern about how a secret agency with special authorities fits within an open and democratic society. Endeavoring to resolve the tensions between the need and the concern has been an important part of the Central Intelligence Agency (CIA) culture.[20]

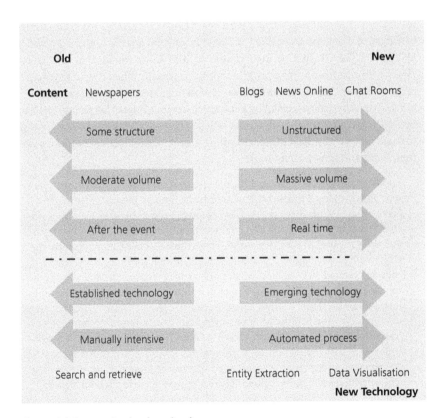

Figure 1.1 Content/technology landscape

---

[20] Available at <http://www.cia.gov.com>.

Between 1954 and 1962 the French intelligence service, the DST, formed the Organisation of French Algerian Resistance whose strategic purpose was to act as a counter-terrorist operation against Algerian militants. This 'false flag' or covert operation was designed to carry out direct 'terrorist' attacks with the aim of countering political discussion, negotiation, or compromise. During the nineteenth and twentieth centuries Irish nationalism helped to justify the forming of a new Branch of London's Metropolitan Police and in 1883 they created the Special Irish Branch to counter extremism and terror from the Fenians who were operating in London. In 1909 the Secret Service Bureau was formed, again in London, to focus on German spies thought to be operating in Britain. This intelligence process was later to initiate a split in the secret intelligence service between local and international. The national, internal, counter-espionage group was headed by Captain Vernon Kell; it became MI5 and was internally called Kell's Secret Service. The overseas and international aspect of the service were headed by Captain Mansfield Smith-Cummings; subsequently he and later heads of this operation were often referred to as 'C'. When writing the James Bond books Ian Fleming changed this to 'M' but 'C' is still used. This operation became responsible for international intelligence operations, became the Secret Intelligence Service, and is known as SIS or MI6. The UK split between national (MI5) and international intelligence (SIS or MI6) has not always worked smoothly, especially when they spied on each other believing there to be double agents working for one or the other agency.

The first public speech given by a currently serving Chief of SIS was on 28 October 2010, just after the organization's official centenary. Sir John Sawers's speech to the Society of Editors outlined how the UK's main intelligence operations view their focus and how they interact:

> The Secret Intelligence Service, MI6, operates abroad, dealing with threats overseas and gathering intelligence mainly from human sources...The Security Service, MI5, works here in the UK, protecting the homeland from terrorist attacks and other threats. GCHQ produces intelligence from communications, and takes the lead in the cyber world. These three specialised services form the UK's intelligence community and we operate in what the Foreign Secretary has called a 'Networked World'. Technology plays an ever-growing part in our work, for SIS as well as GCHQ, and the boundary line between home and abroad is increasingly blurred. The three agencies work increasingly closely together and the next five years will see us intensifying our collaboration, to improve our operational impact, and to save money. [According to Sir John Sawers, intelligence is]...that [which] others wish you not to know; it's information that deepens our understanding of a foreign country or grouping, or reveals their true intentions. It is information that gives us new opportunities for action.[21]

However, as discussed earlier in this chapter, often definitions and theories of intelligence differ depending on the perceived outcomes that are being explored, analysed, and actioned. This is because of the different focus and

---

[21] Available at <http://www.sis.gov.uk/about-us/the-chief/the-chief's-speech-28th-october-2010.html/>.

views of the threat, the timescales, and solutions being suggested and used (see Figure 1.1). As an American intelligence practitioner phrased it to me: 'So, if we were to look at the whole process afresh, I think we might come up with new sets of methodologies and a different intelligence focus for each different threat.' What we require is new ways of viewing the future horizons and a clearer understanding of how and why certain questions about the current situation are being asked and expressed. The tasks and questions should be reviewed both from the user's and the analyst's points of view, as well as from an independent, broader perspective. Given our information availability and the sophistication of our digital software and technology we are capable of far more sophisticated analysis than was the case even a decade ago. And yet even when questions have previously been asked, it was not the technology or the data that was lacking, it was an understanding of the client's expectation and reasoning.

One aspect of these issues, especially in the area of expectations, was high-lighted by a discussion between President Bill Clinton and the CIA Director at the time, James Woolsey. As his predecessors had done since the 1950s, the CIA Director presented the President with the *Daily Brief*—a news and analysis report on the current security issues confronting the USA. At one of their early, but infrequent, meetings Clinton asked Woolsey for analysis similar to a magazine article in *The Atlantic Monthly* of February 1994. It ran for 24 pages, contained over 10,000 words, and was entitled '*The Coming Anarchy*' by Robert D. Kaplan. Clinton had recently studied the piece and annotated it heavily, and the article was offered to Woolsey by way of example of the type of intelligence that Clinton found useful. Later James Woolsey criticized the piece directly to me in the spring of 1997, as coming from a small-staffed, open-source, liberal magazine that lacked rigour and clear purpose, unlike the CIA's tested processes. Clinton had highlighted the piece because he thought it provided him with a perspective on traditional West African social groupings that, as Kaplan the author had argued, could be applied to understanding future inner-city problems in the West. However, Clinton never made clear what his purpose and strategy for this type of 'intelligence' actually was. And here we have a pertinent example, which Jim Woolsey explains as one of the problems between the relationships of the policy-maker with the analyst. Clinton was averse to having focused meetings with his CIA Director and was apparently concerned about aspects of his own secrecy, which seemed to be a personal issue that he never made clear. Woolsey wanted to give the President clear intelligence and assistance but was often left out of the loop and he never had a one-on-one, face-to-face meeting with Clinton. What Clinton probably wanted from the example of '*The Coming Anarchy*' piece was open-sourced or non-classified intelligence that, as President, he could use to develop his geopolitical perspective and in open speeches. However, as Woolsey pointed out, the problem with using pieces like '*The Coming Anarchy*' is that they have a bias of their own and are not given a broader validation and review process.

New Views on Strategic Intelligence

The theory and practice of national security has begun to alter for many nations since the end of the Cold War, mainly brought about by the changing international threats from insurgency, terrorism, and international crime. However, from a historical perspective, there has always been a series of transnational threats. Each operational aspect of the strategic intelligence picture will give its view of the threats and how these can be addressed. However, if we step back and look from a theoretical hilltop over the local, national, and into the global horizons then a potential, mosaic theory of intelligence is suggested. To be effective this new approach would include the current news and intelligence analysis, a traditional intelligence-cycle model, strategic perspective, a forward-looking scenario-planning process, and a post-modern 'mosaic' of background, which links and networks to the other intelligence processes and their understanding. The aim is to give a clearer understanding of the types of issue requiring action and consideration, offering the policymaker potential ways forward, and some clarity as to how the problem or advantage came about and the influences that the past exerts on the potential solutions.

This analysis is not a straight-line, conclusive outcome and must be used to stimulate a planning process that engages with different aspects of the organization structure and the changes that might be necessary. It should review the current external landscape, scan the past for lessons and understanding of different cultural bias, and explain the different future outcomes and possibilities. This process should be on-going and challenging whilst continually producing current intelligence for management understanding and the decision-making process. However, when all of these strategic-planning, intelligence, and analytical processes are employed the picture, the thinking, and the options become much clearer, not only to the decision makers but within the intelligence organization as a whole. There is more engagement and, importantly, a clearer way forward, which can constantly be reviewed. The old cycle of narrow, 'conservative' planning cycles and layered structural management would be challenged and broken. It means a more collective and inclusive approach but, and let us be clear, this is not about democracy for its own humanistic benefit, this is about making better, clearer decisions that will be implemented in a more decisive, time-considered, and effective way. These processes have ramifications for decision making, discussion, and the review of reasoning within an organization. There should be regular reviews of the very nature of how an organization is intellectually and physically structured. It means much more sharing of information, and reward for process of achievement and effective teamwork, as well as individual achievement. Focusing these intelligence methods on semantic news, traditional analysis, scenarios, and background models is the reason for the changes; not change for change's sake but because the old methods have ceased to work effectively in a changed environment. This analysis should become the standard parts of the strategic and intelligence process no matter where it is used: in government, in policing, in business, and in the non-profit sector. These methods, and the potential outcomes and ramifications of these methods and others, are more deeply researched in Chapter Twelve.

The Cold War paranoia—the Old World view—still exists and it is not going to go away quickly even if there is a generational adjustment to the current, post-modern, global perspective, in which engines and centres of change merge and move frequently. To put the post-modern views into focus we first have to deal with the underlying shocks to the cultural perspective and the globalization of the media. Importantly, the world economy is changing the landscape and since the end of the Cold War this new globalization has started the process of remaking economic boundaries, which has also been directly affected by the links and networks of the Information Revolution. All of this has recently changed the intelligence paradigm.

Now it is time to go back and review the past and its different histories and influences that still resonate in today's electronic, 'temporary' environment.

2

Information Revolutions and their Effects on Intelligence Methods

Every time new media are created this alters the way in which individuals, society, and business operate. It changes the way in which individuals and groups engage with others and understand themselves.

New media technology and delivery are also used to engage and change current conflicts, crimes, geopolitics, and economics. New information and communications processes offer different ways of communicating, marketing, and entertaining but they also alter the way the world is perceived and analysed.

The Effects of New Media

By the late 1990s 24-hour news channels and the effects of web news began to have their globalizing influence and as we moved into the new century they began to change the more traditional economic model of newspaper delivery and print. A more global economy had other competitive effects that reduced costs and improved delivery. There has been a dramatic doubling of the world's population in the last 25 years and this has brought with it growing global numbers of literate individuals as well as a significant increase in numbers of poor people. During this period everything from satellite television to traditional print still found an audience because of the increase in the literate population, and most aspects of the media continued to grow. But electronic social networking and mobile connectivity were growing at an even faster rate and being used by different social groups to effect change in the moment, as can been seen by social monitoring of some of the more radical effects.

Now let's begin this media review by going back to near the end of Shakespeare's life, a century and a half after the radical changes and outcomes brought by the Gutenberg press. 'One of the great diseases of this age is the multitude of books that doth so overcharge the world that it is not able to digest the abundance of idle matter that is every day hatched and brought into the world', wrote Barnaby Rich in 1613. Born in the 1540s, Rich was a writer and soldier who had fought in the Low Countries and Ireland. The advance of movable type and the growing number of books during his lifetime made him feel unable to recall all he had read and to say that a lot that was being published did not warrant the privilege of being bound as a book. Rich saw the dramatic growth of print as a major generational problem.

Arguments about the media have been going on a lot longer than this. For more than 5,000 years people have been organizing and recording their thoughts and actions as pictures, data, and information for retrieval and searching at a later time, or as a memento for future generations. These recordings have been achieved by pictures in caves, marks on tablets, the compiling of records, hieroglyphics, the storing, organizing, and indexing of papyri, gazettes, books and all new forms of media. At different times throughout the last 3,000 years libraries and index systems have been constructed. The oldest known library was created in Elba, in the Fertile Crescent, between 3,000 and 2,500 BCE and by 300 BCE, Ptolemy Soter, a Macedonian general, created the Great Library at Alexandria. Even after the inception of electronic transformation libraries that can be accessed in most countries, in 2009 5.3 billion non-virtual items (books, information records, CDs, DVDs, *et al*) were checked out from libraries in the Americas, Canada, and Europe, an increase of 11 per cent over the previous year.

Nonetheless, this traditional use of information and knowledge is being overwhelmed by the electronic revolution, which experiences a far higher rate of growth. And one significant intellectual by-product of the increasing use of web technology, and its lack of easy verification, is that many beliefs in the 'truth' of information's content are now considered a post-modern, internet idea, which lights up and fades as the power is switched on and off. Similarly, in modern times what constitutes an individual has been defined and argued about and the traditional psychological patterns have been analysed in different ways by philosophers and psychologists. There is a lot of debate about what constitutes an individual and what acts to make individuals change: from Descartes' 'I think therefore I am', or Sartre's 'you are what you do', to Wittgenstein's belief that the way in which you use language defines your 'reality'. The cultural concept of reality and the understanding of different languages have an important effect for intelligence. When analysing the opposition it is required to understand the interpretation of different languages and the way individuals act when using language, and it is especially necessary to translate cultural use and slang. The current reality, of course, is often argued to be more complex than past ones, since 'electric information' or the web have a tendency to fragment events and on each search to offer some different information about an event, and it is often unclear whose point of view is being offered. And of course similar effects, beliefs, and practices have had an impact on the intelligence process throughout history. It is important to consider and discuss how these different media technologies have affected our own understandings and our interpretation of those of others.

In the developed world what are still considered traditional print media conform to machine and production time. This breaks process time into linear functions and departments, in which the industrialized process and the products being made are considered as one part of the overarching technology and repetitive machine industrialization. Critics of mass industrialization say these production processes are now just part of our physical and psychological make-up. Advocates suggest that this allows single sets of activities to be completed efficiently and effectively to unified standards. Some will say that this is one of the major manufacturing reasons why capitalism is so successful and should be protected and defended. Others who have followed this argument from a media perspective have concluded that one outcome from this development is that the process and products of print are often more important than any information contained within them. This argument suggests that even the delivery vehicle, the bound, printed paper of hard-copy books, newspapers, and magazines, is sometimes considered more important than the information contained within it. Instead of raising intellectual discussion often the media have fixed meaning and solidified thought while still apparently giving the impression of intellectual freedom. They appear to represent the ideal of free speech even though in reality this is sometimes what they restrict. What they often represent and symbolize is the writer's status, the owner's political and economic preference, and their cultural position, not necessarily their understanding. But in contrast to traditional print products, electronic information is often said to offer a new and burgeoning idea of freedom of expression and open information sources. And this argument is often used at the launch of any new media creation.

The different ways human perspectives adapt to communication and different forms of medium often produce fundamental misunderstandings about media's potential. This will often be caused by lack of applied system knowledge. These problems go to the roots of our attitudes and the analysis that we bring to many of the more complex issues of cultural understanding, and the effects they have on understanding different national intentions and beliefs. This process of course has an enormous impact on our understanding of our opposition and our enemies and therefore how we should collect and interpret the information used to create intelligence. These are not new problems but if we are to bring some clarity and real understanding to them then we have to get under the surface and revisit the circumstances that have built and instilled the understandings and misconceptions within our human outlook. Before going back to the roots let us consider a few recent examples.

Radio was initially disliked by the more traditionally oral parts of the community as is testified by an unnamed American farmer in Ken Burns's documentary about radio from his television series *America*. The farmer is heard to say harshly, 'I don't hold with it. I don't hold with furniture that talks.' Amusing as his comments may now sound, the farmer is not alone in this discussion; he does not like, and is morally shocked by, the 'furniture' he can have no argument with or control over. This he felt was especially true when the furniture tried to tell him what to think about and what the answer is. He engages daily with his own self-belief and sense of personal ownership, and thinks that the radio is an attack on his individualism and beliefs, which of course to some degree it is. Intellectually, he would have been supported by the Scottish Enlightenment, which America followed and used in part to ground its revolutionary break from the monarchical, social, and legal aristocratic hierarchy of England. There seems little doubt that, if they could have been asked, Socrates and Plato would have agreed wholeheartedly with the farmer's comments. Today, a significant number of intelligence analysts, commercial technologists, and government officials believe that the web is changing social groups, commercial organizations, and individuals and that none of us will ever be the same as we and our forebears were in the twentieth century. All of this, they believe, will have enormous implications for beliefs, culture, art, commerce, politics, and economics as we go forward. This electronic revolution within information and knowledge has only just begun and therefore, they would argue, it is difficult to tell what this might mean for the future. Yet some areas of human activity might provide suggestions of what this implies for our future and to see this we need to review certain aspects of our past and our intellectual beginnings.

Environmental Gossip

Early in their history humans, like many animals, made rudimentary verbal exchanges along with some more sophisticated communications using hands, feet, body, and localized environmental signals including stick rhythms, rock beating, shouting, chanting, singing, hand signals, mime, branch waving, rock throwing, smoke signals, and body painting. Then about 200,000 years ago there appears to have been a small radical change in a renegade gene FOXP2 that allowed and encouraged humans to start talking in a more structured way. FOXP2 can be found in a number of animals and the difference that is found in humans is apparently quite small—probably only two amino acids are different—yet when combined with other physical attributes such as being able to join the thumb and forefinger in a dedicated and (compared to other primates) very sophisticated way this attribute adds advantage and range to what humans can do. All of this and more combine with a sense of time, pattern recognition, and the imagination to see the future as a possible event. This meant that humans could join and hunt in groups with a clear sense of direction and possibilities.

Once successful the hunt gave them a store of meat that bought the tribe time for thought and creation.

Humans seem to have left the western coastal areas of Africa in a number of waves of migration that were probably initiated by tribal disputes, fights, changes in their understanding prompted by language, and also importantly by increasing numbers of humans and reducing food supplies, and by the movement of hunted animals and changes in the weather. All had an impact on and encouraged migration. As with all species some individuals take to experimentation and imaginative ideas quicker than others, while the majority tend to be developers or followers. This happened with speech, which was a step change in human development and rapidly began to separate humans from the pack. Not only did this biological accident alter communication, it also began the long process of improving memory and building tribal history. This process is still expanding and will continue to develop. It took thousands of years for the limited ancient languages to become the more sophisticated languages of today. We continue to make many improvements to the rudimentary elements of language and its written structure, to expand and improve its usefulness. One of the more obvious is the active creation of new words to expand our subtlety and descriptive understanding of reality and our intellectual and emotional responses. Within most people there is still a belief that language and speech are fixed and not to be played with or changed except perhaps in more playful and scatological ways. It took generations for languages to become embedded and primarily fixed and like all major changes this was both positive and negative: positive because faster development took place as they became more focused and culturally fixed but negative since the original creation becomes too procedurally managed and rooted in convention and constrains later innovation.

Originally, one, almost independent but very necessary, element is required to allow imaginative innovation to begin and that element is economically rich free time. This probably coincided with the beginnings of speech among the hunter-gatherers of eastern and central African savannahs where food was plentiful and the climate more temperate than today. This allowed tribes free time for consideration and creation. Circumstances add to these developments and there were individual and environmental reasons why speech development would have taken off faster in some tribes and individuals than others. On the edge of the savannah the course of rivers, the positioning of animal waterholes, and the height of hills or direction of mountain caves and shelters all contributed to some individuals' faster development. Some language and dialects would have been generated as descriptions of pathways, to outline the terrain as well as to articulate plans for the hunt. The cooking of vegetables and animals would have been mimicked, discussed, and sung about. Speech of course has its limitations, most obviously because it can only be used over relatively short distances, and dialectal issues restrict cross-tribal communication. Also, it only partially stored memories, which could easily be lost when a knowledgeable member of the community died, especially if this happened relatively early in their life. This was one of the reasons for building rhyming sentences, to improve the community's collective memory. A form of oral poetry was first used not for artistic purposes but to improve historic memory and to record how to solve complex practical problems that require each element to be started and finished in a particular sequence. Singing, beginning as chants during the hunt, stems and builds from this memory process. New communication methods rarely eradicate early ones and yet they tend to alter the old methods in ways that it is difficult to predict. The limitations of speech created new inventions, which built upon older markers that had been part of humanity's view of landscapes and geography, such as particular shapes in rocks or trees. This identification was used by humans long before speech and probably developed to indicate paths and significant sites. These ideas-as-markers started to be used to communicate history, events, important ideas, or places of significance and took on shapes and understandings associated with particular tribes. The development of counting followed a similar development through the allocation of stones for quantities and later the marking of trees, sticks, or rocks with strokes to represent numbers and the use of fingers to communicate them. All of these creations began to be formalized into what we now call symbols: representations of concepts, the most obvious of these like stars or crosses being later used for religious purposes.

The first recorded human thoughts and images have a very long history. They were presented in the artistic form of marks and images going back probably a lot further than what have come down to us as Stone Age cave paintings. Currently the oldest known cave paintings are at Chauvet in France, the age of which is debated and may be in the region of 35,000 years. Likewise, the purpose of this art is disputed but it may have been recorded so magic might increase the numbers of animals for the hunt, or to shock young hunters and engage them in the reality they were soon to experience. Deep underground, firelight would have been necessary both for their creation and for their dramatic appreciation. The cave paintings are still very potent and offer a picture over great distances of time of an artistic and past reality. However, they do not aim to systematically record events. Forms of sound communication developed very early in human history with different types of drumbeat being created in different locations. Perhaps because of its geographic isolation the drum did not develop in Australia, although sticks were used to produce a beat. The interesting thing of course is that the methods may differ but the underlying sense of rhythm for communal feel and memory was still required and invented. In some African tribes drums were and still are given a status similar to that which the later developing nations gave to manuscripts and books by putting them in libraries. Often tribal drums have their own drum house in which they 'live' while not being played. If you wish to upset a 'drum' tribe or cultural group you destroy their drum house, just as in the developed world you burn the tribe's books.

Humans have used many methods of indirect communication, from the development of petroglyphs—rock carvings—to arrangements of stones such as those used by the Inuit in Northern Canada where human-like statues are used as territorial boundaries or markers for significant places. In different places and at different times the human world went on to create pictograms, which represent objects or events by an image. This is an early form of writing. This was a technique of carving an idea or an event into, or painting it on, a surface. Later, pictograms were linked to tell a story over time. By 15,000 BCE there began to be links from symbols to writing with the creation of calendars and lists. And later still ideograms appear which develop communications by allowing far more subtlety to be captured in the symbol and these can represent concepts such as cold or night. The connection of images with words is also apparent in some of the early communication techniques of Ancient Egypt, where a pictorial symbol becomes a word and is used to represent an idea. All of this took place before the appearance of Chinese proto-writing around 6,000 BCE and the Middle Eastern, fully fledged writing system which is believed to have been invented in the Bronze Age, after 4,000 BCE. This Middle Eastern invention developed into cuneiform by the late third millennium BCE. The earliest forms of writing were based on exploiting elements of pictograms and ideograms to produce at least four major writing types: logographic (which is thought to be the oldest), syllabic, figural, and the later 'segmental', or alphabetic. All four systems tend to borrow and use elements from each other. A pictogram is a symbol often representing an object, an activity, a place, a concept, or an event. This is an idea being sent through drawings. Gradually pictograms evolve into ideograms or graphic symbols that represent an idea and so can pass on more abstract ideas such as a dark, open mouth conveying a sense of fear.

Academia has separated prehistory from history, defining writing as the catalyst for the change. The original Sumerian writing came from the use of clay tiles used to record a commodity. Account keeping developed as society and communications developed within villages and gradually memory was partially separated from the imagination and clearly represented as a collection of records and accounts. For the first time past activity was clearly modelled and value and debt put into symbols of local record. The first pure alphabet was created in about 2,000 BCE in Ancient Egypt, where they had been using elements of this alphabet for over a thousand years. For many centuries the alphabet spread (north from Egypt; in ripples from China) but most alphabets stem from these origins. More importantly, alphabets lend themselves to faster reproduction and ultimately the development of printing, something that held back the development of movable type in Korea (whose printers first created this innovation) where the writing was based on logographs, single characters representing a whole word. In Korea, as in Europe, the ruling classes saw printing, even in less sophisticated form, as something that would reduce their control: but that control was stronger in Korea than in Europe. This issue has affected every innovation in communication and is now part of web culture. Governments of all persuasions want and do control the media and the 'message' as far as they can. The important, underlying catalyst of Western development was the adoption of the alphabet. Different alphabets emerged from the Middle East and spawned

Hebrew, Greek, Cyrillic, and Roman versions. Not only did these alphabets make writing more accessible, they also gave printing with movable type far more mass development potential.

In 105AD the Chinese imperial court announced the invention of paper; by the sixth century AD Chinese engravers created a technique of wood-block printing; and by 850 AD they had made books with hardback covers and printed pages. By the twelfth century AD Pi Sheng, a Chinese alchemist and inventor, had created movable type; in 1157 the first paper mill was built in Spain; and in 1428 Laurens Janzoon printed the first prayer books with wooden typefaces. By the time of Gutenberg's European invention of mechanical printing using movable type and oil-based inks in the middle of the fifteenth century it is obvious which alphabet he would select from the number of languages he had from which to choose. Perhaps surprisingly, he did not choose a vernacular language, which would have opened up a much larger potential audience. He printed his Bible in the Latin alphabet, which meant it was positioned for a traditional audience—perhaps because he was hoping for acceptance by the church, the cultural elite, and also the traditional purchasers of bibles. Gutenberg also took care to create type designs for his Bible that ensured it had both a modern and a traditional look. These were to become known as Schwabacher and Textural typefaces. The printed version, which had 42 lines of print on each page, contained 1,282 pages and was bound in two and sometimes three volumes. Before completing the print run he showed some early bound copies to a group of aristocratic sympathisers at a fair in Frankfurt during the summer of 1455. His audience was very enthusiastic, giving him added confidence for his approach—this city later became the venue for the now famous Frankfurt Book Fair. In 1605 Johann Carolus created the first newspaper as a regular scheduled publication in Strasbourg, which was then part of the Holy Roman Empire. The first modern newspaper was the *Avisa*, which was published in Wolfenbüttel, Germany in 1609. As can be seen, the effects of German commerce and intellect on the early media were very significant. The Gutenberg invention triggered a printing revolution across Europe. German printing expanded to over 270 towns and cities by the beginning of the sixteenth century. The European output of printed books expanded from a few hundred in the latter part of the fifteenth century to over 1 billion a century by the end of the eighteenth.

Over the centuries we have recorded many types of information and understanding to create knowledge and beliefs and much of this information has been used to give governments, the military, and commercial organizations understanding and intelligence. We have used open and closed sources of information and have adapted and focused these using discussion, technology, and conversations with contacts. We have consistently collected, collated, and indexed information in large libraries, organizational files, and their data records. Individuals also, of course, have collected information and cultural records in many forms from books to CDs to electronic downloads and connections to music, television, film, and spoken news, views, and the arts. It is clear that for many centuries we have been engaging, using, and recording the ebb and flow of our thoughts, news, and understanding of the world within which we engage, although our individual analysis of its purpose is more modern.

By 2007 there were over 6,500 daily newspapers being delivered globally (of which nearly 1,500 were in the USA) and they were selling a combined total of nearly 400 million copies a day. The effects of the web and related technologies are now creating sharp declines in Western paper-publishing circulation and economics and many newspapers are in decline or have already closed, although others have taken on aspects of the new technology and economics and are surviving and growing. However this comes after other attacks on newsprint from radio and television, from which some of the press learned. All of these different modes of communication have played their part in the globalization of the media and the changes to the way in which we understand and view ourselves, and although the more traditional methods of delivery will certainly reduce, history suggests they will not go away.

Electronic Media and Modern Intelligence

Today, the vast amount of information supported on the web is far in excess of anything collected in the libraries of the past. From an intelligence perspective, the sheer quantities of the available imagery and data and of information are arresting. Estimates of the approximate size of the web currently run from around 15 billion to 1 trillion pages. And like your everyday thoughts that only partially run over highlights of your memory, most search engines trawl only the surface tides and waves; they rarely search the inner depths of the Deep Web. A search engine like Google searches only about 3 or 4 per cent of the entire web's content. Therefore 96–97 per cent of the Deep Web, most of which is free to use, is often unexplored. The Deep Web will be reviewed in more depth later, in Chapter Four.

Currently, analysts and intelligence practitioners have to engage with this information overload, which has expanded at an explosive rate and is altering their views, but the theoretical models for intelligence creation remain largely unaltered. Within the intelligence process, the organization that reviews the information, analyses the data, and creates intelligence, and its secrecy are often considered the defining elements that separate intelligence from information. Throughout the ages different types of information, different media, different informants, and changing methods of technological collection and analysis have been employed, and these have altered the perspective over what has been interpreted as intelligence. Defining intelligence in terms of secrecy has obvious advantages in conflicts and has proven useful when targeting people considered potential threats and in countering imminent surprises; as well, secret intelligence about the enemy or competition is useful in difficult negotiations. However this has also tended to reduce the larger possible perspective of the intelligence picture. One of the major purposes of intelligence is to give short-, medium-, and long-term perspective to policymakers' understanding of a current situation, and to offer them specific, perhaps secret, advantageous knowledge. It is to give advantage in competitive, pre-conflict, conflict, post-conflict, and macro-economic situations. The broader definitions of intelligence have often been lost or ignored, while policy and current politics take the foreground. Often the reasoning is that time is of the essence and history does not apply, since the current situation is different and changes the thinking.

Intelligence processes do not just aim to ensure national security, as is often claimed; sometimes they are deliberately shifted to help ensure that a particular government's foreign policy is supported or a strategic viewpoint is maintained. The intelligence at the outset of the Iraq war surrounding weapons of mass destruction and the 45-minute warning are still debated. Here UK government policy to support the USA and the potential need to protect the gathering of oil supplies played their part. The UK intelligence services and the UK government collided over which policy and which intelligence to follow, and over what aspects of different intelligence supported which policy. The cultural influences within intelligence organizations have always attracted debate and argument, as they do within the staff of any large organization. Bias and saying what others want to hear are major issues. The recent appointment of General Petraeus to head the CIA is interesting to note, as he made a point of speaking to his new, large team of people immediately after he was appointed, and he soon hit this long-standing debate in particular:

> We don't do the President any favors unless we give him the clearest picture possible of whatever issue he's facing. ... please feel free to tell it to me straight; in fact, feel obligated to do so. There should not be a case when someone walks out of my office, or the deputy's, or any of the other senior offices, and says, 'Man, I wish I had said ...' whatever. That should not happen.[1]

Today's intelligence analysis can also become overwhelmed by the sheer quantities of available information. There is now an overload of information and data tending to make collection sometimes seem more important than analysis. New software and different technologies are and will be used to analyse data, but intelligence never was just about the collection, analysis, and dissemination of information. Certainly policymakers see judgement as their part of the process, and one that is often more relevant than the information or intelligence itself. Both from the analyst's perspective and that of the policymaker, these processes are rarely seen as just set pieces of academic analysis. The intelligence outcome can be as much an art as a science and unfortunately can sometimes include propaganda, unintentional, and intentional bias as well as clear, objective judgements. Given the decision timescales involved, all of these elements need to be balanced

---

[1] Excerpts from remarks made by David H. Petraeus, Director of the Central Intelligence Agency, at his first agency address, 6 September 2011. Available at <http://www.cia.gov>.

quite quickly in order to reach a decision. Within an intelligence organization's structure and culture process tends to reflect the times and purposes for which the organization was constructed. Every discipline, as Nietzsche said, and I purposely repeat, is constrained by what it forbids its practitioners to do. Disciplines and the internal culture of any organization have implicit, often unspoken rules, on the way operations use thought and creative imagination, and the rules surrounding intelligence and the organizations that attempt to produce it are no different. We often tend to look at the world through the eyes of our parents, friends, and grandparents, and the structures and organizations of our larger bureaucracies continue to have an underlying similarity to the past. Today a broad range of policymakers, from country leaders, politicians, and law enforcement commanders, to CEOs of commercial organizations now use what they term intelligence. The objective is still seen as to gain advantage in everything, from war to commercial competition. This kind of thinking and action goes back as far as society. Although individuals might not necessarily call it intelligence, they seek advantage by using information gleaned from gossip and conversation, as well as from whatever media, technology, or covert methods are available.

In discussion with myself after meeting at a conference in Belgium in October 2011, Ilan Mizrahi of Mossad Intelligence summed up his viewpoint as follows:

> Circumstances, technology, and human nature are the three important pillars when dealing with intelligence. Currently circumstances and technology are changing rapidly, yet human nature is not. The present problem of radical increasing information and therefore increases in the growth of intelligence will continue to get bigger. Therefore as a starting point we need to clearly define national security. It seems we need a broader definition of what we mean by national security as what now tends to get incorporated within this arena has significantly increased. From this we will need to receive more precise PIR (Precise Information/Intelligence Requirements) from decision makers. Open sources will contribute to decision makers' beliefs that now when they are much more educated they need less analysis from intelligence organization[s] but at the same time their dependence on intelligence organizations will increase to supply them with more information. Intelligence organizations will continue to prefer secret information because professionally they are well aware of its biases and manipulations but also because to not promote it threatens their unique position with decision makers. Open sources today have the potential to contribute to tactical-operational and strategic trends and processes. And this will alter some organizations as giant quantities of information in Twitter and Facebook will need those youngsters who understand it much better than the traditional manpower but still are we really ready to recruit 16 to 18-year-olds to the services or outsource their services? The weakest point standing in front of these oceans of information will be the human nature aspects of collecting, analysis and dissemination.

3

The Written History of Intelligence

Since social history has been recorded, the collection, interpretation, analysis, and actions based on different forms of intelligence has been seen as part of government, the military, and more recently business.

This chapter discusses military intelligence and some of the many prominent books and concepts from the Chinese military classic through to the traditional intelligence cycle and the more recent business intelligence model.

Military Intelligence

Military intelligence (MI) is considered the original creation and purpose of the intelligence process and is defined as providing information and analysis to help the commander make more effective decisions in times of conflict. Historically, therefore, warfare was seen as the birthplace of intelligence. Yet the methods used to attack and counter and the attempts to predict enemy actions probably go back originally to our tribal ancestors and their organized hunting strategies.

The first recorded and published intelligence methods and processes that are still available to us are Chinese. These documents give a background to a long history of MI and information use. Much of it is still relevant today, especially to understand conflicts in developing nations and societies. In China the mounted farmer became a warrior. These new armies used knives, bows, and spears from prehistoric hunting. Usually the object of the conflict was to maintain or get control of hunting and agricultural states in order to grow the area of dominance and become increasingly self-sufficient. Often the underlying objective of the conflict was to be able to look to the horizon with knowledge of and a sense of secure control over the whole area.

Through the centuries different methods were explored and employed, which have been formalized into three levels of military intelligence: strategic, operational, and tactical. These are broadly separated by the time, the distances, and the intentions being viewed. Traditionally, these understandings are based on a current or intended battle environment. The first of these three types of intelligence is *strategic* and this is intended to be a planning process and a way of getting a large picture of what might be of concern within the broader aspects of war in general rather than specific battles. The process will consider the political perspective, the intended outcome, and how this can be achieved. Intelligence can be used to form a strategic, broader understanding of the current reality: the geography, society, government, and particular organizations, groups, or individual intentions, their probable actions and potential threats. Intelligence might also suggest counter-methods, espionage, or prevention and what might be the outcomes if nothing is done to stop or change the enemy's intentions and actions. Aspects of this broader strategic vision may be longer and considered over a number of years, and in stages this will feed into the operational and even into some aspects of the tactical intelligence operations. In the strategic outlook everything from the operational environment, the seasonal weather, the geography, the hostile, friendly, or neutral forces, to local communities and the supply chains, the commanders, and the intentions of the enemy, will be considered. Strategic intelligence therefore is often focused on the broader issues of the state, down to personalities and preferences, faults of the command, the size of the population and the support systems, the state's technology, and the defence and attack weapons available.

The second type of military intelligence is *operational* and this usually examines a much shorter period: a few weeks, perhaps a few days. It is focused on particular and specific aspects of the broader strategic operation. Operational intelligence is used to support large groups of troops. The commander is briefed and will ask for intelligence and once in operation will be expected to offer information and intelligence back to headquarters and the senior command.

The third type of military intelligence is *tactical* information/intelligence, which is often laid over operational intelligence. It is faster and often 'of the moment' within an action or battle taking place. It is about current enemy actions and presumed intentions. Tactical intelligence aims to support military operations on the ground and is short-term and precise in its effectiveness. Intelligence will be given to patrol and attack groups and, once they return or can access communications, then exchanges of information and intelligence will take place. Tactical intelligence is tasked to support a force commander and is there to assist and support battle operations. Communication and surveillance systems (or lack of them) often play a significant and crucial role in the way in which this process is used and what affects it. Often the time frame may be the only real difference between operational and tactical intelligence. At times in a combat zone the emphasis on tactical and operational intelligence may change and be quite fluid as the nature of the combat alters.

Since the beginning of organized warfare the role of intelligence has often been seen as crucial. Understanding the landscape, the weather, the local communities, the numbers of opposing troops, their equipment and their commanders, their protection systems, and their fighting history—all and more are important for the commander and his officers. And from these observations of the area and the enemy, spying and talk with the locals (data collection), intelligence has been traditionally created for specific actions.

Chinese Military Intelligence

The Art of War is attributed to Sun Tzu who is also referred to as Sun Wu and Sunzi and was thought to have been a senior commander in the later part of the 6th century BCE. This is the most successful book ever published about military strategy and tactics and is still read and referred to in many military academies, intelligence circles, and business schools today. It suggests that war is a combination of strategy and tactical understanding, and even its title suggests that warfare is closer to an art than a science. The reason suggested is that, unlike science, warfare sees personalities and groups attempting to interpret and control the environment, the enemy, and the military mix. Planning and understanding the changing environment within which you are working is very important. But Sun Tzu's view of planning was not to build a strategy and then blindly overlay this on the environment within which you are working, but to react and change with that environment and the people you are working with and are up against. In this environment planning is continuous adjustment, reconsideration, and action. Static strategic planning works in a longer-term or more controlled landscape, but when you are faced with a continuously changing environment competing plans collide, refocusing and completely altering the engaging and surrounding reality. *The Art of War* contains 13 chapters or sections. These include planning, war, offensive attack planning, tactical positioning, power, weakness and substance, combat, nine changes to tactics (which include moving the army), understanding the weakness and strengths of the enemy, the use of different weapons, using the environment as a weapon, and the use of intelligence, information sources, and spies. As often happens with older texts, *The Art of War*'s writing history has been challenged and argued about, but versions of the book exist in roughly its current form since at least the later part of the Warring States period, which ran from roughly 475 BCE to about 220 BCE. Battles using 1,000 chariots and over 100,000 men first took place within the Warring States, but this was after Sun Tzu's time (see below) and so the book was probably changed and added to at least up until the period of these major battles. And intelligence, as a concept, is often considered to begin with Sun Tzu, a general and strategist who wrote the book in the late Spring Autumn Period of the Chinese civil wars around 520 BCE. The Spring Autumn Period began in 771 BCE, lasted until 476 BCE, and was linked to the first half of the Eastern Zhou Dynasty.

Warfare for Sun Tzu was an art. It has five factors that he believed should be reviewed when beginning a war. They are moral law, Heaven, Earth, the commander, and method and discipline. Moral law aims to ensure that the soldiers and the people completely support their ruler even when in danger. Heaven is the requirement to take the seasons, the time of day, and weather into account. Earth means understanding the geography and its dangers (marsh, mountains, rivers, narrow passes, and open ground): all should be considered and included in plans of attack or defence. The commander must be seen to be virtuous, benevolent, strict, sincere, and courageous. By method and discipline the army will be well maintained and organized into divisions and ranks. Good roads will support the supplies and there will be a system accounting for expenditure and budgets to keep track of the economics.

For Sun Tzu spies were a very important part of the art of war and he classified five types of spy in his book. For him these are important aspects of foreknowledge or intelligence. This foreknowledge does not come out of the air or from spirits, but is factually based and only comes from other people. And therefore spies are used to obtain and communicate this information and potential intelligence to the commander. The five types of spy are locals, and inward, converted, doomed, and surviving spies. When they are working as a system for the commander they can be seen as a 'divine' or perfect system. Local means the inhabitants of a district. Inward spies are within the opposition's organization. Converted spies are enemies that can be turned into double agents. Doomed spies are purposely meant to come to the enemy's knowledge, so that the enemy gets wrong information from them. Surviving spies bring back information about the enemy's camp.

After the invention of movable type *The Art of War* was included in the *Seven Military Classics* and published as the military textbook.[1] Subsequently and more recently as a well-known text it has been used as the basis for analysis of other disciplines including business, negotiation, and law. However, the book's reputation comes from a variety of famous leaders quoting or saying they had been inspired by Sun Tzu, from Napoleon and Mao Zedong to Douglas MacArthur. During the different conflicts in Vietnam, the Vietcong claimed to have implemented tactics from *The Art of War* against the French and then against the Americans, and General Vo Nguyen Giap, the Vietcong's principal commander, said he used the thoughts of Sun Tzu to win in the Vietnam War that stretched from 1955 to 1975.

Although Sun Tzu's *Art of War* is usually referred to as the start of military intelligence, it was one of seven books that put military intelligence into effective government use in China. The Seven Military Classics of China are *Six Secret Teachings of Jiang Ziya*, *The Methods of the Sima*, *The Art of War*, *Wuzi* by Wu Qi, *Wei Liaozi*, *Three Strategies of Huang Shigong* and *Questions and Replies between Tang*

---

[1] Ralph D. Sawyer, *The Seven Military Classics of Ancient China* (New York: Basic Books, 2007, p. 38).

Taizong and Li Weigon. Published military intelligence begins with the *Six Secret Teachings*, a treatise on civil and military strategy traditionally attributed to the legendary military strategist Jiang Ziya, who is also known as Tia Gong Wang, of the 11th century BCE. Jiang Ziya discusses the Six Secret Teachings with King Wen and the book is written with revolution as its purpose. It describes how the kingdom can be organized to create future growth:

> Moral, effective government is the basis for survival and the foundation for warfare. The state must thrive economically while limiting expenditures, foster appropriate values and behavior among the populace, implement rewards and punishments, employ the worthy, and refrain from disturbing and harming the people.[2]

Most governments would claim these as their value system and often ignore the effects of their own bias when they vary these principles. The first two sections of the book are discursive and strategic, forming a background to the next four chapters, which are tactical. The book begins with a broader picture in an engaging, story-telling style that an intelligence analyst might still use to engage the policymaker. The text discusses how the economy and the future can be improved whilst the future rule and role of the king stabilizes. The second section, called 'Military Strategy', suggests that an attacker must try to overwhelm the weaker parts of the army and society associated with the enemy using propaganda and manipulation. This is the 'hearts and minds' scenario. This strategy, which of course has been employed by all governments and organizations in many forms and with varying degrees of success, teaches commanders to achieve victory without warfare. It teaches commanders to outwit opponents through diplomacy, news control, and manipulation. The next chapter, 'the *Dragon Strategy*', talks about the different military operations, how commanders should operate these processes, and how to create a system of rewards and punishments in order to maintain a commander's authority. This chapter also discusses military communication, the need for secrecy of command, and how to get intelligence about the enemy. This is the first published reference specifically about intelligence.

The fourth chapter of the book, known as 'the *Tiger Strategy*', talks about equipment, tactics, and the most important aspects of command. Much of the chapter talks about effective retreat from difficult situations. It puts high importance on counter-intelligence techniques and emphasizes the use of speed and manoeuvrability. This section emphasizes that a commander must guard against laxity within the ranks and must be constantly engaged with and act in accordance with ever-changing conditions. A commander must observe and utilize the effects and interactions of variables such as weather, terrain, and human psychology in order to achieve success. The fifth section, 'the *Leopard Strategy*', discusses geography and how tactical planning must really engage with intelligence about the landscape of the battle space. The final, sixth section is 'the *Dog Strategy*',

---

[2] Ralph D. Sawyer, *The Seven Military Classics of Ancient China* (New York: Basic Books, 2007, p. 38).

which discusses a range of different strategic and tactical operations. Probably one of the more profound parts talks about the use of chariots, infantry, and cavalry, both tactically and strategically. Like other sections this chapter stresses the need to understand the enemy's weaknesses and how these can be effectively turned to advantage. Also discussed is the importance of the choices of your own troops and that these choices must be accurately based on their effectiveness and talent, particularly on how effective they are as cavalry. The Dog Strategy also emphasizes that as a commander you should never attack an enemy whose morale is high; that the commander must time a concentrated attack for when the moment is right.

The second book in the Classic series, entitled *The Methods of the Sima*, lays out government and military administration, laws, and strategy. The book was written during the 4th century BCE during the Warring States period. This work describes how to build a military administration rather than strategic command. It suggests that war is a necessary outcome to maintain peace and power. It says that there is a balance of power to be maintained between peace and war and that to ignore the need for the military will result in the state failing, just as too much warfare will destroy peaceful growth. The lord or king must find that balance. It explains that the purpose of war is to achieve a civil working life for the average citizen and that ceremonies at the outset of war should make clear how significant this approach to peace is. People must act and understand the differences between how they act when they are civilians and how they must act when they are soldiers.

The fourth Classic, *Wuzi* by Wu Qi, is thought to have been written about 440 BCE and is considered to be one book from a two-volume work. *Wuzi* contains six parts, each analysing different aspect of military strategy and tactics: planning for the state; evaluating the enemy; controlling the army; the *Tao* of the General; responding to change; and stimulating the officers. Wu Qi is thought to have spent three years as a Confucian student. He puts a lot of emphasis on the training and use of cavalry (chariots and horses). The *Wuzi* explains that the commander should apply different strategies and tactics based on geography, the local weather, the equipment, training, and social outlook of the opposing army, and the enemy commander's background and personality. Collecting and analysing this information and intelligence should remain secret. The fifth Classic, *Wei Liaozi,* suggests that the ruler use both a social and a military strategy. It states that people and agriculture are the driving forces of a society and that these should be built and provided for using social and humanitarian values and practices. The structure of the sixth Classic, *Three Strategies of Huang Shigong*, is (as the title suggests) in three parts. The first states that once in command a leader must be followed without question or interruption; must be heroic, clear, and fast in action; and should treat his people well. The second requires him to respond to changing reality and not assume knowledge from other experiences in his past. He must use current intelligence and change actions where and when necessary. In the third he must understand the people and commanders around him and use the most useful and experienced in official positions. The argument in the book is similar to some of the other Chinese Classics in saying that long-drawn-out campaigns must be avoided. Speed and efficiency should be the driving forces of military engagement. Finally, the content of the seventh Classic, *Questions and Replies between Tang Taizong and Li Weigong*, seems to be based on a real discussion of experiences of battles between Li Jing (571–649 AD) and Emperor Taizong (599–649 AD). It is more modern in date than the other Classics, coming from a period when weaponry was made of iron and steel and the use of chariots had stopped (or in which they were not considered as important as they had been in the earlier books). The book is an analysis of strategies and tactics that had been used and employed in earlier battles and discusses particular tactics (speed, flanking, and frontal attacks).

After the *Seven Military Classics* of China one of the next most important early Chinese books on military strategy is the *Art of War* by Sun Bin, who is supposed to have been a descendant of Sun Tzu. The book was apparently composed of 89 chapters with a selection of pictures attached, but a complete version of the book does not exist. The sections of the book that we have stress tactical issues for success and talk about respect for the commander, understanding and practice of the arts of war, and the sensible use of spies.

Ancient Mediterranean Military Intelligence

The Egyptians, the Greeks, and the Romans all used different types of intelligence to maintain their position, extend their control, and to review each other's activities. And all made significant and focused use of spies. Egyptian hieroglyphs suggest the presence of court spies and that Pharaohs employed spying techniques to entrap foreign agents. The Egyptians also employed spies to research and to gain information and intelligence on foreign countries' governments, commerce, and social groups so they might conquer them, and gain land, trade routes, and slaves. The Greeks employed spying and deception as a common method of operation and this practice was translated into their literature and became part of their traditional story-telling (such as the Trojan Horse). During the period of the Greek city-states intrigue and spying was often employed to understand the enemy's defences and capabilities. Later, the Romans learned from Greek military history. They also spied on their neighbours and aspects of this intelligence helped them gradually to create the largest state in ancient times. They created a secret service known as the Frumentarii, uniformed individuals attached to a legion whose main work was to ensure the legion had enough supplies. They travelled and used spies to understand local communities, and find out where supplies could be taken or bought. This process was used to assess resistance levels within local communities and inform the military's engagement practices. Gradually the Frumentarii became the secret police of the Roman military and thus important in the implementation of propaganda, news restriction, and censorship of information. They mapped the geography of the areas through which the armies would travel, and would research the size of the enemy army and its capabilities. In the 3rd century AD the 51st Roman emperor Diocletian closed down the Frumentarii, which gained him a lot of popular support since they had become a feared institution that spied on friends as well as enemies. However a new group was created, known as the Agentes in Rebus, which became more organized and effective. Originally these were couriers but gradually their work became far broader, their service became militarized, and they were divided into five ranks. The 6th-century historian Procopius wrote in his *Secret History* that the emperors used the Agentes as intelligence officers, ordering them to gain enemy information as well as geographic, social, financial, and cultural information about local governors and the community they governed. The Agentes became known as 'sheep dogs that had joined the wolf pack', a description created by the 4th-century philosopher Libanius. As their experience and intelligence operations increased they were given wider roles and responsibilities, including Customs and the supervision of large government building projects.

The military intelligence process is generally driven by instruction and understanding of the commander's information requirements and aims to offer information, intelligence, and analysis that helps them view, decide on, and direct effective actions. The process, which is the beginning of the intelligence cycle, should also help to clarify and focus future information requirements. As others had done before and since, the Romans borrowed ideas from the Greeks and the Egyptians. Always the purpose has been to gather and analyse information that contains or can be made into intelligence about friend or foe. The object is to be able to understand the current picture better, to operate with it more purposefully, and occasionally to map or 'predict' the future. The process is about gaining an understanding of the present with the aim to improve current plans and actions. Some of this analysed data may help us to know and predict the intentions and potential future actions of friends or foes.

Machiavelli's *The Prince*

In the early 16th century Niccolo Machiavelli, an Italian diplomat, historian, and political theorist, wrote *The Prince*. It was a treatise intended to explain to a new leader the strategy for staying in power and Machiavelli hoped it would serve as a tool to get him back into aristocratic and government favour. The book says that immoral or criminal behaviour by the prince should be understood in terms of effectiveness for maintaining power and that such behaviour should certainly be used if considered necessary for staying in power. The general theme of the book is to promote a type of scientific reality rather than a mystical idealist philosophy, but the way in which this is done in *The Prince*, which was not published in book form until 1532, five years after Machiavelli's death, meant that it was criticized for immorality. Aspects of this criticism seem justified but the realism with which the author approaches the subject is striking: he does not leave outcomes to fortune and chance but is rigorously analytical and directly practical in his methodologies. The book does not discuss ethical righteousness or virtue but suggests what is best for the ruling elite, at that point in time the Medici family. Machiavelli promotes the idea of effective fortification of cities, so that if they are attacked they can be defended well, and warns against using mercenaries which he believes are not as effective, and more cowardly, than troops engaged from the prince's own citizens. He says that even if they win mercenaries will expect financial benefits that become progressively more difficult to afford. The book had a direct effect on many of the rulers of the time and soon after its completion the new publishing technology of movable type allowed books to be published far faster than previously, and distributed internationally. The book exerted influence on Charles I of Spain and Henry VIII of England.

Machiavelli also wrote the *Art of War*, which was written after *The Prince* and echoes many of the themes of the previous, more influential book. *Art of War* is written as a Socratic dialogue promoting the use of the military as the roof on the princely palace without which the contents and personnel inside cannot be protected.

Carl von Clausewitz took part in the Napoleonic Wars as an officer and an analyst, and later defined military intelligence as 'all the knowledge which we have of the enemy and his country'. The commander has to select and sift intelligence in the thick of war and this calls for an experienced, analytical, and historically aware person. Clausewitz says 'what is required of an officer is a certain power of discrimination, which only knowledge of men and things and good judgement can give'. It is the combination of intelligence, and the commander's understanding and judgement, that Clausewitz viewed as the crucial requirements that together offer some clarity in the fog of war. He defined strategy as the way battles and scrimmages are planned, since they form a crucial part of the overall military involvement with the enemy. He said strategy was 'the use of engagements for the object of war'. An experienced soldier and officer himself, he held that war was an important way of extending politics using a different method. He did not believe that, as some in the Enlightenment had argued, war is a form of chaos that is without structure. He said that war can and should be a systematic and controlled use of an overriding argument. For him intelligence was military in nature, extremely relevant and necessary, although some of it could be inaccurate or false because it is often coloured and tainted by the fog of war. It is also very dependent upon who is collecting and analysing the information that becomes intelligence. It is vital that the commander understands the bias and character of the information collectors and analysts when making choices and selecting which intelligence will be used and what questions and other interpretation might be needed to clarify its use.

> By the word 'Information', we denote all the knowledge which we have of the enemy and his country; therefore, in fact, the foundation of all our ideas and actions...[A] great part of the information obtained in war is contradictory, a still greater part is false, and by far the greatest part is of a doubtful character.

This is part of the opening of Chapter VI of '*Information in War*' from Clausewitz's *On War*. It suggests how far the author's experience of war, including the Napoleonic Wars of 1805–12, defined his views on strategy and intelligence, making these very much part of the moment and rarely something that is complete at a time of contemplation. War, strategy, and intelligence were for Clausewitz part of the same intellectual conundrum. However, he also saw intelligence as providing a defensive advantage:

> We shall only notice one point, which is of the highest importance in war, that is intelligence, not so much special, great and important information through persons employed, as that respecting the innumerable little matters in connection with which the daily service of an army is carried on in uncertainty, and with regard to which a good understanding with the inhabitants gives the defensive a general advantage. *On War*, Book IV, Chapter 6.

The Intelligence Cycle

The intelligence process has traditionally been seen in two parts: the policymaker asks for information on a particular subject and a subordinate provides the relevant 'intelligence'. The purpose of the intelligence is to offer a unique insight into the issue being discussed. Therefore the intelligence process or 'cycle' (as the process has become to be known) has at its start the commander or policymaker requesting particular information and the analyst then collecting and analysing data and information and hopefully bringing back what is perceived to be the answer to the master's earlier request. This will include information classified as 'intelligence' and it is this unique, often secret, information that potentially gives the commander advantage over the situation or the opposition.

The intelligence cycle, as shown in Figure 3.1, comes from an American model created in the 1920s and is a production-based process, which has a mechanical sequence similar to a manufacturing production-line principle. By 1926 military intelligence in the USA was said to operate by requirement, collection, utilization (analysis), and dissemination. The commander set the mission and this determined the direction of the collection effort, which moved from collecting to processing to use of information. As an overarching model, for most command structures there is little wrong with the theoretical outline. In practice the sequence can become cross-connected and is occasionally broken during the working process. This is of course true of most theoretical models when reality meets theory and the intelligence cycle is no exception: it is operated to suit the players and the particular actions being undertaken. Also, the cycle model does not suggest any problems with the relationship between the analyst and policymaker, who are traditionally seen as commander and assistant, or in some instances master and servant, yet these relationships have had their share of disputes and personality clashes. As one former US intelligence agency director said when discussing the relationship between policymakers and agency analysts, 'we be's—

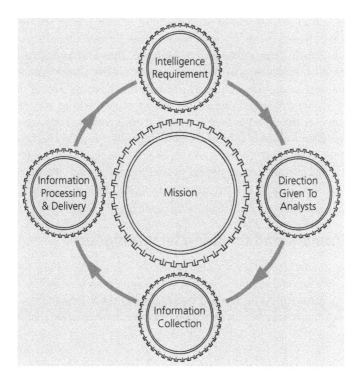

Figure 3.1 The intelligence cycle

we've been here since before you got here and we'll be here long after you're gone'.[3] This relationship and the lack of it between policymakers and analysts, along with their preferred bias and opinion, will be discussed in Chapter Seven.

In recent times the intelligence cycle and the definitions of intelligence have broadened and the word intelligence has been used when giving government or commercial policymakers a strategic picture of the national political or commercial situation. Today the theory and concepts of intelligence are used in many other fields and are not restricted to the military, government, the corporate sector, and the intelligence agencies. Often the commercial perspective includes international markets and the geopolitical and macro-economic landscape, and the discussions taking place are focused by what has been termed Business Intelligence methods. Now police and law enforcement, non-government organizations (NGOs), and smaller commercial, non-profit, and charitable businesses use many of these strategic and tactical intelligence and planning techniques. But to understand the basis of what intelligence is attempting to achieve we first need to understand the original intention and purpose of the intelligence cycle.

---

[3] William Nolte, 'On-going Reform in Intelligence Practices' (2008) *Harvard Journal of Legislation*, p. 211.

The cycle is a formal master–servant relationship model, which has been given a production-based process. It has a mechanical sequence similar to a manufacturing production line. And as an overarching outline there was, and still to a reasonable degree is, little wrong with the theoretical outline, even despite the objections raised above. This model was formalized into a theoretical process at the end of the Second World War and during the early years of the Cold War. Today, the linear aspect of the cycle has been interrupted, reversed, and cross-referenced to a degree that has thrown this model into question. With the changing nature of potential and current conflicts and issues and policymakers' need for prompt and accurate information (brought on by the Information Revolution), the intelligence cycle is now in need of assistance and additional material.

Government and Commercial Intelligence

Stepping forward from military intelligence we can see there have been many genuine debates and arguments about what constitutes intelligence outside a battle environment. At other, more peaceful times the information and intelligence requirement might be for a national or broader international strategic perspective and this type of intelligence has become something that commercial organizations use to understand the current environment, to anticipate market changes, and to bring about their own commercial and organizational changes.

In the government environment different types of intelligence will often be used to review the political and economic realities being faced. These will include the effective military capabilities and intentions of foreign nations, whether friend, neutral, or foe. Intelligence agencies, governments, and policymakers will use intelligence methods to look at the overall international space and to plan their future initiatives. Traditionally, government intelligence originated from open, diplomatic sources and covert, spy material; only later did it include technological, cultural, or sociological sources. This information may imply environmental, geographical, and industrial capabilities and within the collected data and information some will be secret. All of this interpreted data is what is used to support a political leader's decision-making process and will often be termed intelligence.

More recently, the business and commercial world has begun formalizing the use of intelligence in its strategic planning and has started to use the term Business Intelligence (BI). This type of specific intelligence may come down to information that offers competitive advantages, local marketplace discussions, or arguments over pricing policy. A senior IBM researcher, Hans Peter Luhn, wrote an article in 1958 in which he defined BI as 'the ability to apprehend the interrelationships of presented facts in such a way as to guide action towards a desired goal'.[4] Adding to this, in the 1960s Luhn created the concept Selective

---

[4] H.P. Luhn, 'A Business Intelligence System', (1958) *IBM Journal* Vol 2, No 4, pp 314–319.

Dissemination of Information (SDI). He sent different, personalized, specific, work-focused information to a large group of army scientists and engineers. Each received aspects of the information base that directly related to their work. At the time the information was sent by post and the whole process proved too expensive, but the concept of SDI is still very important and we will return to it later in the book.

BI came out of the 1960s and through the 1980s was seen in terms of computer models that aimed to engage with management decision-making and strategic planning techniques. More recently Howard Dresner of the Gartner Group described BI as an umbrella term used to improve business decisions by using fact-based analysis. Currently the Business Intelligence Channel has stated what they see as the aim of BI: 'Business intelligence is the process of making better decisions in an environment that provides data and reporting that is timely, reliable, consistent and understandable in a useful format or presentation.'[5] Chapter Ten focuses on BI and discusses different elements and methods of BI in far more depth.

As can be seen from the different uses of the term intelligence, there is no fixed definition for it and its construction has been the subject of debate. As Julian Richards has argued in his book, *The Art and Science of Intelligence*, as a concept intelligence is not a science, concerned solely with data collection and analysis of the secret and available information, data, and imagery. Nor is it solely an art, perceived as an interpretation of the current situation viewed from a particular analytical perspective. It has elements of both factual and psychological perspectives. This debate is similar to the arguments and discussions surrounding definitions of philosophy, which Bertrand Russell considered was neither a science nor a religion, but floats somewhere between the two. Like science philosophy is based on reason but like religion it tries to find answers to larger and broader questions and test meta-theories. So, intelligence is not seen just as data or information nor is it seen solely as interpretation or opinion—yet it certainly has elements of both.

In 1964 Sherman Kent, one of the fathers and primary technicians of US intelligence practice, discussed the problem of language usage in the intelligence cycle. In *Words of Estimative Probability,* Kent discussed the problems of agreeing what particular words like 'probably' or 'almost certainly' mean in terms of the likelihood that something might or might not happen. He distinguished the gap between different thinkers and analysts, likening some differences to that between 'mathematicians' and 'poets'. Definitions of intelligence and how it might differ from information or opinion have a long history and have created a number of arguments surrounding definitions. However, its purpose is more generally agreed and most observers often reflect consciously, or not, on Sun Tzu's book. In doing so they regard the prime purpose of intelligence as being to

---

5 Available at <http://www.information-management.com>.

counter surprise by forewarning, as summed up by Arthur S. Hulnick: 'Nothing is more important in the world of intelligence than preventing surprise.'[6]

Over nearly 65 years since the US formal inception of the intelligence cycle the threats to the USA and to all developed and developing nations have altered considerably and what was efficient and effective in the Cold War is in need of new and additional methods to stay in touch with policymakers' changing agendas and for the intelligence process to stay effective. We now have mobile phones and an interconnected civil and military aviation industry. We have insurgency, international crime, and terrorism as well as more traditional types of conflict and warfare and the Cold War's atomic and hydrogen bombs, and of course we now have drones that use electronic bomb targeting, and cyber attacks. Now the public and policymakers get information, news, gossip, and advertising at the touch of a screen or voice connection as they travel extremely quickly around their country and the globe. And far more frequently than in the past the public distrusts the established areas of authority and are concerned about not only the areas mentioned in this paragraph but also such global issues as the environment, financial crisis, people trafficking, computer hacking, and privacy.

In part the traditional, strategic enemies have changed and government control has been brought under enormous and conflicting pressure from the tsunami of information and technology that continues to expand its influence. This has brought pressures on the capacity of the intelligence agencies, the military, the police, and commercial strategic organizations to analyse and understand the vast quantities of data now available. And all of these changes are again altering the nature and dimensions of many intelligence organizations' purpose and process. One of these broader changes is a new version of globalization and the significant effects of this on the intelligence process will now be discussed.

---

[6] 'Indications and Warning for Homeland Security: Seeking a New Paradigm', (2005) 18(4) International Journal of Intelligence and Counter Intelligence, pp. 593–608.

PART TWO

Post-modern Information, Knowledge, 'Truth', and Intelligence

The second section of this book reviews the current changes that intelligence and its strategic perspective are experiencing and some of the background that often is not made clear enough to current practitioners. This is an aspect of mosaic intelligence; a background that is required to put current intelligence into perspective.

Chapter Four discusses the changes to globalization that have altered relationships or made other realignments come to prominence since the apparent ending of the Cold War. The reshaping of the political landscape and the way in which this has altered the global economy, the macro-economics, and the geopolitics, along with linked and networked communication and information, have altered our perspective and actions. The global economy has an interconnected variety of law, cultural and commercial practices, political concepts, and working practices that tend to make trading fluid, difficult, and restricted, depending upon your national government's relationships, your company's country's status, and who you are as individuals in the senior ranks of your culture.

Chapter Five reviews some of the new information sources and the darker side of globalization, as President Clinton described the increase in global insurgency, cyber warfare, and terror. There are also the Deep Web and the Dark Web. The Dark Web represents the largest share of the electronic information on the web and amounts to between 96 per cent and 97 per cent of the web's content. Popular engines such as Google and Bing each in their different ways find some different results but together they and other popular search engines only cover 3 or 4 per cent of the web. The Deep Web contains vast quantities of unstructured information and data that is mainly unsearched, yet may easily be penetrated if only different search engines are employed, and is mostly free to access. Chapter Five also explores the Dark Web (the criminal web).

Chapter Six reviews the cultural bias and different perspectives within government, commercial organizations, and individuals. Chapter Seven reviews counter-intelligence, covert action, conspiracy, and propaganda. It looks at the ways governments, agencies, and commercial organizations aim to alter or change public understanding of and preference for a wide range of issues from national security to ethics and morality, and the public's views on the government and its policies. Finally, Chapter Eight reviews some of the supervisory roles that monitor the intelligence communities.

4

Global 3.0: A New Geopolitical Intelligence Landscape

Alfred Rolington and Sam Wilkin—Head of Business Research at Oxford Economics

This chapter reviews the background to the ways in which the expanding global economy has taken on a new, post-Cold War perspective and is far more interconnected, and yet still partially fractured in the different ways in which it operates. The global economy is characterized by fluid multiple centres of trade employing a range of different business, economic, and some new geopolitical models. This landscape requires a broader, more effective intelligence model if these changes are to be understood clearly and engaged with effectively.

This new 'Global 3.0' is having profound effects on the way individuals, governments, and corporations operate and accordingly they should change the way they perceive their position and roles. Additionally, these global changes affect what is perceived to be future competition, threats, and the intelligence perspective.

This is a mosaic chapter in the style of the new intelligence process outlined in the Introduction and detailed in Chapter Twelve.

Often in the worlds of national or global politics, macro-economics, or local commercial activity policymakers and senior management want the facts; need them now; then will reach a decision and the action will begin. Often this immediacy is how they see what is required and they do not want what they see as peripheral detail. However, in order to understand a current situation clearly, it is necessary to have a clear background to the history of particular events, processes, or a policy's focus, and this should be offered from different cultural perspectives.

These different cultural perceptions need to be reviewed and discussed with current policymakers. Time constraints and access to policymakers may make this difficult to achieve. Nonetheless, aspects of the cultural and historical background can be included concisely in briefings. What follows are the authors' views of the background to globalization and from this longer report—written as an explanatory chapter—short pieces of what is considered background perspectives could be supplied to policymakers, giving them the focused view or mosaic context that is required to make clearer decisions. From an analyst's point of view it is also very important to understand what the policymaker knows and so this perspective is aimed at the policymaker and is not meant as a precise historical record but as a particular interpretation from a European intelligence viewpoint.

The new global economy has altered the ways in which intelligence operates, just as it is changing the way in which different cultures interact and exchange ideas. The new, electronic, multi-integrated environment is dramatically increasing individuals' interconnectivity. Social networks over mobile phones and the internet, and new information sources have changed the way people exchange ideas and this has been enhanced by the ease and relative cheapness of travel. Since the end of the Cold War there has also been a lowering of trade barriers by reductions and elimination of export fees, import quotas, and tariffs. Gradually a transnational flow of popular culture has occurred through a kind of acculturation—an exchange of cultural preferences as different societies come more directly into contact with each other, while remaining relatively separate in their cultural beliefs. This is having an effect on what is considered nationalism and what constitutes being French, Brazilian, Canadian, Malayan, or Australian.

The Economics of the New Globalization

The developed world's new economics of globalization was often at the forefront of politics especially in developed nations after the end of the Cold War. Presidents like Bill Clinton made globalization an important argument for improving US exports and this became a crucial part of US foreign policy and intelligence. Even the CIA was seen as an assistant and analyst in the fight for an improved, economic, foreign policy strategy. However this changed to a large degree with the events of 9/11; and even Bill Clinton, who left office in January 2001, has called the outcomes of 9/11, 'the dark side of globalization'.

The ending of the first Cold War and the rising tide of geopolitical globalization have altered the strategic intelligence outlook for all developing nations. The global economy is expanding from a contained version of capitalism, which northern Europe, North America, and Japan controlled, to one in which many countries, organizations, and corporations have a growing influence, and networked dependency. We have moved from the G8 to the G20. Some authorities would argue that the world is changing from a geographically modelled economy to one characterized by fluid, multiple centres of trade with different business and economic models of capitalism. They see corporations, sovereign wealth funds, and stock markets as shifting the economic power from government control. Many of these new growth engines are using new forms of capitalist economics and communication to create innovative growth and new markets. At a local level this has had a profound effect on a lot of people but as yet many are unaware of the changes. Jobs, education, and livelihoods have been altered and the old ways will not return. What was once manufactured in your country, giving jobs and a degree of economic security, has now moved overseas and the jobs will not come back. New work paradigms are being created that make the average white collar worker less likely to see employers the way in which their forebears did. Increasingly, people see their jobs as temporary. Unlike their grandparents they do not see their working life as being spent with one or two employers and ending with a long-term, job-related pension. More data related to their work will be delivered whilst the employee travels to different, networked working environments and monitoring effectiveness and efficiency will become more analytical and accurate. The idea of the workplace will alter and it will centre on the person rather than a specific building or work site.

Changes to Working and Networks

As the idea of the workplace alters, management and organization structures will alter, individuals' work will be monitored on an ongoing basis, and management from a distance will be more common. The effects on individuals will differ with individual psychology and training but isolation will be more frequently felt and become part of the new paradigmatic social problems. This process, which now runs 24/7, would have been far slower and would not have been pushed in this direction without electronic network technologies. It often bypasses government control, although this will fluctuate and some governments will encourage the independent use of global networks while others will attempt to restrict or control their use by domestic or other populations and governments. The web and electronic communications and connectivity have made an enormous difference and it is difficult to see how this new global commerce could have happened without the electronic under- and overground. All of this activity is making the traditional, economic and geopolitical, global intelligence models look outdated. All corporations and other bodies, including underdeveloped nations, are themselves under pressure to adapt to challenges from frontier economies that are beginning to make their presence felt.

Globalization is usually defined as the process of transforming local or regional phenomena into global communication networks. The word has also been used to describe the international transformations brought about by commerce, technology, and politics connecting and networking people, cultures, and their economic futures. Globalization is altering the internal drivers of the world's economic system and, as more diversity takes root, the overall dominance of the West is apparently coming to an end. The dominance of the United

States, Europe, and Japan is giving way to a wider dispersal of economic power. The GDP of developing countries has risen from less than 20 per cent of the overall world economy 40 years ago to over 40 per cent in the first decade of the twenty-first century. However, the ways in which this growth has taken place do not conform to the traditional definition of globalization and this has confused the discussion, definitions, and arguments about capitalism and its global impact.

Five Global Drivers

There are perhaps five main drivers of this new landscape.

The first is the enormous influence and size of the emerging nations and their need for expansion, and this has altered the dynamics of the global market. Countries such as China have now become far more integrated into the Western conception of capitalism, leaving aspects of their communism behind or at least to one side. The list of emerging nations has been joined by India, parts of Scandinavia, South Korea, Brazil, and Russia and the list is growing. The BRIC—Brazil, Russia, India, and China—are a group recently defined as the most important advancing national economies by Jim O'Neil in a paper called *'Building Better Global Economic BRICs'*. Oxford Analytica has defined a group of nations as *'Pivotal Powers'*: Turkey, Mexico, Egypt, Iran, Indonesia, and Nigeria. These are countries that from their growing population size, strategic position, political balance, strategic policy goals, and economic growth potential are considered likely to influence the coming changes in geopolitics and global economic growth.

The second driver is the enormous growth of the financial markets and institutional investors. Financial markets have evolved over several hundred years but became much more significant during the last 25 years and particularly since the end of the Cold War. Over that period they have improved the liquidity of capital by means of derivatives and currency markets, although who has benefited from this apparent liquidity is an argument we will return to shortly. Also, institutional investors have large sums of money to invest in the share markets. These institutions include banks, insurance companies, pension, hedge, and mutual funds. Once again, in recent decades their influence has grown enormously.

The third driver is the increasing influence and reach of multinational corporations. Some of the larger corporations have become incredibly important. Because of their size and influence some are as important as countries, or more so. Shell, Google, and Microsoft are perhaps more important than Bolivia, Bhutan, or Luxembourg. These companies are becoming culturally and intellectually more global in their operations and understanding and they are beginning to hire senior and middle managers from many different nations and cultures. While they search for managers and executives, of course, they are actively searching for new markets and technologies and for different places from which to source product and services. This has meant that governments have had to respond with increasingly innovative tax and legislation incentives to attract corporations to their jurisdictions. It has also meant that corporations have to develop an understanding of their reputation in different cultures and regions and this has made them aware of potential conflicts of interest between their activities in one part of the world and those elsewhere.

The fourth driver stems from the interconnectivity of communications technologies and information, which has given an impetus to the exchange of ideas and knowledge as well as commercial communications and engagement. This business process was rarely possible before except in contained small areas where local markets operated; the price and availability of products and services were negotiated face to face in real time. This gradually began to change with the use of telephone communication, but the cost of this, even into the 1950s meant that it was rarely used, except for large contact negotiations. But now thanks to the electronic networked world, such transactions are now taking place on a worldwide 24/7 basis at far more economically acceptable rates.

The fifth driver is that national borders, in the established sense, are becoming more fluid. Governments are taking a more consciously open, rather than closed, approach to their borders and the trade crossing them and this debate has altered the right *versus* left political landscape. Different regions within countries have had their local politics changed by this debate. For instance, a country's stance on whether to allow foreign companies to own traditionally local firms, or whether as a nation to join an international trading agreement, has altered their domestic politics. Generally this has tended to make the political landscape more open and accepting of negotiation and international cross-border agreements. However, this debate still stirs intense political discussion about everything from who owns a port or a car manufacturing company to what effects the outsourcing of services or manufacturing will have on the local economy.

Expansion of Crime

One of the results of the opening-up of societies is that local, cross-county or state, and international crime have increasingly become interlinked. Local crime is undertaken by the active few, who are usually well known to the local police, and who break, enter, and steal. However 'local' can also mean that certain crimes are broader and networked. Cross-county or cross-state activity is pursued by larger criminal groups who understand that, if they commit crime in a state or county other than their own, they are less likely to be investigated or charged, because few state and county police forces share information about crime or criminals, since there is often no benefit to the local police to do so. And now the third layer of crime is expanding. This is the area of international crime where millions of dollars, euros, and pounds can be made by electronic theft, people trafficking, drug distribution, prostitution, and a range of other activities such as child slavery. In the developed world international crime was between 4 and 5 per cent of GDP during the 1950s. Today it averages 9–11 per cent of GDP across most of the West. In western Europe, Italy (where conservative estimates put it at more than 21 per cent of GDP) is an exception. However, the problem is potentially deeper than this since there are no clear ways of describing and calculating crime. What is considered crime in most nations and regions might or might not form part of the way law enforcement will determine crime. The definitions of crime, what is recorded as crime and populates the police and law enforcement statistics, change over time. Frequently what is currently recorded and used as guidelines for the public's perception of crime, and its increase or decrease, is out of date with the real, current, criminal activity. Chapter Eleven goes into more depth on this subject. And of course criminal activity has also been fuelled by easier, cheaper travel and improved information systems. Improved communications and web use have changed and 'improved' the activities of insurgents and terrorists.

As Marshall McLuhan suggested it would, this interconnected global world with its five major drivers has become a kind of multi-layered, global village. The effects of the drivers on individuals will continue to be transformational. Issues of nationalism will reduce for the middle classes as their jobs take them overseas for large parts of their working life or mean they travel internationally far more than previous generations ever did. International commercial understanding, culture, and languages will become far more important and the education to support them will increase.

Understanding the new strategic landscape is vital for all policymakers and is therefore part of the broader role of intelligence analysis. Globalization is a process in which economies emerging nationally and regionally both influence and are influenced by the process in far more interrelated ways than ever was the case in the past. The objective of these emerging economies is to improve economic interdependence and political recognition and this is achieved at present by a number of interrelated activities. Some of the capitalist 'village societies' are similar and function on agreed lines, while others take quite different legislative and cultural foundations as their starting point. However, virtually all have a broadly capitalist approach and China is a good example of a country in which government control of the markets and over banks, some major institutions including the web, and the press is greater than you might expect from a centralized and controlled but expanding, partly capitalist, economy. Globalization has reinforced capitalism's purpose but has also changed its characteristics. And in the early twenty-first century globalization is not about the decline of the United States, Europe, and Japan, it is about the rise of everyone else. To model the changes to government and the effects of globalization using an example of the newly networked economy would be to review aspects of the recent Western and then more global economic crisis and the underlying, cyclical financial problem.

Financial Crisis

The financial crash of 2008 was largely created by changes in America's banking and financial systems and in the way government treated the financial market's ability to raise and borrow money. This stems from different economic arguments, which began after the First World War, were fuelled by the Great Depression, and raged throughout the twentieth century. Government's ability to control the economic environment came into question and gradually two types of broad economic theory came into play: Keynesian intervention by government *versus* the *laissez faire* Austrian School and the monetarism of Milton Friedman's School of Economics at the University of Chicago. The first broadly argues for governmental and legal controls on financial institutions and the second suggests that free markets will balance themselves internally.

From a democratic government's view, and certainly from that of a new government, or one that is attempting to be elected, the current and recent financial position of the population is a very important aspect to focus upon, and voter support has an enormous impact on policy and government messages to the electorate. Governments in the West are often elected after what is seen as a financial crisis created by the previous government that the new government claims it will resolve and put right.

After the Great Depression the US government passed two laws to control financial activity; collectively these have come to be called the Glass–Steagall Act. The first came into force in 1932 and the second, more effective *vis-à-vis* the financial community, came into force in June 1933. Together they effectively kept America out of another deep depression for over 40 years. The repeal of this Act came in part through the Depository Institutions Deregulation and Monetary Control Act of 1980, which removed the Federal Bank's control of interest rates, and then through the 1999 Gramm–Leach–Bliley Act that removed the separation of investment banking and commercial banks. Thus the Act also removed what had been seen as a conflict of interest between investment bankers being able to direct, decide policy for, and control commercial banks. The Gramm–Leach–Bliley Act directly contributed to the financial crisis, which began to play out in 2008. A number of financial sector players and academic promoters were invited into aspects of government and financial control committees and boards in the USA, which tended to mean that senior layers of government around the world received at least partial intelligence as to what was actually taking place before the financial crisis began. Many senior government decision makers were unaware of, or did not understand, what credit default swaps, collateralized debt obligations (CDOs), and sub-prime mortgages were and the rating agencies, which were largely paid by the financial and banking sectors, gave high ratings to these hedging and gambling derivatives. From an intelligence point of view the essence of the problem has largely remained, even after the apparent worst of the financial crisis was over, since the legislation has not altered to any great extent and the banks have reduced in number and are therefore more powerful than they were before the crisis. Their power to influence government to their own advantage has increased and the amounts they spend on government lobbying just in Washington DC runs into billions of dollars every year. This issue, and similar ones in future, are a global intelligence problem that is not going to recede, and these problems will require intellectual focus and continuous review.

One example that helps to explain the problem from a more focused perspective is to review the financial crash of 2000 in Iceland. Traditionally Iceland had three banks, which were controlled by the government, and the country's economy performed extremely well up until 2000. The government privatized the banks and then allowed mining and other, external corporations to operate without traditional supervision. After deregulation and as the crisis began the banks were given triple-A ratings by rating agencies. The population of Iceland, some 350–400,000 people, contains a large middle class (in Western terms) and the national economy had a gross national product equivalent to between £9–10bn/$13bn in 2000; after the crisis this fell to less than £7bn/$10bn. Hardly anyone in the whole of Iceland was unaffected by the crisis. However a third of Iceland's pre-crisis financial regulators have been given jobs by the privatized banking and financial sector and the problem has not receded.

From an intelligence point of view these broader examples of crisis should be taken into account when advising governments. And it is not as if there was no warning from academics and aspects of intelligence before the 2008 crisis. Even the FBI issued a report concerning mortgage fraud as part of its *Financial Crime Reports to the Public 2004*. However, the problem is not easily resolved as, given the mass of information that is available, how do the intelligence agents advising decision makers filter information relevant to potential or current threats correctly and on what basis do they make their assessments? We will returm to this issue in Chapter Twelve but for now this chapter will give a broader, background mosaic to globalization and its wider strategic effects. The purpose is to suggest different ways in which strategic intelligence should be considered and constructed. The problem that needs continuous discussion and review is identifying the threats and opportunities available to the nation that the policy and decision makers should consider and prioritize. These of course range over a broad area depending on whether this strategy is being looked at from commercial or government, intelligence, military, or law enforcement perspectives.

Modern Globalization

We are going to argue from a particular and partial European intelligence perspective that in the last 600 years three fundamental, geopolitical revolutions have completely altered international macro-economics—which we might call Global 1.0, 2.0, and now 3.0. These are partly based on Thomas L. Friedman's *The World is Flat: Brief History of the 21st Century* (2005) and, although the historic analysis can be, and of course is, debated, this would form part of the discussion with policymakers. The change element we will focus upon comprises the media and the political aspects of innovation.

In the West the first, Global 1.0 (1450–1800), can be argued as being the invention and use of movable type that gradually changed sixteenth-century communications and altered the way people thought about their intellectual freedom, their cultures, and religious beliefs once new kinds of information and knowledge gradually became far more available. After Gutenberg had tried to use his new printing invention to help reunite the Catholic Church, others saw it as a way of breaking Rome's control. Movable type allowed the Bible (and books in general) to be printed far quicker, reducing the costs of production, and transforming the economics of translation. All of this allowed the Bible to be published in the vernacular, encouraging more interpretations of biblical texts to appear, which helped to put a match to the Protestant Revolution. This in turn gradually gave life to a capitalist mode of thinking and expression, fuelling the development of Western economies. It also gave more life to humanism, creating a new intellectual and scientific Renaissance.

At the same time as Gutenberg was working in Mainz new types of ship were being developed in Europe, particularly by the Portuguese and Spanish. The carrack, a three- or four-masted sailing ship, allowed the size, capacity, and distance travelled by ships to increase substantially. The Portuguese and Spanish used carracks to map and explore large parts of the world, particularly the far shores of the Atlantic. The main aim was to find alternative trade routes to the Indies, since explorers were driven by the search for gold, silver, and spices. The consequence of this new ship design was that large quantities of goods could be transported across far greater distances. This reduced costs and increased supply creating the conditions for the Dutch and English East India Companies of the late sixteenth and early seventeenth centuries to flourish. Within a relatively short period economic confidence and revolutionary media technologies changed the ruling and merchant classes' ways of thinking about themselves and their societies. In other words, they had time for the intellectual life, and to engage in it outside the narrow confines of traditional religious life. The innovations and the wider thinking that went with them began what we now describe as 'modernity'. A new understanding and an application of science, technology, commerce, and capitalism were developed that began both an agricultural and an industrial revolution. This in its turn engendered social, cultural, and political assurance, creating a new Western culture and economy that operated over and above national or local markets, towns, and villages. Adam Smith and David Ricardo developed the strategies and theoretical models for capitalist economics. They helped to move the focus from national monarchs and rulers to more of a mercantile, trade-based system.

The second significant global development—Global 2.0 (1800–2000)—began to blossom in the late eighteenth century within the nation that had engaged most successfully with the ideas and practices of capitalism: the United States.

US-style economics had been in its infancy until the end of the nineteenth century. In the later part of the 1880s it took off and became more expansive and global in its efforts. However this rush of capitalism took on more problematic aspects with the ways in which it lent capital on short-term contracts to parts of Europe, particularly Germany, after the First World War, and then in the ways in which its government dealt with the stock market crash of 1929 and the subsequent Great Depression. Nevertheless the USA dominated the world economically, culturally (in part through its cinema), and politically through ideas of individual freedom, which took root more globally after the end of the Cold War.

Now, in the twenty-first century, we are seeing the playing-out of the third significant change—Global 3.0 (from 2000). This is globalization driven in part by the internet, 9/11, and emerging nations but backed by corporations and developed nations. These countries, corporations, and institutions and the financial instruments they have spawned (the EU, the IMF, the World Bank, sovereign wealth funds, pension funds and other institutional investors that created the market for derivatives), are changing the nature of globalization and making it a far more genuinely worldwide activity. Although the United States is still very important in this Global 3.0 world it no longer dominates: prosperity is more widely spread.

Between 2004 and 2007 the average annual growth rate of 100 countries was over 5 per cent. In 1978 people below the poverty line represented between 40 and 45 per cent of the world's population, or possibly more. Today some experts put the figure at around 25–30 per cent, although these figures are heavily contested for political bias. Because of continuing world population growth, the effects of AIDS and other pandemic illnesses, and changes in the ways in which poverty is recorded and analysed, the consensus figure is probably closer to 35 per cent. However, perhaps for the first time in the last 1,000 years, we are experiencing real global expansion and a reduction in poverty. This has brought with it all the gains and problems that a local community experiences but on a much larger scale. In an interconnected global environment most of the difficult issues that individual countries had to deal with in the past are now crossing borders. Disease, various forms of crime (money laundering, prostitution, people trafficking), and terrorism now require countries to work and act together. As Richard J. Aldrich says, there is a paradox since post-industrialization puts privacy at risk while overlaying anonymity. He does not believe that globalization has delivered a 'global village'. Instead, it has produced a global mega-metropolis in which exists vast anonymity and diminished privacy.[1] Globalization has changed the intelligence landscape and reorganized the risk profile. The picture is more like a mosaic or jigsaw of differing threats that need to be acted upon and strategically explained from different focal points.

---

[1] *'Transatlantic intelligence and security cooperation'*, (2004) 80(3) *International Affairs*, pp. 733–55.

Crisis of Capitalism

Looked at from this broader perspective even the capitalist world economy has no single political centre. At different times and for different reasons certain places and some networked processes are more important than others. This networked economic culture has found ways to flourish precisely because it is not bound by one political centre. These interrelated economic attributes tend towards longer-term stability. For instance, they help to maintain the interdependence of cities and more rural and peripheral areas within the overall culture. Generally, this overall economic structure is spreading to many countries and regions other than those that constitute the developed world. However, as Marx and many subsequent critics and analysts argued, capitalism produces damaging cyclical crises. These often occur as periods of innovation and expansion that lead to short-term profits but subsequent calamitous losses; recent examples include the bursting of the dot-com bubble and the 2008 credit crunch recession, which was so bad that in Britain senior parts of government were within days of shutting down the commercial banking system, even to the point, still not generally realized, at which cash machines and personal banking would have been suspended. The relatively frequent crises in capitalism are often characterized by an exhaustion of the market leading to recession and stagnation, which is then often followed by new periods of accumulation. These are the capitalist cycles that are reflected in the waves of increasing or decreasing growth rates over many decades. Such roller-coaster rides have always been part of the capitalist system and now exert a global effect. Traditionally, however, they have affected some areas of the globe while other places continued as normal, or were less affected. Today, with Global 3.0 most, if not all, cycles affect larger aspects of the world's commercial activity in different ways over the same period.

With Global 3.0 there will be shifts in dominance, moving power from one country and one region to another along with advances in productivity, technology, the fragility of monopoly, and particularly through expansion, successes, and losses in war. This process has been added to by the rise of corporations, which in many ways have acted almost as independent states or small countries as they have become part of the global capitalist system. The debate about globalization in politics is now more about open *versus* closed systems rather than left *versus* right political positions. Often, within the same country, disputes will range between those who advocate open and closed positions. This has happened everywhere including the EU and the United States. Emerging markets are themselves under pressure as their economies have improved and they now are also a significant source of outward investment. This had increased to US$140bn by 2004/5 or around 18 per cent of global foreign direct investment. In 2005, it was US$160bn From the beginning of 2000 sovereign funds based in emerging-market economies have been investing in both developed and developing markets, which have attracted about US$330bn in inward investment or around

35 per cent of global financial flow. Most of this capital has gone into Asia, the Middle East, or Central and Eastern Europe—Poland, Slovakia, Hungary, and the Czech Republic. All of this activity has led to an increase in emerging market corporations. More than 60 are now present in the Fortune 500 Global List and 20 of these are from China. An interesting outcome is the growth in cross-border mergers and acquisitions and national regionalization. The overarching investment and tax benefit arising from membership of supranational institutions has encouraged many countries to seek membership of the EU. In just a few years, the EU has grown from 15 to 27 member states, faster than any other global institution, although during 2012 it was under severe economic pressure brought about by the 2008 financial crisis, and it remains to be seen what consequences this will have.

A more open government approach is only part of the picture. The EU is not a *laissez faire* organization: on the contrary, in some respects it favours a controlled state's approach and incorporates a good deal of nationally 'selfish' politics. Within some developed nations—particularly in the so-called 'strategic' sectors of their economies—there is still enormous opposition to foreign investment at the 'expense' of local industry, even though such investment promises much-needed renewal. These pressures and the growth in world population have significantly increased demand for resources and this will continue to grow. Since the beginning of the twenty-first century energy demand has increased by 80 per cent. Naturally, it has been difficult to meet this demand and price increases and financial speculation have been the results.

Significantly, throughout history ownership and supply of water has triggered disputes and territorial debates. Water disputes are expected to increase and may affect over a third of the world's population by 2030. Elsewhere on the environmental front, the issue of carbon footprints and greenhouse gas emissions will appear on the international taxation agenda. It is clear that countries that experience an increase in average temperature and lack the infrastructure to cope with this will slow down, economically. This will affect the poorest countries the most. Generally, the environmental agenda will bring recyclable goods and energy increasingly to the fore. Over the medium term oil companies will rely on high prices to cover their investment in exploiting less accessible supplies. Such resources will remain attractive. These high prices have changed the forecasts for oil supply and will continue to do so for some years to come. This will also encourage methods of modifying petrol and diesel to improve and increase fuel efficiency. Rapid growth in different markets is fuelling rising employment in areas that, until recently, would not have had a middle class. These emerging economic models will be well established in many more countries by 2020 and emerging economic models will account for 50 per cent of global consumption by 2020–25, if current trends continue. As the mature markets slow down the future economic growth and prosperity of nations and multinationals will depend upon their ability to engage with emerging economies.

New Phases of Globalization

China is already the largest purchaser of mobile phones with nearly 400 million subscribers at the beginning of 2008. It will overtake Japan and become the world's second largest car market by 2014. This trend is similar to that taking place in Mexico, which is now the world's largest soft drinks market. Few would have dared to predict these developments 20 years ago. The implication for business is a battle for talent, which will be played out globally. Competition for senior management will intensify. There will be severe pressure on the internal cultural identity of organizations and this will have an impact on their core values and cultural aspirations. Continual review of these drivers and restrainers will be necessary to stay current and clearly focused. The challenges for corporations and any organization having to deal with the implications of globalization is finding new, networked and often virtual, ways of electronically operating across borders and cultures. These globalization effects are being realized and absorbed into reorganization strategies. The ways in which organizations are responding to this new environment must also be taken into the intelligence community's thinking and strategy. If the community is to be really effective in its responses to the new, networked, global society and to offer politicians and policymakers their future intelligence requirements these changes should be made.

The challenge of continued management control over disparate elements of the expanding network will increase. Multinational organizations already have to deal with changing social fabrics and localized issues relating to the expanding workforce. These trends will need constant monitoring, as the workforce of multinational companies will fragment more and more. Multinational organizations will be required to develop flexible operating systems that anticipate and adapt to the sources and types of challenge now facing them. Governments and corporations from both developed and developing economies need to understand and see the ramifications of these issues for their own strategies. Improved performance and better long-term strategies will require specific planning and research to fully understand the inherent benefits and pitfalls of this world. Old national boundaries are less relevant in this new global economy and the players will increasingly organize themselves in ways that benefit their clients rather than working within borders. Although this new phase of globalization does not represent a departure from the globalization of the last three decades, it is a more complex and deeper phase of it. This new phase has major implications for policymakers both in governments and corporations. It affects conventional assumptions about strategy, policy, and tactics. Viewed from senior management's perspective a multi-polar world is one in which resources, employees, technology, innovation, and finance are far more geographically dispersed. Global 3.0 is now forcing a fundamental reappraisal of assumptions about communication and its effects on leadership, government influence, corporate strategy, and particularly the ramifications for intelligence.

81

The next chapter will review the changes that have taken place in the web and the way in which enormous amounts of content are unstructured and are not scanned by most of the popular search engines. This has created the idea and the reality of the Deep Web and one element buried within it, the Dark or Criminal Web. Both of these will add to the mosaic intelligence picture that is gradually being constructed.

5

New Information Sources

Here we review some of the new information sources and what has been called the darker side of globalization, which includes the Deep and the Dark Webs, and examine the reach and scope of the popular search engines.

Throughout the centuries intelligence sources have always included people who offer specific information, intelligence about the situation and the enemy, but the range of sources has changed over the centuries to include everything from spying and diplomatic contacts to maps, photography to communication monitoring. A list of traditional intelligence sources is laid out in Chapter Eight but in the new arena of information, the internet and the web have become increasingly important and this is where we will begin this review.

Internet

In the open-source arena the Internet Revolution is by any estimation an over-whelming communications success, certainly as important as Gutenberg's printing by movable type, and it has been implemented and gained influence far faster. Also, like Gutenberg's idea it makes humans think in new, transform-ational ways. It is more significant than the national post, telegraph, or tele-phone and, with all its applications, will prove to be substantially more important than radio and television as a social networking tool, since it allows personal connections, discussion, and argument in a current and continuous, broad and sometimes international way. Of course, the web in its 3.0 form allows far more different types of media to be exchanged, including all previous types of media delivery. It is the electronic world's underlying road and rail network and is a powerful, far-reaching extension to each individual's nervous system, giving disparate people their own communal and very personal under-standing of the world. The applications that flex upon this electronic skeleton, like the web and email, act like luminous, continually moving plants climbing around the internet's expanding trunk and branches. There is general agreement that the net was the powerful outcome from research into packet switching by the US government, US businesses like the RAND Corporation, and US and UK academics. Packet switching is a method of circulating data in coded packages around a network of computers until it finally arrives back at the computer that generated it. This process breaks the 'full' data message up into smaller pieces and then sends it in random order to be rebuilt by the target computer, copied, and then sent back to the host.

The recorded history of the 'original' beginnings and influences that produced the internet is still being discussed and argued about, and is as diverse and tangled as any other difficult history. Historians have never had a fixed philosophy or method that was generally agreed upon and certainly E.H. Carr's *What is History?* has intelligently added to this 'post-modern' view. As a discipline history is founded on a number of different cultural and political principles and it will differ with the particular themes and 'facts' that seem important to individual historians and the 'school' or politics to which they belong. These views can differ widely, even on subjects where generally people were previously thought to agree. How much historical emphasis is given to a particular individual, for instance, and that person's influence or 'genius' over the years, differs greatly as people come and go from historical focus. What role does the background play to any event, such as the weather, commercial growth, war, art, science, or agriculture? How much emphasis should be given to the supply-and-demand push-and-pull within a particular economy and the effects of this on the way particular people or groups react, or the way in which certain technologies have developed? And of course, in their deep love for finding new evidence, historians are similar in psychology and interest to detectives, archaeologists, explorers, beachcombers, and some refuse collectors.

All of these effects apply to intelligence as a process. In the West governments no longer 'authorize' views of history, to make them difficult to challenge; at least not most historical subjects. However, what is 'happening' and being reported from (say) a particular war zone will come under immense scrutiny and will be censored by government officials and politicians. In the summer of 2005 Donald Rumsfeld, then US Defense Secretary, censored the Pentagon's daily newspaper *The Earlybird*. This publication is put together by cutting and pasting current press stories. Because Rumsfeld did not like what some of the weekly and monthly magazine press (particularly publications like *The Economist, Time,* and *Newsweek*) were saying in analysis and comment pieces about the conduct of the Iraq conflict, he announced that no hard-copy magazine formats would form part of the Pentagon's daily mosaic summary of the press. He was reasonably happy with current news stories, which were mainly fact-oriented, but did not like comment and discussion pieces that took a view on the conflict.

The history of the internet is no different and there are almost as many views of its events, people, and influences as there have been articles and books written on the subject. There is no suggestion that there is a conspiracy within the writings about the net but there is intense disagreement as to how much of the internet was a military vehicle and an experiment to counter a communications blackout during a nuclear attack. Many of the perhaps more mundane and straightforward histories of the net begin with the developments in electronic communication networks in the 1950s and 60s. But some historians have said that we should look back to a paper presented to the Royal Society of Industrialists in 1847 entitled '*An International Industrial Network of Steam Gulleys and Mechanical Actuators*' by the American E.H. Beardie. His paper describes the building of a network of silk and cotton mills over a wide area. The idea was to fix a textile pattern and then to transmit this design and the weaving instructions via pressure pulses through a series of steam pipes to each remotely located loom. The title of Beardie's paper was later shortened and the long name abbreviated to *Internet*. Of course one can trace Beardie's ideas back a lot further, if less directly, and other academic authorities go back to the beginnings of calculating machines and Charles Babbage's (1791–1871) design for a Difference Engine (1822) which was to be powered, like Beardie's network, by steam. Of course interesting or well-connected people and anecdotes creep into the picture, often with a sort of fashionable flourish. One such is Augusta Ada Byron, Lord Byron's daughter, who became Babbage's assistant. She described Babbage's later invention, the Analytical Engine, as weaving 'algebraic patterns just as the Jacquard loom weaves flowers and leaves'. This machine has been described as a mechanical computer that employed punch cards.

After Babbage, the discussion often moves to Herman Hollerith, an American statistician from Buffalo, New York. He received his doctorate in 1890 from Columbia University and was immediately employed by the US Census Bureau to analyse the use of water and steam power in steel and iron manufacturing mills. The revolutionary forefront of the second Industrial Revolution in mass production was powered by steam and Hollerith was positioned to understand its working process practically and theoretically. He was believed to be aware of Jacquard's loom, because his brother in-law was involved in the silk weaving industry where the loom was very important. Hollerith also knew of the technology being used in the railway industry where, to record passenger information, the ticket collector routinely punched tickets, as happens on trains today. Hollerith created punch cards, which were sorted using a variation of the Jacquard loom. His major invention was to introduce electricity rather than steam mechanization into the process. Hollerith's creation placed far more information on one card than the railway example, and whereas previously a number of cards had been required for each person, Hollerith's method could use one card for each individual. His invention reduced the time taken to count the entire population to six weeks and the whole census process was reduced from ten to two-and-a-half years. Later, in 1896, Hollerith founded the Tabulating Machine Company, which in 1924 became part of the International Business Machines Company (IBM). In this version of internet history Vennavar Bush, who developed a calculator for solving differential equations (which had been the bane of mathematics for centuries), took history a step further in July 1945 by publishing an article in *The Atlantic* called '*As We May Think*'. This article was a reworking of an essay he had written in 1939 called '*Mechanization and the Record. As We May Think*'. It suggested a number of different technological inventions including personal computers, hypertext, an online encyclopedia similar to Wikipedia, and the internet and the web.

There is something of the philosophic problem of cause in these versions of history. Where do you sensibly stop? Cause will finally take you back to the beginnings of everything. However if you are too short-term in your thinking you will begin too late and you will undoubtedly miss elements that later become very important. Your understanding will therefore only be partial.

If one is to bring this brief glance at the internet's history closer to the present, to where the focus and immediacy are more obvious, then networking of social interactions was captured and created within a series of memos written by J.C.R. Licklider of MIT in 1962. He talked about a 'Galactic Network' concept which captured the principle of the net. In October 1962 he joined ARPA—Advanced Research Project Agency—and rose to head its IPTO—Information Processing Techniques Office. ARPA had been established in 1958 in a classified atmosphere of surprise and response to the Soviet launch of Sputnik in 1957. The intention was to regain the technological 'high ground' that had apparently been lost. The agency was renamed DARPA—with Defense being added—in 1972. At the same time as ARPA began researching and writing about packet switching, the RAND Corporation had been developing similar ideas: in 1964 it published a paper on packet switching for secure voice transmission in the military. Neither group claimed to know about the other's work or the work being undertaken at MIT and the National Physical Laboratory (NPL) in the UK, all of which institutions were working on aspects of packet switching technology.

In October 1972, Bob Kahn of DARPA organized a demonstration of ARPANET, which was the first successful public demonstration of a new network technology. Things moved fast with Kahn's idea of open-architecture networking and was called 'Internetting' from work he had done using a packet radio system aiming to ensure effective transmission and reception even during blackouts. '[If] Web 1.0 was [about] making the Internet for people, Web 2.0 is making the internet better for computers,' said Jeff Bezos, chairman and founder of Amazon. com.[1] This definition expresses one of the conceptual differences between the first generation of the Web, on which only humans can make searches because

---

[1] Web 2.0 conference, 5–7 October 2004, Hotel Nikko, San Francisco. Amazon is the online merchant that has played a key role in the growth of e-commerce. Since its inception in a garage in 1994, is has become the model for online sales and is now the largest retailer on the Web.

the system's structure needs human intervention to work, and the second, or as it is also known the 'semantic web', based on a vision of the Web in which computers automatically link and connect information. The terms Web 2.0, or 3.0, are typical media ideas that shout for attention and clarification. A different argument from that of Bezos, which is equally controversial, is that Web 1.0 existed for publishers to exploit—some did and some went bankrupt—whereas Web 2.0 exists for individual users and their 'blog' communities and is positioned against commercial publishers and hard-nosed retailers. As a phrase Web 2.0 was coined by *O'Reilly Media and MediaLive International* as the title for a conference in October 2004 and ever since there has been controversy as to what it means. One minor part of the difference is described as the gap between *Britannica Online* (Web 1.0) and Wikipedia (Web 2.0).

In Web 1.0 a publisher controls the information, general content, and imagery. In Web 2.0 myriads of individual bloggers and free writers—FreeRighters—create their own sites, messages, pictures, and video for a community, which comes to their sites, reads, and contributes. This is a series of online gossip, conversations, arguments, and noisy points of view. This is said to be the difference between publishing and participation—content management systems *versus* blogging. Before the dot-com boom and bust Web 1.0 was an addition to traditional stylebook, magazine, and newsletter publishing. Many publishers misunderstood the Web and saw it as just another delivery mechanism along with hard copy, databases, and CD-Rom. They then calculated the cost of this new 'delivery' mechanism and realized that to transfer hard copy on to the web could be very cheap. Thus copy—information and content—could be made free to the users and the commercial economics, they believed, would be driven by advertising revenues. Many publishers are still living with this legacy. The cost of producing the editorial was all charged to hard copy products and so the recognized costs of the web appeared almost non-existent. However as hardcopy sales reduced once the Web took off so editorial costs began to be allocated disproportionately and it was now realized that any advertising revenue—which had been used to justify the free provision of content—would rarely cover the costs of continued production.

In the early days of the Web advertisers did not flock—certainly not the traditional advertisers in hard copy publications—and many still have not made a significant transition. As an advertising medium, the Web is quite different from magazine or newspaper advertising and it will take time for cultural understanding to encompass it. It took years for advertising to understand radio, television, or cinema. This is hardly surprising, as each new medium requires a different approach. Traditional, full-colour, magazine advertising created a static medium that hangs in the eye's imagination—provided we are interested in the brand, service, or product—with an engrossed, engaged reader. But the Web is not about reading, it is about searching, gossiping, and wandering. It is similar to the early days of television when people watched the machine, not its content. The medium really was the message.[2] They turned on, switched to a channel, and hardly left it for hours. People watched television not programmes. Only later did they begin to look for a particular type of programme wherever and whenever it was playing. Television advertising became linked to particular programmes, just as print advertising was linked to a particular newspaper or magazine.

Web 1.0 was about displays of information and imagery that communicated to people using HTML (hypertext markup language). It was about users surfing, not spending extended time on one site. Web 2.0 is about computers being able to talk to one another using communication software like XML (extensible markup language). It facilitates argument and gossip between users employing blogs and wikis to connect like-minded communities. It does this in a multitude of languages and if it is to succeed advertising will need to be revolutionized in a similar broad, inclusive way. Thus advertising becomes part of the search story in ways that make it far more contextual than it has ever been before. It needs to be linked directly to an individual person's search criteria in such a way as to add real value to research being undertaken and this process can be described as the beginnings of Web 3.0. Once true web access via mobile phones and other communication methods becomes more common, and the focused linkage of search criteria with feedback begins to be commonplace, then Web 3.0 will be seen to have begun. This difference in search and outcome will also start to trigger far deeper searches of the Web and into what is described as the Deep Web.

The Deep Web

The traditional search engines, which are employed by most people to search Web content, crawl the surface of the web of constructed pages. These more fixed pages, although they may appear active to the viewer in the way some elements of the text, pictures, video, and advertisements operate, are linked to other, similarly constructed pages. The established Web search engines, such as Google, Yahoo, Bing, and others, often do not connect with and retrieve content and information from the deeper parts of the Web where content is data not pages, is format-less, and is constantly created without being fixed into what is considered normal Web content. Like the way fishing trawlers often use only small surface nets and reach only relatively shallow parts of the seas and oceans, most searches of the Web collect from its surface and the areas described as the Deep Web are rarely engaged with by most people or their search engines. Much of the Web is not the more static pages that the popular search engines crawl in ways similar to how library books and documents are stored for browsing. However, even though more recently aspects of the Deep Web are beginning to be incorporated into

---

[2] In some cases the understanding of a new medium requires considerable mental adjustment on the part of the user. In 1895, when the Lumière brothers first screened *L'Arrivée d'un train*, a 50-second silent film showing a locomotive entering a station, it was claimed that the audience reacted not just with astonishment but with panic, and people fled their seats.

advanced searches by engines like Google, nevertheless the average search by most search engines only filters 4 to 5 per cent of the whole Web. And so even now the Deep Web still represents about 95 or 96 per cent of the whole Web and the vast majority of it is rarely searched.

Also, increasing amounts of Web content are not accessible through the normal search engines and only available through search interfaces into which the user has to type a set of keywords, often using meta-search engines to make searches from certain unregistered websites. There are relatively few but a very useful number of these meta-search engines. In a simplified way they operate by sending a question to a number of different search engines and then aggregating results based on the original question asked. A list of some of the known meta-search engines includes Brainboost, Chunkit, Clusty, DeeperWeb, Dogpile, Excite, Harvester42, HotBot, Info.com, Ixquick, Kayak, LeapFish, Mamma, Metacrawler, MetaLib, Mobissimo, SideStep, and Turbo10.

The Deep Web contains the contents of databases, stored tables, stock quotations, flight details, and non-text files such as multimedia, images, and now blogs, comment, and discussions on social network sites, and the amount of available information that is free to use is expanding but generally, as has been said, is not searched. Perhaps surprisingly, most of the Deep Web is free to access and does not require a subscription or fee. The Deep Web contains between 1,000 and 1,500 times more information than the surface Web and is therefore very important from a research and particularly an intelligence viewpoint. The surface Web contains between 19 and 21 terabytes of information, while the Deep Web contains (roughly) between 7 and 8,000 terabytes. Over 500 times more public information can be searched in the Deep Web than on the surface web and a quarter of a million Deep Web sites exist that cannot normally be searched (see Figure 5.1). Some 65 Deep Web sites together contain more information than is

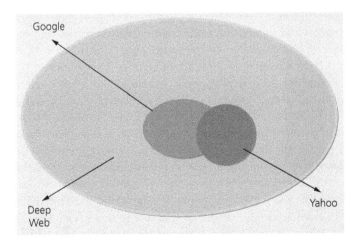

Figure 5.1 Search engine coverage

on the surface Web. The future of Web searching and indexing will make at least part of the Deep Web far more accessible and focused searches will become part of the future of the Web. The problem is similar to the early efforts of humans to map the landscape: even now, with aircraft and satellite photography, much of the detail is not obvious. The major search engines attempt to filter and capture aspects of the Web but lose much of the detail, just as early maps did. And just as secret maps were drawn in the late fifteenth, sixteenth, and seventeenth centuries to offer clearer understandings of where particular mines could be found and specific routes through difficult rocky terrain, so areas of the present Web can be described as the Dark or Criminal Web.

The Dark or Criminal Web

The Dark Web, Darknet, or Criminal Web should not be confused with or considered part of the Deep Web. The Deep Web consists of enormous quantities of unstructured data that sits in the Web and can be searched, but because it is unstructured most popular search engines do not search the parts where it is stored. The Dark Web is partly information that has lost its purpose and intentionally or through misuse become unconnected. Over the decades since the Web was launched vast quantities of data have been created but, like the contents of many household lofts, are rarely looked at or used. However, some websites and large quantities of data are purposely hidden and sheltered within the Web. Parts of this began as military information (called MILNET—military networks) that got neglected, misplaced, and forgotten, and some of this data goes back to the beginnings of the internet's construction. But there is also active use of unconnected aspects of the Web, or purposeful use of it by criminal elements to hack other, legitimate web users, and this is where the criminal web comes into play. Cyber criminals, hackers, insurgents, and terrorists have made use of these techniques to disrupt, steal, promote, and connect criminal groups and activities. Governments and some commercial organizations have used the darker Web techniques to shut down activity they are not happy with, to interfere with legitimate activity, or to change and interrupt activity on the surface Web.

Some elements of this activity were formalized in 2000 by a release of free software called Freenet, created by an Irish artificial intelligence and computer science graduate from Edinburgh University called Ian Clarke. Freenet allows you to use the Web without detection and millions of copies have been put into service, particularly in countries such as China where the authorities will come down heavily on anyone using the Web for unsanctioned activity. The University of Arizona runs what they call a Dark Web Project, which uses supercomputers to search and sift the vast amounts of data difficult to reach or hidden on the Web, as an academic research project and as projects for the US government's intelligence agencies. The project director Hsinchun Chen says the project has been used to establish and analyse the relationships between different terrorist and insurgency groups and to map these clusters for different intelligence agencies.

In a more active criminal area the Dark Web is where drugs, guns, fake passports, child prostitutes, slaves, and pornography are sold. This area of the Web therefore encourages networks to operate that hide crime and are beyond the supervision of the law. Most governments have not changed the crimes they base their crime statistics on for some decades and so often web crime does not receive attention or police observation. As an example of the extent of dark crime, Delft University undertook a study into the use by criminals of people's PCs without their knowledge to send out spam, steal bank details, and mount web attacks more secretly. The figures they reported in 2011 suggest that on average 5–10 per cent of household computers are linked to what has been called 'botnets'. A botnet is a network of hijacked home computers often controlled by a criminal gang, and in June 2011 a botnet with roots in Eastern Europe was discovered to spread over 170 countries. Two years earlier, in 2009, up to 12 million computers were connected by the Mariposa botnet. The FBI and Microsoft, along with a number of other organizations, have worked to disrupt and take down botnets.

And now we will begin to look at what agencies and governments have done and are doing in the areas of counter-intelligence, propaganda, and intentional bias.

6

Counter-intelligence, Covert Action, Conspiracy, and Propaganda

This chapter reviews some of the ways in which message changing and covert actions have been used by governments to change political and public understanding of events. These actions, along with conspiracies and propaganda, enter the collection, interpretation, and analysis of information by refocusing its meaning.

Counter-intelligence

In this chapter we step into some of the mist and fog that (sometimes purposefully) is created around a government's or an organization's activities. We also look at some of the counter-activities that governments and organizations employ against the actions and intentions of others. Counter-intelligence is used by national governments and corporations to identify where a foreign government or organization is using propaganda, insurgents, or terrorists against them. This is done by conducting security investigations by counter-intelligence agents with the aim of understanding how the enemy is changing the message or activity to their advantage. Counter-intelligence may also include actions against the enemy in order to stop or counter the activities of the opposition. It begins by trying to understand how the opposition is using its intelligence services and what their priorities are, and this understanding can be incredibly influential in prioritizing the government's own strategy and tactics. This is the double life of the intelligence services and has been controversial over the centuries. Counter-intelligence can give the government or organization far more effective use of its own resources and can help it to underpin and formulate its own strategy and foreign policy arguments and strategies. Although this may seem an obvious methodology, at least in part, most organizations do not formulate their own strategy after first understanding the opposition's position. In the USA the National Counterintelligence Executive (NCIX) was created for this purpose although criticism has been made of its ability to construct strategic counter-intelligence policies. The basic idea and aim of counter-intelligence is to clearly understand, assess, and counter the intelligence activities and potential actions of foreign nations, insurgents, or terrorist organizations, as well as any commercial organizations that seek to harm the incumbent government or commercial organization.

This then leads to the need for defensive counter-intelligence within the original organization's process. The purpose is to ensure that the intelligence being created for policymakers is not subject to counter-measures by the opposition or enemy. The problem of double and triple agents (like Kim Philby and the Cambridge Five in the UK) has been a source of focus within all intelligence agencies and in the USA has led to examples such as Aldrich Ames, Edward Lee Howard, and Robert Hanssen, all of whom were ostensibly spying for the USA but in fact working or being paid by other governments.

Covert Action

Covert operations are often considered the sinister or interesting aspect of intelligence and counter-intelligence, depending on your particular interest and point of view. They are sometimes referred to as Black Operations (black ops). They include exerting influence on another government or corporation and may include funding to opposition parties within a target. This process seeks to influence the press and media. More recently this includes writing blogs and placing YouTube videos that give different versions of recent events. The obvious point about covert operations is that they should not be traceable back to the source of the fabrication and that they can plausibly be denied. Governments have used covert operations for centuries and many examples have come to light. The British are said to have employed covert operations against the IRA in Northern Ireland and the IRA itself used similar actions against Protestant organizations and the British government. Covert operations are designed to change or influence policy events, individuals, and organizations in ways that assist the initiating power. These operations can include everything from propaganda and theft to assassination. Covert actions are tools that are used to change and affect opposition policy and action or even their existence, and are used in ways that allow the operation to remain undetected or unconnected to the initiator's government or organization, although the event/action itself may well become known. Covert action is different from clandestine action. Clandestine action intends that the perpetrators go undetected: these types of action are and remain secret.

The CIA has had many disagreements about its covert role. Going back to its early days, in 1947 Roscoe Hillenkoetter, the Agency's first Director, did not want it to conduct covert operations as he believed, along with others including Richard Helms who later became Director, that covert operations were so close to policy decisions that they confused the intelligence and espionage process. By their very nature covert actions change the culture of the organization in which they are known to be created and actioned. This of course is often perceptible when actions go wrong or are controversial at the outset. In the USA this is true of the Bay of Pigs and Iran–Contra operations, as well as operations such as Watergate in which some ex-CIA operatives were involved.

Conspiracies—their Unique Facts and Fictions

Conspiracies like village gossip have been part of history since the beginning. They are still extensively used for personal, political, and religious purposes, and commercial gain. A well-known conspiracy that has taken centuries to play out began in county court trials that took place in 1692 and 1693, ostensibly of witches. The hearings were conducted in Ipswich, Andover, and Salem in the State of Massachusetts, USA. Over 150 people were arrested and imprisoned and the courts convicted 29 people of witchcraft, 19 of whom (14 woman and 5 men) were hanged. In the 1930s it was still debated whether astrology columns in newspapers and magazines constituted witchcraft. In 1944 two women were convicted in England under the 1735 Witchcraft Act. The last of the Salem witches were finally proclaimed innocent and exonerated at the end of October 2001. As can be seen with the Salem example, conspiracies often take a long time to be resolved; the problems of communication and bias within the messages go all the way back through our different tribal and cultural histories and often we cannot agree on the reasons for their beginning.

Although our growing electronic media world often claims truth, knowledge, and understanding to be the goals of many communication systems, in the first decade of the twenty-first century the so-called 'electronic knowledge society' offers no recognizable, independent system of validation. It is hardly surprising, therefore, that we have little trust in authority. We have an abundance of conspiracy theories that for many have become, like the stories about the gods told by Ancient Greek orators, the 'reliable truth' we seek. For most, conspiracy is defined as 'attempts to create desired events and or a prescribed understandings of events, actions and people'. A conspiracy usually includes ideas and plans of action, and members are thought to be bound by secrecy. These conspiracies are usually against an incumbent authority or government and are often classified as unlawful by those authorities. However, that conceals the idea that, in order to massage and control opinion, intentionally or not, governments and large organizations help to create conspiracies.

Results opposed to intention can be seen by the reception and interpretation of the UK government's revision of its Prevent strategy.

> The UK government unveiled its updated Prevent strategy for countering extremist radicalization in June [2011]. Prevent, part of the wider CONTEST strategy, has been running for several years but has been re-evaluated and over-hauled. Judging by the reaction of one high-profile activist, some UK extremist Islamists may feel threatened by the strategy, seeing it as a serious challenge to their mission of promoting a militant Islamic 'awakening' (*sahwah*) among Muslim youth...In addition, another Islamist activist is using the government's counter-radicalization strategy to discredit moderate Muslims by trying to play on broader fears that Prevent is being used to gather intelligence.[1]

The original objective of Prevent was to clarify messages concerning issues that were seen to be anti-Muslim and to explain the UK government's balance and what it considered a moderate position in disputes between itself and the Muslim community.

Conspiracy is about the design of a future action. It is an act of working in secret to obtain a desired change to perceived reality. When not carried out by a government these practices are usually defined by that body as having negative consequences. These definitions contrast with conspiracy theory, which is an unauthorized explanation for an event that has occurred. Conspiracy theorists usually attribute the ultimate cause of an event or chain of events, or the conceal-ment of such causes from the general public, to powerful organizations or gov-ernments. There is sometimes also the suggestion of grand conspiracies that unbeknownst to most of us have been running for years, maybe centuries, of which only a few in the know are privileged to understand the significance and desired consequences. Examples of these alleged conspiratorial organizations include the Illuminati, a name overlaid upon several groups, real and fictitious, who were alleged to be controlling many world events. Another example is the Masonic conspiracies, which apparently involved Freemasonry and were tar-geted at government, religious, and cultural control. Another would be *The Pro-tocols of the Elders of Zion*, an anti-Semitic text that was first published in Russia in 1903, which describes a Jewish plot to dominate the world.

In the general public's conception of news and analysis, conspiracy theories are often preferred by many individuals as a way to understand what is happen-ing around them. After all, and to some degree understandably, to many people the media represents a confusing, contradictory, and overwhelming landscape of competing information. The general public and the popular media use the con-spiracy theory to explain events, giving them an answer without the need to grasp some of the complexities of history and political interaction. Along with suspicion and paranoia conspiracy theory is the difficult end of history and literature. Traditionally it tends to be compared to these in the same terms as

---

[1] Jack Barclay, '*Prevention methods—Islamist reaction to UK counter-terrorism plan*' (*Jane's Intelli-gence Review*, September 2011).

astrology is to physics, or new-age herbalism to medical science. It is difficult and has been dismissed as a genuine aspect of knowledge. Yet, while everyone knows that conspiracy theories and stories exist, like the gossip of tabloid journalists and their conflation of fact with fiction and comment, conspiracy theories are given amused but little serious thought. The problem with this position is that in dismissing these ideas many real issues are disposed of at the same time. Conspiracy theories, like local graffiti, are a way of sensing and understanding aspects of public perception. While most is, at best, an interesting fiction sometimes a small amount of it is real and at least partially accurate. Analysts, politicians, and commentators should review and disregard them quite carefully as they give a sense of a general public's belief systems. Like gossip, conspiracy theories are a background noise that do not neatly fit into traditional analysis. They are often difficult to place accurately in the significance of the time in which they operate. As Lord Palmerston, a British statesman who served twice as Prime Minister, ruefully explained: 'Half the world's problems are caused by an error in our choice of conspiratorial metaphor.'

Often conspiracy theory is born from contradictions in official statements or as opinion presented as news and fact. Who controls the information contained within the message? Perhaps more importantly, why were those particular messages created and what purpose are they meant to serve? Every commercial journalist and photographer knows that the most effective way of influencing opinion is by selection and arrangement of the appropriate facts, and additions to them, and this in essence is what most conspiracy theories attempt to do. They present opinion as fact. Page 3 of the 5 May 2005 issue of *International Herald Tribune* carried headlines concerning the up-coming British general election that read 'UK papers offer choice of realities'. The article explained that the public had a variety of different realities on which to base a voting decision, depending on the newspaper they chose to read and believe. In this case news stories were often opinion pieces dressed as facts, that gave particular candidates and parties advantage and promotion, and these apparent news articles were placed in prominent news positions with eye-catching headlines.

There is generally a lack of practical understanding about the ways in which we use the system and processes that produce our content and information. The systems that are employed lack validation and yet opinionated belief is prevalent in the media we read. In reality, our communication history going back into pre-history repeats this underlying problem. Each time we change our information technologies and techniques we change our understanding of the value of information. And alongside, and often embedded within the process, sometimes spin and conspiracies are purposely used to alter opinion and engage the public in ways that enhance a government or large organization's strategic intentions. These are important issues and there is a need to discuss and tease out where the borders of truth and spin meet. Important though this is, it is only the beginning of realizing the deeper problems involved in the information and the technologies we use to communicate and understand our reality. We now have massive and increasing amounts of content and yet we lack the theoretical principles and processes to validate the information with which we will make sometimes quite crucial decisions. For intelligence analysis one of the problems that arises from this lack of validation is, perhaps understandably, the way in which the policy-maker will read and use the open sources of unvalidated information. They sometimes can begin to create policy from these biased sources. This process may also throw some of the intelligence offered to policymakers into question as they often have counter-information (or at least some that differs from the validated material) that they have read, listened to, or seen in the general media.

Today, fewer people believe in the accuracy of information in whatever guise it is presented and from whomever it comes. Truth and belief have been replaced by personal opinion, based either on day-to-day practical logic or a global view that interprets most events from a personal perspective. Over the centuries as a communication culture, we have inconsistently moved from spoken words, physical expressions, and gestures to include singing, signs, sculpture, painting, manuscripts, print, and now electronic communication media in a wide variety of guises. And throughout this long period validation of the presentation systems and the information being presented has never been a consistent or precise requirement. The very idea that newspapers are independent and aim to present facts rather than opinion is relatively new and has a chequered and long-drawn-out history. In the UK it can be said to begin with the printers who used Guten-berg's inventions and intellectual spirit to consistently deliver an accurate Bible in the vernacular, thereby removing at least in part the need for a Catholic priest's interpretation. Individuals believed they could listen and speak directly to God through their own reading of the text and direct interpretation.

Since Global 1.0 the power of understanding has moved more directly towards individual interpretation and opinion. The protest of the Protestant church became the protest of many protestant churches. Once divided opinion begins quickly to fragment and it is still fragmenting within the Anglican and Protestant movements, which see new interpretations emerging every few weeks and cur-rently contain more than 25,000 different denominations. Over the centuries the press as a vehicle for public opinion has divided, built, increased, and attempted to destroy again those politically informed opinions, but who con-trols the press is still of vital interest to current politicians. The owners of the main publishing and media companies are wooed and listened to with interest by all political parties as they of course want favourable publicity for their thoughts, policies, and actions. In the USA freedom of the press, which was guar-anteed under the American Bill of Rights, emerged as a result of a clash with restrictive policies in England. Attempts by the mother country to extend domes-tic policies to the colonies involved an attack on the influencers of public opin-ion at a most sensitive point. The stamp tax of 1765 had imposed heavy burdens on freedom of expression and significantly contributed to the unrest that gave an active role to the press in the American Revolution. This was the first time that a government gave the media freedom to express the truth as they saw it.

Today, the impact of freedom of the press (including broadcast media) is becoming diffused, since even in their heyday media barons generally only paid a half-hearted lip service to any ideas of independent news. Certainly, because of their one-way delivery mechanisms and expensive infrastructures, radio and television largely disregarded alternative views when generating programming. Often publishers, then radio, then television, and now multimedia or online producers, built public opinion and promoted a single political viewpoint. Historically, the radio in particular created singular political voices that were actively used by politicians to promote communism, fascism, and capitalism, often stretching sense and meaning into one message. Today, we now have for the first time a two-way communication technology that for all its faults has the potential for not just two-way but multi-way, serious, discussion options. Wikis and blogs do not just complement existing media,[2] they challenge the purpose of such media through their interactive nature. But the sheer reach and potential of the Web has a downside. Radical ideas mix with opinionated truth. Currently, on the Web, conspiracies have become commonplace and any thought worth the effort to communicate has been used to add to the conspiratorial confusion. Conspiracy theories are now on the increase and are set to grow significantly over the coming decades, since any concept of independent truth has been factionalized.

This was also true of some of the periods before the Web although some were later proved to be accurate. While the stories in *The Washington Post* were about Watergate, other, more partisan media described this as conspiratorial theory. For a long time most of the public did not believe that Nixon or his administration had done anything wrong. It is probably true to say that most of the administration itself believed that the likes of Watergate were actions taken for real reasons of state security and the proper maintenance of the government. Many of the public who were supporters of Nixon still also believe this to be the case. The Plumbers—a name given to the conspirators by David Young, an assistant to Kissinger—were given the task by the Nixon administration of fixing leaks of government policy and actions. They broke the law by breaking, entering, and stealing documents. It was felt and still is believed by many government administrations that if the head of state says to action a plan then, by definition, action taken on behalf of that head of state is a matter of state security and, therefore, is above the law. John Ehrlichman, who was counsel to Nixon, was recorded, when discussing how they would tackle the growing problem of the Watergate story, saying that by reducing its media impact the administration wanted a 'modified limited hangout', which was taken to mean the government should only admit what it is compelled to admit. Generally the more recent US mistrust of governments grew from Watergate and a gradual belief in *The Washington Post*'s reporting.

---

[2] A wiki is a website on which users can add, modify, or delete content. A blog is a personal journal in which visitors are allowed to leave comments ('blog' being an abbrevation of 'web log').

Conversely, the mistrust of elements close to government, which are some-times believed to be conspiring to topple and change the government or its sen-ior individuals, comes from conspiracy theories of a particular type. This is true of the main conspiracies surrounding the murder of John F. Kennedy, which are still strong as are those surrounding the death of Diana, Princess of Wales. Given the current power of the Web to generate and alter conspiracy theories it is diffi-cult to see how these could currently be refuted or clarified for many of the gen-eral public. And it would seem that the conspiratorial view of history will increase, both as a preoccupation that has to be adjusted for and as an element embedded in history itself. However, if we analyse the death of Kennedy, then we can begin to see how the conspiratorial stories take root. The assassination of the 35th US President took place on 22 November 1963 in Dealey Plaza, Dallas, Texas, at 12.30pm Central Standard Time. This is about as far as complete agreement goes. Lee Harvey Oswald, an employee of the Texas School Book Depository, probably assassinated him. This was agreed by many government investigations including the Warren Commission, which investigated for ten months and reported at the end of 1964. This is also what the United States House Select Committee on Assassinations reported in 1979. These conclusions initially met with general support but now polls show that the general public no longer believes the author-ized version of events and alternative theories have emerged, although no single version holds sway. The alternatives come from such ideas as the problem of the bullet that is said to have entered Kennedy and then gone on to hit John Con-nelly. This has been called the 'magic bullet' because it apparently had to change direction after entering and then exiting Kennedy, in order to hit Connelly. Another predominant theory uses the Dictabelt evidence from a microphone mounted on a police officer's motorcycle that was stuck in the 'on' position. The recording lasts 5.5 minutes and apparently begins 2 minutes before the shooting occurred. This, it is suggested, indicates that a fourth shot was fired and therefore a second gunman must have been on the Grassy Knoll. But even the police offi-cers involved cannot agree which recording was made from which motorcycle and it is quite possible that the recording was made from a police three-wheeled motorcycle some distance from Dealey Plaza. According to various recording specialists this would make the evidence null and void. Nevertheless, the con-spiracy is built from the idea of more than one assassin, that Oswald was set up, and that the real assassins were Mafia killers employed by J. Edgar Hoover, the FBI chief, and Allen Dulles, ex-CIA, on behalf of Lyndon Johnson who was then Vice-President.

This is different from the conspiracies surrounding 9/11 which are also still growing and range quite widely in their treatment of the events that took place on 11 September 2001. However, here there is no general agreement within the conspiracy community and its views of what actually took place that day. There is a lot of disagreement about the actual events; everything from planned and deliberate demolition of the Twin Towers and five surrounding buildings, to American Flight 11 and United Flight 175 being used as a spectacular display, to planned non-attendance at the Towers by Jewish employees on the day in question, to the government deliberately using a truck bomb to bomb the Pentagon rather than it being hit by American Airlines Flight 77, to the fourth plane, United 93, being attacked by US fighter aircraft.

Another example of conspiracy theories and the difficulties of unpicking them concern a real conspiracy, which was first identified in a theory that later proved to be correct. In a conspiracy planned and implemented by the oil industry during the 1970s, the 'Seven Sisters'—Standard Oil of New Jersey (which became part of Esso), Royal Dutch Shell, Anglo-Persian Oil Co (which became part of BP), Standard Oil NY (which became Socony and later part of Mobil), Standard Oil California (which later became Chevron), Gulf Oil, and Texaco—met regularly and formed a cartel. The name 'Seven Sisters' was coined by Enrico Mattie, an Italian entrepreneur, and refers to oil companies that, after the Second World War, dominated oil production, refinement, and distribution. The seven included three companies formed from the break-up of Standard Oil, along with four other major companies. The cartel was able to negotiate the rates, flows, and distribution chains they wanted from most Third World oil producers and they did this with the knowledge and backing of the US government, the US military, some European governments, and NATO. It was only over the course of the decade after Arab states formed the Organisation of Petroleum-Exporting Countries (OPEC) that the Seven's influence began to wane. The West's recent interest in the Middle East and in alternative oil supplies from Africa and 'the 'stans' stems at least in part from this change in control of the West's oil supply.

The problem of conspiracy and conspiracy theories is that, unlike most aspects of history, the players are not usually willing to explain and verify. If we look back through history there are of course many examples of conspiracies and the theories surrounding them. I want now to look at one event which still reverberates in England and parts of the Commonwealth, despite being over 400 years old. It is the Gunpowder Plot, an episode in history that includes a host of interwoven elements from covert action, conspiracy, terrorism, and insurgency, to counter-intelligence and propaganda.

The Gunpowder Plot

This plot has all the elements found in many subsequent conspiracies and was actively used by the government of the day in a variety of ways to create a new view of reality in the mind of the early seventeenth-century British public. The conspiracy began as an idea when there was no immediate successor to Elizabeth I—at least she apparently would not announce one. 'The rising sun is what men look to rather than the setting sun,' Elizabeth gave as her reason for not naming a successor. It is said that it was only on her deathbed that she appointed James VI of Scotland. Doubt surrounds whether that decision was in fact taken by Elizabeth or by her inner council once she was dead or just before. James certainly did have some influence within the English court and was certainly kept in the picture by Robert Cecil, the Queen's Secretary of State. James was duly appointed in 1603, but owing to an outbreak of plague he did not formally open Parliament for some time. The opening was delayed for 18 months, during which the Catholic Gunpowder Plot began in earnest. How much of the plot did Robert Cecil, 1st Earl of Salisbury, James's intelligence director, know before it was uncovered?

The discovery of the Plot is said to stem from a letter, possibly forged, sent by Lord Monteagle after, it read, he was told of the plot by Francis Tresham. However there is little doubt that at least two of the conspirators—Thomas Percy and Thomas Bates—were in Cecil's pay, even though in the end he allowed them to be or purposely had them killed. There is also the role of Henry Garnet, an English Jesuit, who was executed for his involvement in the plot. Garnet had been told by Rome that the current Pope (Clement VII) had stated that anyone appointed to the English throne should not be anti-Catholics. Since for 20 years Garnet had been very active in seeking English converts and supervising the Jesuit mission he had a price on his head. Some of the Gunpowder Plotters certainly knew Garnet personally and while on a trip to Flanders he helped them get introductions to Guy Fawkes (and for other conspirators who went to Rome). In June 1605 a Jesuit, Oswald Tesemond, told Garnet about the Plot in confession. Garnet probably also heard confessions from a number of the conspirators including John Grant and Robert Winter.

Historically, Catholic governance had used confessions as a way of resolving and reducing sin and it also helped the local priest to understand the local community, as well as particular individuals' psychology. Confession offered a mechanism for understanding a cultural situation, passing information and intelligence up the church hierarchy, and partially controlling locals, but in this instance it appears that Garnet did not pass on the knowledge he had to anybody in authority. Regardless, the Monteagle letter, which suggested a devastating explosion was planned for James 1's address at the opening of Parliament, was forged or conveniently passed on and gave Cecil a way to inspire James himself to suggest Parliament's cellars as a suitable location for a bomb after he had read the letter.

As was later recorded in *A discourse of the manner of the discovery of the Gunpowder Plot,* [3] it was supposedly James himself who uncovered the Plot by pointing to the cellars: 'I did upon an instant interpret and apprehend some dark phrases therein...'. There were calls for the cellars to be searched and Guy Fawkes was found. Here, it would appear that Robert Cecil actively brought the King on side. He got the King to take part in the action as though the King was solving the mystery and yet much of the action, it seems, was controlled and under the guidance of Cecil. There was a real plot by English Catholics to assassinate the King and the aristocracy of England by blowing up the King's coronation. The conspirators wanted to begin a revolt or civil war and to place James's children (under

---

[3] By Francis Bacon, 1561–1626, English philosopher and statesman who served as Attorney-General and Lord Chancellor of England.

their guidance) on the (henceforth Catholic) throne of England. They believed that once this had been achieved they would receive help from the Spanish Crown. But because of the delays occasioned by the plague the plot, it seems, leaked gradually to Cecil who at the time ran almost a police state in England with many threatened and paid informers. Cecil used the plot to get the King's trust. Cecil did this in a number of ways besides the use of the Monteagle Letter. He used other media available at the time.

Propaganda

Propaganda is exaggeration or lying using selected, apparent facts, opinions masquerading as facts, and different forms of authority in order to influence attitudes within a group, community, region or nation, in order to assist one's own group or nation in its influence and effects. The methods used can range from gossip, to the media, to authoritative statements by prominent individuals or groups, to cultural reinterpretation, to art. Prior to and during the First World War, Woodrow Wilson's government created the Creel Committee or the Committee on Public Information to actively influence American public opinion in favor of US involvement. Earlier in American history, The Marshall House (now a hotel, in King Street, Old Town Alexandria, Virginia) became the place where the first propaganda sign for the Confederate cause was put in place at the beginning of the American Civil War. The sign is dedicated to James W. Jackson who, it claims, was the first martyr to the cause of Southern independence. Jackson was shot dead after he had himself shot Colonel Elmer Ephraim Ellsworth, a northern soldier of the 11th New York Zouaves, for taking down a Confederate flag that Lincoln had seen from the White House. Ellsworth, a friend of Lincoln's, had said he would have the flag removed. The sign, which in 2012 remains in place, makes no mention of the fact that Jackson had first killed Ellsworth.

Now if we go back to the early seventeenth century we can examine the use of propaganda to support James I and his engagement with the incoming English Parliament. Shakespeare worked on a version of *Macbeth* between 1603 and 1606, which was probably first performed in the latter year. It has been suggested that it was originally commissioned by the English government to impress James and to show that his new throne was his by right. It is more likely that Cecil had Shakespeare adapt the play to suit the government's purposes. In 1605 the playwright's position was uncomfortable since his father John Shakespeare had been a friend of William Catesby, father of Robert Catesby, the main Gunpowder Plotter. John Shakespeare and William Catesby wrote some illegal Catholic manuscripts, which were later found in John Shakespeare's home in Stratford-upon-Avon. Just as happens today the past and current beliefs of many middle and upper class people were known or speculated about like village gossip. At the time England had a population of just over 4 million. Today New Zealand has about the same number and people there will tell you they know someone hundreds of miles away or they know their close relative or friends: it is a very intimate place. Not only was a conspirator a possible connection but also both William Shakespeare and Ben Jonson would have known some of the other conspirators, and could have met them in the Mermaid Tavern in London, because some were from towns and villages near Stratford-upon-Avon. Jonson and Shakespeare probably wrote some of the words that were used in the State Prosecutor's speech at the trial of Garnet (see above).

Shakespeare was 40 years old and was well aware of the interest of his audiences. He probably adapted *Macbeth* to suit a performance before James who was also in his early 40s, had a serious interest in literature, and wrote well-respected poems and pamphlets. James also understood and had a shrewd sense of propaganda. He realized how powerful books, masques, sermons, and plays could be in the service of authority and his impact on English literature is considerable, not only because of the dramatists and writers he supported, but also later for the translation of the Bible into English that he sponsored—the *King James Bible*, which added deep literary sensitivity to the Protestant claims of the Reformation.

Shakespeare also trimmed the length of *Macbeth*; it is now one of the shortest plays in the Shakespeare canon. This would have suited James's taste, as he preferred shorter plays and masques. Adjusting the play to suit a royal audience would not have been unusual for Shakespeare; at the time plays were not considered fixed texts, they were an oral work in progress and far closer to a jazz musician's view of music than a printed musical composition. Conspiracy begins the play; MacDonald aims at defeating Duncan, the King of Scotland. Meanwhile Sveno, King of Norway is ready to invade from the east. However the clearest reference to the Gunpowder Plot is in Act II, Scene 3 beginning:

> Enter a Porter, knocking within;
>
> ... (Knock) knock knock
> Who's there, in the other devil's name?
> Faith, here's an equivocator, that could swear in both scales—against either scale.
> Who committed treason enough for God's sake?
> Yet could not equivocate to heaven.
> Come in equivocator...

Shortly after the Porter explains to Macduff, who had been knocking, how 'drink may be said to be an equivocator with lechery'. The whole bawdy, comic interlude is out of keeping with the rest of the play. Some commentators have suggested this was deliberately placed here in order to release the tension and purposely lighten the darkness. However it seems likely that this is a scene added to refer to the treachery of Garnet, who had been executed. Father Garnet knew of the Gunpowder Plot because in at least one and probably two or three cases he had it told to him by conspirators in confession. The scene has never sat well with the rest of the play and feels like an addition that has been squeezed in to give James's frail concentration a topical and humorous relief. The second reference to the times comes because of course James sat on the Scottish throne at the end of a line running from the historical Banquo. In Act IV, Scene 1 Macbeth returns to challenge the witches. The first witch warns of Macduff; the second, 'of none of woman born shall harm Macbeth'; the third, 'Macbeth shall never vanquished be until Great Birnam Wood to high Dunsinane Hill shall come against him'.

Having dismissed all three warnings Macbeth urges...

> 'Tell me, if your art can tell so much, shall Banquo's issue ever reign in this kingdom? [A line of eight kings steps forward with the last, Banquo, holding a mirror to the audience.]... And yet the eighth appear who bears a glass and shows me many more...'

James would probably have been seated in the front row in the first indoor and dark performance to the court and the Banquo character would have held the mirror to reflect James's image, thereby confirming his descent from Banquo. Banquo was James's ancestor but Banquo's royal claim took two centuries to materialize: one of his descendants, a steward in the Scottish royal household, married into the royal family, hence James's family name of Stuart. The issue of legitimacy remains ambiguous yet here in the play Shakespeare and Cecil have ensured the royal line is secure and confirmed James's belief in the Divine Rights of Kings. Banquo and James are directly connected and the ghost from the past meets the real James, probably at night: most of the play is set at night and it might have been performed in a large hall turned into a theatre at Hampton Court. There are many connections to James within the world of the play. James had already experience his father's murder and his mother's execution. He had been the target of a number of death threats including the Main and Bye Plots of 1603. Understandably, he experienced paranoia and suspicions.

The play, and Cecil's defeat of the Gunpowder Plot, helped to strengthen the English and Scottish ties of trust. James had written a book on witchcraft and had attended witch trials. In his book he states that one of the acts that witches could accomplish is the movement of forests and woods, which appears to happen in Macbeth. In the play Lady Macbeth, upon news that Duncan will stay the night in her castle, calls on the black spirits to remove her womanly physique and change her into a witch, and she becomes one of the others, a darker Eve tempting her Adam to evil. The play's historical accuracy concerning Macbeth and Duncan has been reversed. The real Macbeth was like Richard III, the victim of an effective propaganda campaign. Historically, Duncan was the usurper—which is what the rebellion at the beginning of the play is really about. Historically, Macbeth had a claim to the throne. Macbeth's murder of Duncan was a political assassination and Macbeth became a popular hero in the style of Robin Hood for a century afterwards. The legitimate heir to the throne whose rights had been displaced by the usurping Duncan was Lady Macbeth. So when the real Macbeth ascended the throne he was ruling as Protector or Regent until Lady Macbeth's children—it is Shakespeare who deprived her and Macbeth of heirs—should come of age.

The Gunpowder Plot is important as a view into responses to conspiracies like 9/11, and shows how the Western world—that microcosm which often becomes history—responds to a new level of international and domestic interdependency and submerges the age-old boundaries between domestic and foreign relations, fiction and truth, conspiracy and real politics. The problem of analysis is obvious and throughout history distinguishing fact from opinion has always been a major issue. However the process of validation needs to become more rigorous and auditable if we are to expect independent and democratic government to always continue. Methods that have been suggested for testing the validity of conspiracy theories are such ideas as Occam's razor, which asks whether these stories more or less probable than other statements or apparent facts. As we ana-lyse the methodologies, are proofs well constructed? Are there clear standards from which to determine what evidence would prove or disprove the theory? And when looking at a conspiracy are the whistleblowers significant in number and authority? This is difficult territory, for who would have really thought back in 1962 that Operation Northwoods, which conspiracy theorists claim to have been a plan by the US Department of Defense to simulate a terrorist attack on US soil and to blame this on Cuba, was real and was finally rejected by Kennedy, for which (in part) he later fired his then CIA Director, Allen W. Dulles? Government papers confirming the proposed purpose and intentions of Operation North-woods were released on 18 November 1997 by the John F. Kennedy Assassination Records Review Board.

In the broader context of conspiracies analysis some academics I have spoken to believe that it is time we considered the construction of an independently veri-fiable database with linked events, verification levels kept up to date, and con-spiracy arguments assessed clearly with academic and other authorities' probability ratings. This could be done by a measurable, independent, audit trust to check the data and give value to the opinions. This would be a beginning to building an independent valuation and description of historical and current events and actions. It might begin to restore faith in verified and accurate infor-mation, giving it independent status we might begin to trust, and this way inde-pendent academic history might add to and gradually begin to verify what we know, or think we know.

7

Cultural Perspective and Bias Summary

This chapter reviews the cultural bias within nations, organizations and individuals.

What drives the policymaker's consideration and final decision, and the paths leading towards decisions, are often discussed. One important aspect of the decision making process is known as 'cognitive bias', which describes how we tend to make decisions based not so much on empirical evidence but on our memory, thoughts, and feelings. Unconsciously, we make decisions that fit the questions we wish to answer rather than what is in the evidence before us. This process is known as heuristics and it means a tendency to adjust and refocus decisions based on anecdotal short cuts to the decisions that the policymaker unconsciously prefers to make and answer. Such bias is often accepted consciously or unconsciously by the individual, and by assistants and groups that work together, and is known as 'groupthink'. This is a psychological effect that can sometimes occur when groups of people, often employees in the same organization, are trying to make decisions. They try to reduce argument by coming to an agreed decision without geunine discussion and evaluation of the real, different alternatives. The concept was named by Irving Janis in his 1972 book *Victims of Groupthink* in which he discussed the issues surrounding the Bay of Pigs attempted invasion of Cuba and the groupthink that led to some bad decision making.

An example of cognitive bias is suggested by the decisions that George McClellan made during the early part of the American Civil War,[1] apparently based on

---

[1] George McClellan, 1878–81, a major general in the Union Army during the American Civil War.

Allan Pinkerton's intelligence. At the outset of the war, neither the South nor the North had a centralized intelligence organization and individual commanders organized their own sources of intelligence. Pinkerton, a Scottish social radical from the then economically growing Gorbals district of Glasgow, had met McClellan during the 1850s when the Pinkerton National Detective Agency solved a number of mid-western American train robberies. He was working for the Illinois Central railroad that then employed Abraham Lincoln as a lawyer and George McClellan as their head of engineering, and the three met during this period. Pinkerton had developed a series of spying techniques using surveillance shadowing of suspects, and sending his own agents to work for the opposition in order to monitor and pass back information and intelligence. However, after the Civil War started (just after the first battle of Bull Run), Pinkerton and his agents were tasked by McClellan among other activities with estimating the numbers of Confederate troops and recruits. The figures that McClellan apparently received from Pinkerton under the code name Major E.J. Allen were almost three times the real numbers. While it was probable that the Confederates had 70–80,000 troops McClellan claimed that the Pinkerton reports suggested they numbered 200,000. The problem with the figures was probably the combined effect of an overestimate by Pinkerton (since this was what McClellan wanted to hear) and an exaggeration by McClellan (to gain more time for recruiting, training, and strategic planning).

What is Meant by Culture?

Often the culture and bias of an organization is simply accepted within its management structure, just as social hierarchy, class preferences, and decisions are accepted generally within a family, a village, or a town. Older cities tend to operate as a group of interlinked but separate villages and towns: as they often develop from a number of smaller entities (perhaps farms and villages merge to produce towns, then towns merge to become cities), if the communication and transport work well then the city will contain influences from different cultures. Yet cities have their own influence on surrounding culture that can come from different, predominant aspects of the social and authoritarian life of the city. And then each city is different from the others: Paris is certainly different from London, and London is definitely different from New York, and all are different from Beijing, as Beijing is remarkably different from Tokyo, Sydney, Moscow, La Paz, Toronto, or Jakarta.

Just as within a single city social cultures can be quite separate and unique, different cultures can coexist within organizations. For instance, the Seine in Paris and the Thames in London separate areas with different cultural make-up and economics. In a broader sense, cities are affected by, sometimes create, yet tend to follow the recent history and the dominant economic model, the cultural or religious authorities, influential individuals, rules, and their primary purposes.

Similar strategic outlooks and desired effects are often thought of as the underlying influences on any organization's structure. A small business has a purpose at creation, and is influenced by the emotional and economic factors that affect its owner. To some degree this applies to all organizations, no matter how large, but of course, once organizations grow, the influences can be very significant to an outsider coming in but are often unconscious to most of the employees within the organization. People who join and stay usually find ways of fitting into the organization's structure, settle into the culture, and gradually become less aware of what they saw as significant or different when they joined. Like all aspects of human cultural and physical life, different human organizational structures should require a review every few years. However, often this does not take place since the internal workings, the managers, the directors, the employees of a traditionally constructed organization often adopt then reinforce the view that this particular organization is well structured for what it is attempting to do and has the right feel, shape, processes, and methods for the purpose. The belief continues that it was constructed for a particular purpose and, although the reality it is working within has changed, it also has changed (at least in part) to achieve what is now required from it. Often, however, organizations only change when a radical event occurs, throwing them into disarray. This can mean a new government, a new CEO, a change of ownership, commercial failure or success by one smaller part that affects other, influential parts, or (what is more common) a radical change to the environment within which it operates, causing the reality that it knew to disappear or change.

What must be analysed is what the organization's current culture reflects, what its influences are, both internal and external, and how they have changed over time (say, the last decade). What reality was the organization created for and what was its purpose? What have been the traditional influences and why did they originally gain influence? What is the reality that the organization now is supposed to deal with and in what ways have the customers, the policymakers, the managers, and the employees changed with the times? And have they consistently introduced the changes required to make the organization effective in the environment that now exists?

There is something even more fundamental that must be considered and that is the way in which people within the organization treat each other and how they perceive the outside world. What is the current outlook of the organization, how effective is it, how has this changed over the period surveyed, and what has this done to relationships between divisions, departments, and individuals? More importantly, are the operating methods, the levels of authority, the processes, discussion, and argument within the organization still relevant in the current environment? In some instances the very nature of its authority, the 'respect' in which it is held, its social norms, might have become locked into an outdated and traditional model that has continued because this apparently suited an out-of-date structural belief or commercial model. Some older structures still exist in parts of religious bodies or the military: an authoritarian structure, that goes back to a form of ancient, male-dominated, working life is still in place and structurally believed to be an important and effective way to serve. These older structures and interactions often remain unchanged in many organizations because they are built into what the cultural purpose for the organization was and still is perceived to be. There is rarely any serious discussion about these issues as, to get to where they now are, the people at the pinnacle of the organization were required to believe in the traditional methods, seniority, control and promotional mechanisms, points of view, and ways of thinking. They are linked by culture and time frames to another world view and (in the case of the military) to an earlier age or past conflict, the spirit of the time, and remembrance of those who served then. History will often look back and smile or wince at the psychology, misunderstanding, and often arrogance of belief and perceived reality that organizations worked within.

However, within society generally, there are usually two dominant intellectual influences that affect most individuals, families, and groups in different ways. The first is the historical bias of the society within which they live and a belief that this history has determined the current way things are emotionally and intellectually constructed. The second is the belief that there is now a need for change. Often these come in to play (or conflict) at every new change of generation brought on by a political, economic, or technological shift. The rising generation reject the beliefs held by their fathers, mothers, their predecessors, and their daily social and cultural process system. This idea has been taken by a number of different philosophic, religious, political, and economic thinkers as a way to understand and change society. Karl Marx called this process 'dialectical materialism' and argued that traditional cultural considerations and groups are subject to transformation and transition brought on by less considered commercial and economic forces that ply their trade within a society. The concept is that within every society a more fixed traditional superstructure exists, which includes the society's ideas, religious practices, social structure, art, culture, politics, and law, and that these more traditional, deeper layers tend to be embedded into the individual and social groupings. And Marx's theory suggests that every generation or so these superstructures are put under pressure by new technologies, economics, and (importantly) by new thinkers and developing social groups. All of these debates go back to the types of discussion and argument that began in the early days of Western philosophy; some are even found in Socratic argument and debate. Inside any organization elements of these types of dispute can always be found and from an intelligence perspective aiming at strategic understanding these are important to identify, understand, and analyse.

One commercial example of these radical shifts can currently be seen within the world of media, government, and intelligence, where significant change came with the rise of the internet, social media, and networked communications. These changes radically affected different aspects of each organization: some organizations altered their perspective while others changed little or not at all. The ones that engaged with the new media began to understand the changes to the way the public and traditional media customers were beginning to view their own engagement with technology, globalization, information, and communication. These media businesses tended then to be altered by the environment within which they operated. New organizations arise and are created and often these affect the intellectual and commercial outlook and purpose of more established organizations. The traditional and established daily newspaper businesses were hierarchical in management structure (pyramid), they employed a production-line process both to produce newspapers and in the way in which they were managed and operated by senior management. This was driven by traditional, mechanical process, by perceived customer delivery requirements, and by the similar methods used by competing newspapers. The process began each day with an editorial review of the previous day's paper and of competitors, and then that day's editorial meeting would take place, usually in the morning. It would review press releases and photographs, reports by journalists, comment, interviews, sports results, art and cultural reviews, and business, economic, and political information and analysis. By early afternoon the pages would begin to take shape and headlines and comment would be constructed. A review would happen at least two or three times before each page was finished and the process of constructing the mechanical printing plates (and later, electronic pages) began. Samples would be taken, changed, and agreed. Finally, the word would be given to print and the presses would roll for many hours on a national daily paper. Bundles of finished newspapers would be collated and folded, and the delivery process launched to take them via trains, lorries and vans to retail outlets ready for the evening or the next morning's sale. This process required, or so it seemed, a way of operating that was most effective for the required outcome and it produced its own management and worker structures, social and cultural understandings and arguments, and its own bias of operations and understanding.

The new world of networked, primarily electronic publishing and communication had both negative and positive effects on the traditional outlook and opportunities. Potentially, from an individual and organizational perspective, more extensive linkage could clarify some older issues stemming from hierarchical structure, at least in part. Modern communication and information has scope to improve clarity and this might follow more international spoken communication. Social communications and different media alert even the non-traveller to entanglement within political cultures and the bias that social groupings and language creates.

Different languages have different ways of saying similar things but often these words and phrases have acquired different emotional and social ramifications. There are many more complications to the translation process than most people believe and it is often only when we are actually hear another language being spoken that we really begin to perceive the differences. If you mention people who do not have a job to one group in Croatia this will not mean (as it would in some parts of America, France, China, or the UK) unemployed people. In Croatia (and perhaps in other sections of these other countries) this might be taken to mean 'layabout' or even (more likely in large sections of Croatian society) 'criminal'. These differences are not fixed and often change with time. They can also change within certain age groups who will give words alternative meanings, often ironic ones. Younger groups who use a particular word or phrase with a different emphasis to their parents will often assign a quite different meaning to a common word in everyday speech, to distinguish themselves from their teachers and the older generation. Under everyday circumstances such misunderstanding will not mean too much, perhaps, but when a government, corporate entity, or aid organization is negotiating with local authorities the problem (if unresolved) can quite often lead to a serious misunderstanding. In most languages these issues are not easily resolved since, as Saussure suggested,[2] languages are not a mirror image of each other. Ancient Greek had a number of different words for, and different understandings of the idea of truth whereas Anglo Saxon languages tend to assign a conception to the word 'truth' that is almost mathematically fixed within the culture. When we try to understand seriously and negotiate between two cultures we begin to realize these very deep-seated differences, even before we start to take into account the social norms and *mores* that operate in different societies and districts.

What a society understands by and feels about 'strangers' and 'relationships' is often an important question that needs a clear answer. In Thailand if you cross your legs the upper leg's foot must not point to the person to whom you are speaking as this is considered to disrespect the person being pointed at. In some cultures it is thought to be bad manners to step directly between the doorways when crossing a room. For centuries diplomats have had to cope with these aspects of international relationships and of course some have managed better than others. Length of hair, beards or shaven for men, and make-up and perfume for women, have often defined aspects and divisions within a culture. This is before we start to include facial emphasis, body language, and hand gestures, all of which (subtly and sometimes more obviously) mean different things in different cultures. And when you add different clothes and fashions you have potentially quite separate cultures. The current discussions over youths wearing hoods and Muslim female dress are just a recent example of a recurring social argument. Clothing distinctions have been an issue throughout history with many societies finding themselves the nexus of a cultural clash. It happens among Jews, among Buddhists, and among the different religious and social cultures in Northern Ireland. In another way, uniforms from military to medical create a particular atmosphere in which special types of communication are expected. As the American Ambassador (1776–85) to the austere and culturally bound court of France, Benjamin Franklin arrived without a wig. He claimed he had mislaid the right one and was left with one that was too small and fitted badly. So, when announced

---

[2] Ferdinand de Saussure, 1857–1913, Swiss academic whose ideas laid the foundation for many significant developments in twentieth-century linguistics.

at court, he suggested that, like Rousseau, he was a man of nature and the atmosphere changed from one of disapproval to one of amusement. Franklin was made very welcome and the relationship between the governing powers of America and France became closer and was strengthened during his tenure.

Within a culture there are many subtle aspects that help to position you within a society. The way you use language is one of the most obvious. Most countries have a hierarchy based on the sound and adaptation of the language: from Texan drawl to New Englanders' quiet ring, from English Cockney slang to Etonian public-school's casual, clipped authority. Every country has different ways in which it can place, encourage, and classify its population based on the sound, vocabulary, descriptions, and tone of voice used. Oral communication, including gestures and physical contact, hand-shaking, hugging and patting, are the oldest and still the most important forms of human communication and for many people on the planet, still the only direct contact they have with others, although even in a purely oral society symbols, markers, painting, and sculpture play a part in the communication culture. People separate themselves from each other and groups lay markers and boundaries that give rise to family groups and tribal exclusions. This is done in all manner of ways from signs to fences, from marker warnings to carved trees and branded cattle.

These demarcations have been around as long as humans have separated themselves from the other animal groups. When symbols began in some cultures to morph into abstracted, less personalized forms, written communication had very different relationships with the cultures to which it was exposed. The earliest evidence we have dates back over 5,000 years and was usually created for mundane memory-recording and commercial documentation reasons. The divide between individual and collective thinking and its practice is fundamental to many thinkers and philosophers. To many, particularly modern thinkers, individualism is the idea that the individual deals with reality directly and has a real sense of the way it operates, and that other people are just one aspect (usually, although not always, a very important aspect) of that reality. For individualists the whole of reality is important, whereas collectivists deal first and foremost with other people: in their view, a group or collective of people deals directly with reality, not the individuals within the group. Individualism has been growing as an idea in Western culture and goes back at least as far as the Greek philosophers and the break with the divine kingship system of the Mycenaean period. These descriptions are too broad, but the belief systems that were adapted saw Greek culture, and later Western culture, begin to separate individuals from groups. Now it is time to put this into an intelligence context.

Post-modern Intelligence

Since the taking down of the Berlin Wall and the end of the Cold War, Western intelligence services, like the military they partially serve, have had their enemy and their overarching strategy removed. They have lacked a broader meta-theory and their principal focus has disintegrated and been defused. The Cold War gave meaning and a substantial single enemy to the process. Once the Western and Soviet worlds had moved on, thankfully to most, the military view lacked strategic clarity and substantially this was also true in the intelligence services. This was reflected in the political arena as politicians grappled with the new landscape. For some years populations moved in different intellectual directions without focus and the commercial world often seemed to become more important than politics. As the Cold War ended the Information Revolution started, and as the abundance of information and ease of access began to take hold in the West the uncertainty of post-Cold War understanding moved in many different directions. Western intelligence services were asked to change and respond to the new environment but were not given by government or senior military of intelligence officials a clear vision as to how to respond and what or who the new enemy would be. There was no easily recognizable enemy that could be pointed to as the reason for action and consequently governments began to cut budgets for both the military and intelligence. It was said that there was to be a change in mission and roles and that open-source information would become more important to the intelligence process but there was a distinct lack of purpose and direction from senior government and military figures.

History can identify many similar aftermaths to a major war or series of conflict. What history shows is that a radical rethink and deeper discussion are required and that a fast and often unconsidered response is not useful. And if one looks at the Cold War more broadly then the ideological differences and the economic issues that these concepts raise need to be spotted in the new environment, since they had not totally disappeared. Often both sides had quite fundamentally misunderstood their perceived enemy. American intelligence held that there was a missile 'gap', since the Americans partly believed Soviet claims of enormous arsenals when the evidence showed this to be untrue and the Americans to have a massive superiority. The misunderstanding between the USA and North Vietnam about America's presence and purpose in Vietnam and the reasons for the conflict only came to light once the war had ended. The fact that it was more of a civil war between North and South Vietnam and that neither side was truly communist was almost completely missed by American intelligence. In the Cuban Missile Crisis the fact that the Soviets had planted missiles in Cuba was in part a tit-for-tat reaction to American missile deployments in Turkey. As tensions reached a height Khrushchev tested Kennedy by telegraphing two messages of different meaning and tone within hours of each other. The Americans responded to the softer arguments of the first and apparently ignored the second message. This approach was given credence by an American diplomat, Llewellyn E. 'Tommy' Thompson, who had been stationed in Moscow and had direct connection with Khrushchev. Thompson believed that Khrushchev wanted to negotiate, that the first message was from Khrushchev, and that the second was from some of his austere commanders. This turned out to be more or less correct.

What these and many more examples demonstrate is that the use of post-modern techniques and thinking processes might be more useful in a series of confusing and difficult geopolitical situations. In direct warfare on the ground, battle strategy and actions are clearer in their need for specific pieces of intelligence. They require it to make a plan more effective and to give a plan potential in the first place. But in a changing geopolitical situation in which elements of the landscape do not seem to follow expected contours it would be useful to step back and review the different potential scenarios in a post-modern, intellectual way. Traditionally, changes to the strategic intelligence picture can often come from a new enemy being perceived, or a new issue, or from a new technological approach to military equipment and weaponry. Such revolutionary changes as cavalry, the cannon, the rifle, the tank, the aircraft, or the submarine radicalized the intelligence process. But of course newspapers, the telegraph, the radio, television, and satellites changed understandings and reactions as well. However, despite all the recent technological changes and inventions the fundamentals of the intelligence process remain—namely, to provide strategic and tactical warning to policymakers—and the object of intelligence both from a military and a political viewpoint, is to prevent surprises. Warning and analysis is the informative function that policymakers and military leaders need. In order to achieve this outcome intelligence organizations must have access to the information from which to create Sherman Kent's concept of knowledge that is targeted, predictive, and capable of being acted upon. Thus the end of the Cold War, and the Information Revolution and the economic globalization that helped to link up far more aspects of the planet than ever before, have altered our concepts of threat and possibility and have changed our way of thinking in an unfamiliar, information-abundant world.

Today we would say that everything from the proliferation of nuclear weapons to terrorism, to the financial/economic crisis, cyber attacks to global environmental warming, weather extremes, and the lack of water, to a possible large meteor impact or a flu epidemic, are strategic threats. Also included are the issues surrounding organized crime, people trafficking, and drug cartels as well as the wars that still take place: at any time on average there are between 20 and 30 conflicts taking place in which hundreds of people die every year. The problem of course is in part that we are creatures that reflect our own nature, and our organizations are creatures of their times, designed to respond to given sets of historical memory and circumstance. However, once the world had moved to a more fractured, overlaid, and broken-up view of itself, then a non-centralized, more outward, networked operation was now required, at least in large part.

An Intelligence Review

This final section of the book includes Chapters Eight to Twelve and discusses the intelligence process, beginning in Chapter Eight with the intelligence cycle: the policymaker's role in supervising the analyst, the bias and presumptions built into the process, and the structures used to organize the work and the employees. Other forms of the intelligence process are also discussed from a business and law enforcement perspective. Finally, the proposed new group of intelligence methods called the Mosaic Method are reviewed and discussed.

Chapter Nine reviews the traditional methods of collecting information and the processes, analysis, and assumptions used to create the intelligence cycle. It details many of the collection techniques and some of the changes in collection that have taken place over time. It looks at collection using diplomats and spies, at signals and measurement, and at signatures intelligence. Secret intelligence is discussed, and how some failures in the intelligence cycle come about. Chapter Nine also discusses how the relationship and potential misunderstandings between the analysts and the policymaker can cause real problems in the intelligence process.

Business intelligence is reviewed in Chapter Ten and the history and origins of some of the concepts and practices are discussed as well as the methods and processes used in business intelligence in the present and recent past. Chapter Eleven looks specifically at one large aspect of current policing and the intelligence methods and the assumptions built into the United Kingdom's police operations. This chapter is written by Sir David Phillips and Dr John Phillips, and is specifically intended to give a broader view and a different perspective from the author's on the issues surrounding the current intelligence arguments.

Finally, Chapter Twelve analyses and considers the new information, networked communications, and potential intelligence methods that can now be incorporated into the changing environment. The purpose is to give an understanding and critical view of the new ways in which intelligence and new organization structures can be created and used to give a clearer picture through the fog and mists of the new electronic reality.

PART THREE

An Intelligence Review

8

Traditional Intelligence

This chapter will review the traditional methods of intelligence collection, the analysis that is used, and the assumptions that are built into the collaborative structures and processes employed, and reviews how some of the structural reviews and supervision work.

The Intelligence Cycle

In the traditional intelligence model the collection of information, the analysis methods, and the structure and composition of the organizations will depend upon the strategic outlook of the government (or sponsoring organization) and its intended operations. The strategy should be the process driving the request for information and this strategy should have been constructed by considering what the current and perceived interests, options, and threats are. These will alter as events and the opportunities for the decision makers change. This process alters with time, events, actions, and personalities. A first and continuous step is to construct, consider, and review the strategy and the actions perceived to stem from this strategy. Then, as shown in Figure 3.1 (page 63), those responsible for decisions and policy use the process to enable them to consider and action operations and so at the outset they will ask the analyst for specific, relevant, information and intelligence.

The Intelligence Review and Strategic Threats

In order to get some strategic clarity I have looked at a review of the intelligence process by the Intelligence and Security Committee in the United Kingdom. This body's purpose is to consider and review the intelligence process, its resources, and changing threats. This can be seen as one example of supervision: it gives a picture of the process and what are assessed to be threats to an individual country at a particular moment, and discusses these, interviews players, and reviews the process. The Intelligence and Security Council publishes an open-source document once a year in the form of an Annual Report. The Report for 2010–11 begins with its Key Theme, which in this case restates the Council's underlying intelligence aim, the security and protection of United Kingdom citizens. It then explains in outline the issues that need to be considered in relation to how this will be achieved and some of the results and considerations going forward. In 2010–11 one important issue was a financial review and planned spending reductions of 11 per cent in response to the current economic crisis. The committee discussed the changes to budgets and the effects of these on the intelligence services, as well as the effects these financial cuts would have on security arrangements for the London Olympic Games.

The report then reviewed the nature of the current threats to the United Kingdom and its local and foreign interests. These threats were stated to be terrorism, hostile foreign activity, and nuclear proliferation. Terrorism was seen as coming from international groups like al-Qaeda and local groups in Northern Ireland. Cyber attacks aimed both at government and commercial organizations were highlighted, and considered very important. Nuclear proliferation, particularly in the Middle East, with particular focus needed on Iran, was considered a very important issue. Iran required attention because it was thought that if Iran became a nuclear state this would encourage other countries in the region to do the same, heightening tension and the risk to the United Kingdom. Next, the report focused on the amount of money the three major intelligence agencies in the United Kingdom (MI5, MI6, and GCHQ) were to receive after the current financial spending reductions were taken into account. Over the preceding decade the total amount that the intelligence agencies cost per year had more than doubled from £800m to £2bn. This was caused by changing terrorist activity since 9/11 and this requirement for nearly £2bn was still in the budget after the current financial reductions had been taken into account. What this tended to mean was that annual expenditure would not increase over the next few years and therefore inflation would reduce the amount available for other heads of expenditure by around 10–11 per cent. Finally, the report put forward recommendations and conclusions. This can be seen as a supervisory review that is broad and aims to engage Parliament or the government in the intelligence process and offers in most democracies a way of informing the press and public. In most democratic countries this process is generally reported openly. In Chapter Nine we delve deeper into the supervision process.

The Collection of Intelligence

What of course takes place within the intelligence services themselves when the intelligence cycle is applied, is a process of understanding the threats in detail, analysing how the service will tackle them, and then getting the job done. Methods used to gather information and intelligence have changed with technology and understanding, since information can come from open as well as closed sources. The different methods of information and intelligence collection are generally considered under the following heads:

1. *Human intelligence (HUMINT)*—this can come from spying, diplomacy, politicians, government officials, specialists and contacts on the ground, academics, commercial organizations, and journalists.

2. *Signals intelligence (SIGINT)*—this can come from intercepts, telephone calls, email, ships, planes, ground sites or satellites, wiretaps, and other electronic intercepts. This is sometimes referred to as communications intelligence (COMINT).

3. More recent versions of signals intelligence include electronic intelligence (ELINT), telemetry intelligence (TELINT), radar-transmitted intelligence (RADINT), and cyber intelligence (CYINT)—this is data intercepted and gathered from computer systems, electronic databases, and broadcast material.

4. *Imagery intelligence (IMINT)* or photo intelligence (PHOTINT)—this can come from pictures taken by aircraft, satellites, journalists, and photographers using different types of equipment that might take pictures in the dark or from a great distance.

5. *Measurement and signatures intelligence (MASINT)*—this means the collection and analysis of traces of biological, chemical, or nuclear materials. It is also concerned with the collection of data concerning industrial activities and manufacturing of potential weapons, and of data when weapons or equipment testing takes place.

6. *Geospatial intelligence (GEOINT)*—this is information and intelligence gathered from satellite systems and other airborne systems that can analyse and picture terrain, buildings, or military forces on the ground.

7. *Technical intelligence (TECHINT)*—this term covers detailed technical data gathered from computer systems and other records or analysis.

8. *Open-source intelligence (OSINT)*—this is information and intelligence gathered from the media, the Web and the Deep Web, and professional, public, and academic records.

9. *Social media (SOCMINT)*—this information is captured from social networks like *Facebook, Twitter,* and *Douban* and can give a view on public perceptions, beliefs, intended actions, and reviews of actions taken. This can be used to help identify criminal activity, insurgency, and disorder. (The term SOCMINT was created by Sir David Omand, Jamie Bartlett, and Carl Miller and published in a report for DEMOS in April 2012.)

Secret Intelligence

Secret intelligence can come from many different sources and be collected using many techniques. The most common understanding for this term is of spies who have been given a large audience through spy fiction and, however important they are to the process, they are by no means the sole players. Independent technology interceptions all the way to outright theft all play their part in the gathering of secret intelligence. Often secrets are found and gathered independently of human sources by means of superior intercept technology or, for instance, a particular understanding of the enemy's use of a specific technology. This was true of the Enigma machine, which had been invented by German engineer Arthur Scherius towards the end of the First World War. The machine was commercialized in the 1920s and a number of different models were created; the German navy and then the army, along with a number of other organizations, governments, and their military, began to use different versions of the Enigma. At the end of 1932 the Polish Cipher Bureau broke the German code and gave the answers and technique to the British and French intelligence operations a few weeks before the outbreak of the Second World War.

Human intelligence, spying, is the employment of agents and informants who often feel they have been mistreated by their government or governmental service and, at least in part, also operate for payment and a physiology of secrecy and adventure. Others have found themselves compromised (perhaps by blackmail about their previous actions) or are offered sex, threats, and/or money. Intelligence gathered from such sources is problematic, since a sense of trust and purpose has to be established by the receiving intelligence service. The intelligence can come in the form of documents that have been stolen, downloaded, copied, and then passed on. This whole process and its broad techniques go a long way back in history and, along with prostitution, spying is often considered as having the oldest job description in history. Throughout the history of intelligence there have been ruptures in the strategy and cycle brought about by unexpected events that have caused a change of operations or technique. In worst cases, the intelligence failure has led to the defeat of the organization, military, or government.

Strengths, Weaknesses, and Failures of the Intelligence Cycle

Intelligence is often considered a process, not simply a product. And the process is often broken down into five sub-processes, that are briefly as follows. The first step is to define the intelligence need of a policymaker, commander, or manager. The second step is to review and consider the types of information and intelligence that are required to get the best results. Other intelligence analysts with specific skills are often used to clarify and separate the different types of information and data. The third step is when collection of information takes place: resources (computer data and analysis, covert operatives, diplomatic sources, satellites, etc) are matched against the requirement, collectors are given the task and go to collect the data, and different technologies and specialties will be required. Fourth, the information is analysed and intelligence created. This analysis, which has probably been going on as part of the process, can engage a number of different analysis techniques, technical and electronic software systems for analysis as well as specialized individuals who finally create the intelligence in a format matched to the requirements and ready for the policymaker. This may require translation, film development, and/or hiding some identities. Fifth, the intelligence is delivered, disseminated, and explained to the policymaker, commander, or manager. Finally, decisions are made, actions taken, and the processes begin again. In reality often this sequence does not work as a circular process or linear method. Events happen and might get reviewed, elements get changed, and different parts of the process will happen at different times and at different rates. Overall, however, this process is what is traditionally considered the intelligence cycle. This is not necessarily an easy process as sometimes different agencies have responsibility for different aspects of the cycle and they will not necessarily agree.

The intelligence cycle can and occasionally does fail at each stage in the process. Defining the requirement is the first part of the cycle and the definition can be incorrect, or too broad, or not specific enough, and this can mean that the wrong information and intelligence is collected and analysed, or that the analyst does not clearly grasp what was being asked. This can come about by mistakes in discussion, or misunderstanding, or bias on either part. Sometimes the requirement being too broad will mean that information and intelligence will be created that would have fitted another priority. Sometimes decision makers will add considerations and knowledge of their own to change the requirement from what is really needed and, of course, the analyst might do likewise.

The second type of failure can come during the collection process: any of the methods being used can be faulty. This is particularly true of human intelligence where the fault can lie with the agent, diplomat, or spy offering information or intelligence that they think might impress their minder. They might do this for a variety of reasons, ranging from a need to stay in the operation, for more money, or to raise their perceived importance. However the fault in collection might also come from the use of a particular technology that is partly misunderstood, misused, or faulty. It also might arise because information or conversation intercepts are misunderstood, misinterpreted, or mistranslated. Other reasons can be a misinterpretation of imagery or messages. Open-source data gathered from the media or the Web can be misleading or intentionally wrong, and second- or third-sourcing is necessary to validate the information. Naturally, wherever possible this should always be done.

The third source of failure is in analysis. There is frequently too much information and the methods for reviewing and focusing massive amounts of data might not be as effective as they could be. Sophisticated technologies for reviewing data to identify specific issues and points are not always available.

The fourth problem leading to failure is that there is always a bias in the interpretation and focus of the analyst. This can mean that the analysis is too narrow, or aims to support a previous view and has what has been termed 'cognitive bias', which is similar to thinking in a particular pattern or making particular assumptions, and is often unconscious. Often this unintentional thinking might have elements of groupthink, where the team doing the research and analysis come at the problem from a particular point of view that is unconsciously built into its thinking and mental acceptance of the reality being analysed.

The fifth type of failure in the cycle might come with faulty dissemination of the analysis. This can occur because it arrives too late for the required action. It could be sent to the wrong recipient: with current technology it might be intercepted and forwarded somewhere else. Where the report is presented directly to the decision maker the recipient might misinterpret or misunderstand it, or the analyst might fail to be clear or specific. Feedback between the analyst and decision maker should regularly take place but sometimes this is not done effectively and misunderstandings continue. One specific example is that of Jean Chrétien, the twentieth Prime Minister of Canada (1993–2003), who suffered from a form of dyslexia and hearing difficulties. This meant that he got a better understanding of issues from visual and verbal presentation, delivered more loudly than usual, than from reading a detailed report.

These issues are not infrequent and much of the analysis of the way people absorb information is not well understood, but if a decision maker is to receive and understand information it is vitally important that their methods of acceptance and intellectual clarity are considered and worked within. For instance, dyslexia affects somewhere between 5 and 10 per cent of the human population in different degrees and is often perceived to be associated with low IQ; but the two are not related and people with dyslexia can have high IQ (as did Jean Chrétien). To complete this chapter we now briefly review the role of democratic government supervision of the intelligence process.

Supervision

In the USA, the Department of Defense (DOD) Intelligence Oversight program supervises intelligence operations. The objective of this supervision is to ensure that all intelligence and counter-intelligence business conforms to US law, DOD regulations and directives, and Presidential Executive Orders. DOD supervision has two broad strategic objectives that it legally sets out to ensure are met. The first is to make certain that jobs and tasks get done and the second is prevent these activities from countering the constitutional rights of US citizens. (See Chapter One (page 28) for discussion of the Church Committee.)

In the UK, the supervisory role is undertaken in large part by two groups the first is parlimentarty, the Intelligence and Security Committee (ISC), which was set up by the Intelligence Services Act 1994, the second is governmental, the National Security Council, which was set up by Prime Minister David Cameron in May 2010. It is governmentally tasked to oversee all issues relating to the UK's national security and has as its aim to give ministers a clearer insight into the intelligence services.

For some time the Intelligence and Security Committee has been arguing for extended powers and that instead of reporting directly to the Prime Minister it should be a Committee of Parliament, with necessary safeguards reporting both to Parliament and the Prime Minister. In the Justice and Security Bill of 2012, some of their requests will be legally put in place. (Intelligence and Security Committee Annual Report 2011–2012).

The Committee and the Council are given access to highly classified material and their members are cleared under the Official Secrets Act 1989. Their responsibility is to review the policies, actions, budgets, and expenditure of the SIS or MI6, the Security Service or MI5, and GCHQ. The committees interview and are briefed by senior officials from the different agencies and related departments within government and Whitehall, and have reviewed and discussed operations and processes with some foreign organizations and key officials from intelligence operations in the USA, Canada, and a number of other states. These are usually secret meetings and the ISC produce reports on particular issues they believe to be relevant and important and they may also produce reports on issues raised by Parliament or by particular ministers. The ISC also produce an annual, unclassified report, which lays out their role, actions, and requests and suggestions for action.

The National Security Council has now brought into question other supervisory bodies like the Joint Intelligence Committee (JIC), which is part of the Cabinet Office, has traditionally attempted to direct the different national intelligence organizations, and has offered advice and intelligence to the Cabinet on security—related matters. The JIC has been there to oversee priority setting for the three intelligence agencies (MI5, MI6, and GCHQ) but, as a senior intelligence officer explained to me, the problem is that each of the different roles within JIC has its own agenda and they are more inclined to argue and politically influence their perceived role and case than to oversee a coordinated intelligence effort. A similar issue arises with the Joint Terrorism Analysis Centre (JTAC), which is there to give government and corporations intelligence relating to security and foreign affairs with special reference to terrorism. JTAC's aim is to set priorities relating to terrorism for the three intelligence agencies and its scope now includes cyber terrorism.

The issues surrounding the relationship between policymaker and analyst are reviewed in Chapter Nine.

9

The Relationship of Analyst and Policymaker

This chapter reviews the issues, relationships, and problems that the different roles and personalities of analysts, managers, and policymakers produce.

The relationship between intelligence analysts and senior government policymakers needs to work extremely well if clarity, understanding, and integrity are going to be possible. As Sherman Kent said: 'There is no phase of the intelligence business which is more important than the proper relationship between intelligence itself and the people who use its products.'[1] He went on to explain that the relationship requires a lot of attention and work from both sides and that, if not attended to, it is easy for it to fall apart.

The potential problems surrounding analysis and policy become more obvious when the probable issues are assessed and examined. Policymakers' purpose is to change, build, or rebuild aspects of the nation they represent. They are there to carry out the tasks that were set and some they had personally planned when getting elected. Often they perceive the job they have to do from political, economic, social, and personal perspectives. What else is included will be based on the understanding, intelligence, personality, and behavioural patterns of the policymaker.

However, because of the sheer quantity of information and data coming in floods this affects most policymakers. Few individuals can take on a policymaker's role and actively keep a clear and accurate understanding of all the information flows that are available and often necessary for a clear decision-making process. Accordingly, the policymaker relies upon the work, explanations, and filters of the

---

[1] In *Strategic Intelligence for American World Policy*, Chapter 11, 'Producers and Consumers of Intelligence', p. 180.

analyst. But as with all relationships there can be better and worse times between them and understanding, help, and assistance can give way to problems, argument, and hindrances.

In government one of the obvious issues between the policymaker and the analyst is the different ways in which they are employed. Generally the analyst is in regular employment and, instead of having to get elected by a large group of political voters, as a policymaker does, analysts have to pass tests and interviews. They often have a job with a time-span not necessarily based on the political election process. In business, the managing director or financial director are often directly affected by changes in the share price, which tends to shorten their perspective. The problem of the relationship of between the analyst and policymaker can also be described using Wittgenstein's later philosophy, in which he writes of the different ways in which the same language is used by different groups of people to mean different things. Different groups change the meaning of the words to suit their practices. How words are used in a scientific context may alter their meaning from what is understood in business or religion. This can frequently be seen in the average boardroom when the sales director, the finance director, and the CEO are discussing potential growth strategies, the outcomes, and potential actions and tactics. Each director comes at the problem from different perspectives based on their own personalities, the views from within their own departments, how they regard the others at the meeting, and an opinion about the background and the issues being discussed. Often and most importantly, the outcomes or agreed actions they and their departments want from the meeting may well determine their understanding of what is discussed, argued about, and agreed. This is again different for the military, in which the structure and relationships are determined by the hierarchical ranking and officer structure, which was historically first put into use by the Roman Army. The Roman structure has broadly been used into modern times with one modern difference being that the managerial head may be a political appointee. For instance, in the UK this political appointee is the Minister of Defence, who reports to the Prime Minister; and in the USA the President is the Commander-in-Chief. In the business world the managing director or finance director are usually in charge of strategic policy and the head analyst will report to them.

So, in each case, one of the major issues that should be specifically addressed early in the relationship is how different are the analyst and the policymaker's understanding of the strategic perspective and what particular words about the possibilities and options mean to each player in the process involved to arrive at that intelligence. Often they do not use the information-gathering processes and intelligence outcomes in the same ways and have quite different perspectives on the information/intelligence and the processes involved in its direction and outcomes. This is understandable as they come from different perspectives and often have different reasons for using the intelligence process. Also, when doing their job different external pressures will be exerted on analyst and policymaker from other parts of government/employing organization, and other national players, and the policymaker especially will get pressure from other governments/competing organizations and international figures.

Often policymakers will enter their position with a limited knowledge of the historical baggage that goes with the job. What are the underlying economics of the nation or organization? What current agreements affect policy going forward? What are the management issues within the organization that they are to run? What are the relationships and what are the personalities that this policymaker will have to deal with? What is the current government's/management's strategy on all of these issues? And naturally there will be many more of these questions. Naturally policymakers will also bring their own agenda and be influenced by promises made, people they know, and relationships they wish to improve, begin, or reduce. Alongside all of this are the current internal staff, the management, and the intelligence analysts who would like time with and influence on the policymaker. Often the agenda of the policymaker make it difficult for the analyst to get adequate time with them. This has been true since management and political structures began. The policymaker will probably have met the analyst just before or at the time of starting the job and will ask for information/intelligence on subjects that they probably know something about. This might be to test the system, to get a new opinion, or just to see what the analyst is like to work with.

The beginning is crucial to ensure that the relationship has a chance and will work for both parties. In the UK the Cabinet Secretary will be one of the first to meet the new Prime Minister as she/he enters 10 Downing Street on the first day in office. One of the first things that the Cabinet Secretary will do at this meeting, once the doors to 10 Downing Street are closed and they are alone together, will be to explain that the new Prime Minister has to make an immediate decision about how the government should respond to a nuclear attack should he/she have been killed. The Prime Minister must sign papers stating what the response would be so that the nuclear task force and whoever might then be in charge of the country can be alerted to whether to immediately respond with a nuclear counter-attack or not, and to whether the new head will be asked to make the decision or to negotiate. The relationship between policymakers and their secretary/analyst begins immediately and very similar events take place in most Western governments on the outset of new heads of government. This process has been played out on stage over the centuries, from Shakespeare's *King Lear* to Sir Tim Rice's amusing suggestion of some of the relationship issues in the lyrics to 'The Morning Report' over Sir Elton John's music for *The Lion King*. The relationship is described as a privileged honour done to the king every morning when news is given to him about the state of the animal tribes, which is given with sensitivity but also a degree of sycophancy.

Others with direct involvement whom I have spoken to have clearly laid out the problems in the day-to-day relationship between the intelligence officer and the decision maker. The system of intelligence briefing and the intelligence cycle depends upon the relationship between the decision maker and the intelligence officer. The officer needs to understand clearly where the policymaker stands on particular issues, what that person is trying to achieve, and in what time frame. Both should relate to the subjects and to each other in a positive manner. Intelligence officers must promote their information and intelligence so that it is understood, its nuances appreciated, and engaged with the policymaker's thoughts and actions. The objective for the intelligence officer is to explain what is known. The hard evidence about the situation and people being discussed should be explained and then the officer should offer possibilities, scenarios, the opposition's intentions, and potential outcomes. However the decision what to do is in the hands of the decision maker and not the intelligence officer and it must be understood by both sides that each will have their preferred information and intelligence sources and their preferred outcome. Intelligence officers should know that sometimes their information and intelligence will be used and at other times it will apparently be overlooked or incorporated within another decision process. During the Second World War the head of British Scientific Intelligence, Reginald Victor Jones, warned against the practice of putting self-interest or the interest of the organization before the needs of the decision maker. He called this 'Very Senior Officer Veneration Syndrome' or telling the commander what one thinks they want to hear in order to promote their interest. The problem goes to the heart of the need for independent intelligence analysis and briefing and has been at the root of intelligence and policy relations since the activity first began. Intelligence can give clarity and facts but also an understanding of the background and potential ways forward. It is not a fixed view and it is not precise fortune telling, it is an overview with some clearer aspects and other partial or complete unknowns. It is a backdrop, a painting of the background and a staging of the action and potential action. It is a stage-play, not a precise photographic enactment of the guaranteed future.

Some intelligence officers I have spoken to will occasionally grimace when asked to discuss the relationship with policymakers. A senior member of SIS or MI6 explained this, often tenuous, relationship as one of the most demanding and problematic aspects of their job. This can be because policymakers often already have an agenda that they perceive the 'civil servant's' role as enabling the policymaker to fulfill, and because, at least in part, they often see the intelligence role as being to support the proposed actions and outcomes. The issues that surround intelligence and the organizations that create it are subject to sometimes intense pressure from senior politicians and their staff who wish to find intelligence to support their own strategic, political, and immediate purposes. There are a number of examples of this in all generations, from many different countries, and in organizations that include governments, the military, law enforcement, and commercial firms. The British government under Prime Minister Tony Blair denied the allegation that it had favourably edited the intelligence leading to the invasion of Iraq. However it is now very clear that parts of that government put a large amount of time into, and argumentative pressure on, the intelligence services in order to get the story the Prime Minister wanted. Some of this came out in the Chilcot Inquiry, which found that during the early stages of the Iraq conflict issues and information were identified as supporting the required case even though it did not find direct manipulation of information to help to justify the war. The former Deputy Prime Minister Lord Prescott told the Inquiry that he was nervous about the intelligence being presented, some of which he said was based on 'tittle-tattle'. One MI6 officer who gave evidence to the Inquiry (identified as SIS2) said: 'The pressure to generate results, I fear, did lead to cutting of corners...I think a fair criticism would be that we were probably too eager to please.' Another MI6 office noted as SIS1 said the 45-minute claim was 'based on wishful thinking...before it was fully validated'.

However one of the main problems with the analysis of weapons intelligence on Iraq was that the data was wanting and the time frames for decisions, as is often the case, were quite short. Nonetheless, more balanced analysis was available and some governments made more accurate and balanced choices based on evidence that was seen to be unreliable. For instance, the Canadian government under Jean Chrétien did not immediately sign up to and support the Iraq invasion although put under severe pressure by the USA. This now seems a sensible conclusion to have drawn in quite difficult and time-pressured circumstances.

Discussions between the policymaker and the analyst should take place regularly but this relationship should be neither distant nor too close. Too distant and mutual understanding and clarity will easily be lost; too close, then groupthink can easily become part of the analysis and decision making which will then lose objective perspective. In *Bedmates or Sparring Partners* Tony Campbell, the former head of Canadian intelligence analysis when Chrétien had to decide about Iraq, linked intelligence to the media, a group he had to deal with frequently. Campbell observes that 'broadly speaking' both intelligence and media are in the same business—both are collecting, analysing, and disseminating information. But there are 'crucial differences' between the institutions in terms of ownership (public *versus* private), customer focus (policymakers *versus* the public), and *modus operandi* (closed *versus* open). These differences, he says, naturally establish a tension, one that has taken on 'vastly greater importance and sensitivity' in recent years because of, among other factors, the global Information Revolution and 'increased temptation' in democratic governments to politicize intelligence.

And now we move towards the issues that Campbell is talking about, where intelligence and business meet, and we review the commercial marketplace and its use of business intelligence.

10

Business Intelligence

This chapter reviews the history, processes, and intentions of business intelligence and how these processes have created methods of intelligence that have far broader uses.

Before the widespread introduction of computer systems, with their recording and analytical software, there were real difficulties in trying to create timely, in-depth commercial intelligence. Prior to these electronic innovations there was generally a lack of easily available business data and therefore its collection and analysis was not particularly effective in most businesses. Therefore many business decisions were made from a fairly superficial market and commercial understanding, using sales and purchasing records, experience, hearsay, discussions over lunch, and intuition made by a very small percentage of the business employees usually, no more than 2–3 per cent of the total workforce.

Some of the larger manufacturing operations used their accounting records to give a broad view of development. However, this was usually after events that it would have been very useful to have partially predicted and to have currently analysed. Usually this type of analysis relied heavily on internal systems like production processes and was used to drive the business forward, which tended to work adequately in growing markets but not when the competition and/or the marketplace was changing. The basics of a production process begin with the collection of raw or refined material and in part this was then monitored through the time-driven production line. This narrow, inward-looking, clock-on-and-off, schedule tended to make views of the work and the workers' production line repetitive, discouraged creativity in analysts' actions, and recorded little feedback about how the process might be affecting the company's market position. This production methodology and focus continued until the end of the line when the finished product was completed and put into store. Often, far too much or too little product was stored as sales; demand and delivery were not adequately married up. This process can be seen as a variant on the traditional agricultural production process—sowing seeds, watering, tending and watering, harvest, storage, milling perhaps, or delivery to food manufacturer or flour mill, sale to the customer, and then on to the next stage in the crop rotation cycle.

In business over the last 50 years there has been a radical shift in the use of data and how this can be turned into information, knowledge, and business intelligence. At the outset of this period, just as the production line had driven the earlier business process, the newly emerging computer hardware and software gradually took over the recording processes of the production line, and larger elements of the routine accounting functions. It took a number of decades for this new technology to emerge, along with the functions it could be adapted to perform, before broader and more strategic data began to be collected and reviewed. In the commercial world this has subsequently meant everything from analysis of customer buying-patterns and how these can be related to marketing, service, and pricing data, to deeper commercial analysis aimed at helping to form a broader, global strategy for the whole business and related to the competition's activity, changes to the markets, and potential growth opportunities. Improved decision-support systems were created in the 1960s and developed throughout the next three decades. Gradually these were put into practice and improved by the decentralization of the computing process when individuals began to analyse their own and others' data. This broader view of business intelligence is still used as a definition of its purpose by the information technology (IT) area of business. The applications that aim to assist this type of massive data analysis are often expensive to buy and very expensive to install. Business intelligence is often considered part of the IT function, although the definition of business intelligence has changed outside the IT arena and even IT managers' perspective is being altered. We will return to this later in this chapter. Gradually over the last two or three decades business information and intelligence has shifted from depending solely on the IT department's techniques and methods for analysing data to a more incisive, supporting set of techniques for creating strategy, operations, and action at all levels of management. It has moved from being considered as data processing to broader techniques that can be used to analyse different aspects of business activity. The aim is to offer more clarity and direction to separate departments within a commercial concern and a broader but strategically focused direction and planning process for the business. Business information now covers a wide range of data and analysis activities, from improving profit and reducing loss to growth forecasting, new product creation, design and marketing to an overarching corporate strategic direction. The process often begins with a vision statement, which is set by the policymaker (managing director, chief executive officer, chief operating officer, finance director, or senior strategic manager) and it can now be referred to as the business intelligence cycle.

The Business Intelligence Cycle

Once the business objectives are defined and a vision statement is agreed the strategy should be considered, discussed, written down, reviewed, and internally publicized. From this grounding business plans and new projects for different parts of the organization should be commissioned and written. There should then be an internal presentation, a publishing process, and questions, suggestions, criticisms, and review should be encouraged before the plans are submitted back to the senior management team for consideration, changed, and approved for action (see Figure 10.1). Within set times the actions should begin, developments recorded, and the outcomes analysed and recorded before any changes and improvements to the vision are considered. Then the process begins again. One of the major problems and criticisms of this process is that often it lacks in-depth employee involvement. This is very important for buy-in, learning, and to gather and use their experience. Often, however, in businesses these crucial aspects—discussion and criticism—are not as welcome to senior management as they could be. From the senior management perspective this process could be seen as time-consuming, inward-looking, and thought unlikely to produce new or relevant intelligence. However, if done effectively, it would give a clearer understanding of employees' feel for, comprehension of, and engagement with the market, the internal structure, and the client base. And senior management perspective would find it useful to engage with the company's more recent history and understand which previous strategies worked, which did not, and why.

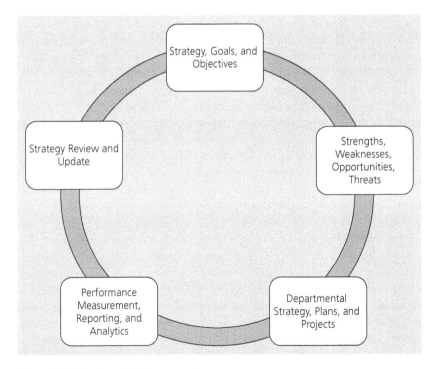

Figure 10.1 Business intelligence cycle

Business Intelligence Case Study

The changing electronic environment became clearer to me when I left university in the early 1980s, where like others I had been using a typewriter to write essays required towards the degree I was pursuing in philosophy and literature. Most of us had little to do with or any understanding of the new personal computers: in the Warwick University library there was a new, computerized, library database of academic papers and relevant information and this I did use.

After university I got my first full-time job as an assistant sub-editor on a new weekly computer magazine and it soon became apparent that the electronic world was dramatically altering with the introduction of the personal computer. Some of the largest effects on many workplaces occurred with the development of these computers during the 1980s. Only later did I realize some of the broader effects that this technology had when I reviewed the PC's history going back to the early 1960s, which most of my parents' generation had been unaware of at the time. At the beginning of the 1980s in the world of publishing the PC was still seen as something to replace the typewriter and quicken the process of delivering publishing copy by supplying articles for newspapers and magazines in a page format directly to the printer rather than to a typesetter. Nothing more radical occurred to most publishers.

The world of publishing still saw the whole process as one of manufacture and production lines but, with the introduction of the Web, everything began to change although only some realized the potential. By the early 1990s business shifts had begun to occur and, when I arrived at Jane's Information Group, we began the process of changing a traditional book publisher, whose main revenues came, like many others, from book and magazine subscription sales, conferences, and a substantial amount of advertising, into an electronic information company. In 1992 advertising for Jane's was nearly 40 per cent of total revenues and on some of its publication products it was over 80 per cent. Jane's book publishing was very traditional with the yearbooks (such as *Jane's Fighting Ships*) in an annual cycle. The very experienced and engaging editors, who took professional interest in the changing world of defence since the end of the Cold War, were still publishing information a year after an event at the earliest.

Soon after 1993 we began to publish a monthly newsletter for each yearbook and then I, and a senior Jane's product developer and researcher, visited the offices of the *Encyclopedia Britannica* in Chicago and got the story of their commercial trouble and how they intended to improve the situation. *Encyclopedia Britannica* had begun with the Scottish Enlightenment in the 1750s. It was initially published in three volumes and was a response to the French *Encyclopédie* of Diderot and others. *Britannica* grew in volumes and sales and successfully adjusted to the markets of the twentieth century. After the Second World War Western upper and upper-middle class families who wanted to give their children an educational advantage were encouraged to buy *Britannica* and the children's edition. The Britannica organization played on these concerns. The reality was that, once bought, *Britannica* was only partially read and remained on bookshelves almost as museum pieces. The Britannica company relied on an adept sales force that worked by going door to door in likely residential areas and used guilt about children's education to encourage purchase. The sales force began to take control of the company and demanded bonus and commissions for every sale: this became the driving force in the company's success.

However, when the PC became more common and electronic software for home use began to be developed, new competition in many markets became the business focus. *Britannica* did not respond well as the sales forces were asked to accept lower commissions if sold as a software package. Microsoft discussed buying *Britannica* and others, but selected Funk & Wagnalls encyclopedia and called their software package Encarta. This and other software encyclopedias were sold to parents in ways similar to the old encyclopedia sales. It was suggested that parents could buy their child a personal computer with an encyclopedia installed for less than the cost of a printed encyclopedia. This was one of the major deelopments that caused *Britannica*'s demise and something I witnessed in part in their offices in Chicago. *Britannica* printed its final hard-copy edition in 2010 and went fully online. Encarta ceased to publish in 2011, citing Wikipedia's growth and cost-free usage as one of the reasons for its commercial failure.

From this experience, and from some of our previous understanding, we rewrote the strategy for Jane's Information Group and began to turn the business from an old-school publisher of print and advertising into an online, electronic database and consultancy company. It took a number of years to achieve the outcomes we wanted but we trebled the revenues and dramatically reduced the reliance on advertising, to below 20 per cent. Because we had increased the rest of the business, this revenue figure was still higher than it had been in the traditional Jane's publishing model. We took the business from loss to just under 20 per cent consistent annual profitability, without spending large sums on restructuring or capital purchases. The lessons I had learned from my previous experience at Lloyd's of London Press and *BBC Video World*, and particularly from our analysis of the new electronic publishing world that originally was based in part on the *Encyclopedia Britannica* and other case studies we reviewed, changed Jane's from the traditional publishing print model into an electronic, networked, information publisher and consultant. The methods were central to our restructuring and were based on our understanding of business intelligence and the analysis methods in this chapter.

The outcome for the business as a whole was to reduce the number of individual employee offices and move to an open-plan office environment, placing coffee machines strategically to get people from different departments to talk to one another, but we also increased the global reach by opening offices in the USA, Australia, Singapore, Paris, and other countries. We flattened the management structure and made it more interactive and discursive across different parts of the organization. We organized meetings and question-and-answer sessions, more management presentations, arguments and discussions over the strategy and planning of products and services, and for each publication we aimed to have an electronic email or web news update, reports (electronic and hard-copy), an updatable database, and still (where required) a hard-copy print publication. However, we were well aware of the continuing changes going on and we created new products and methods to deal with the new environ- ment our customers were experiencing. We also invited our customers into our offices to give them a view of how we operated and to have them present to us about how they saw their work, where our products assisted them, and where gaps were still apparent, and during this process we promised not to try selling to them. By the turn of the century the business had been transformed: the whole restructure process had taken just over five years.

We encouraged individual employees to take personal training and re-education along the new electronic network lines. What we discovered was that the age of the employee was not the dominant factor in this new experience and training environment. Similar proportions of the older and younger staff generations understood and engaged with the new working practices. Some from each of the different generations did not want to change their ways of thinking or working and it took longer for them to adjust. Mainly, we attempted to transform the existing employees with new training, engagement, and discussion. Only as we grew did we bring in new employees and we dismissed very few of the traditional management or existing employees. From the staff's experience, cus- tomer knowledge, and using our strategic and mosaic planning techniques, we built a new commercial model for Jane's.

Strategy Development

To briefly go back in time and review the progression of strategy and the differ- ent approaches that have been used is useful as it offers a greater understand- ing of how current business strategy was developed. After the Second World War business strategy in the West became far more professionalized as indus- tries moved from wartime requirements to a growing and more sophisticated market. Business intelligence (BI) became more formalized when, in 1958, Hans Peter Luhn, a researcher and manager of the information retrieval research division for IBM, wrote an article for the *IBM Journal* in which he said that BI was 'the ability to apprehend the interrelationship of present facts in such a way as to guide action towards a desired goal'.[1] This remains an excel- lent definition of intelligence itself, although, because it was created by IT research, BI has tended to focus on technologies, particularly the computer and electronic technologies. It tended to review the technical changes of data into information, how this might change information into knowledge, and then (by adding more analysis) potentially into business intelligence. Over the next two or three decades Luhn's definition was refocused into 'a broader

---

[1] H.P. Luhn, 'A Business Intelligence System', (1958) *IBM Journal* Vol 2, No 4, pp. 314–319.

understanding of usable intelligence that has been used to help steer commercial decisions and actions'.

Luhn's article '*A Business Intelligence System*' said that BI should 'supply suitable information to support specific activities carried out by individuals, groups, departments, divisions, or even larger units'.[2] From this it can be seen that Luhn already had a broader definition for BI as he realized that the focused use of recorded data, consideration, and analysis would enable businesses to understand their needs and their potential in far greater depth than just working from production cycles, senior management's experience and intuition, and internal discussion.

Business intelligence should begin from an understanding of the business and its recent history, its place in the market space, and its position *vis-à-vis* the competition. This will help construct a strategic understanding of how the business has got to its present state and this will offer a clearer understanding of aspects of the potential for the business going forward. Even on a government level, this is relevant. On 3 May 2012 on BBC Radio 4's *Today* programme, Mervyn King, the Governor of the Bank of England, said that he wished he had spent more time reviewing the history of previous financial crises as this would have given a better view of how to deal with the 2008 financial emergency.

Traditionally, this review process has not been dealt with as well as it could in all markets and large organizations, since the business intelligence cycle, often without realizing the connection, has tended to follow the traditional intelligence cycle model and both tend to operate too much in the present environment. This means that directors/managers create the perspective and the questions and then ask the analysis for the information and intelligence they require in connection with a particular, usually current, issue. As with the intelligence process, this is useful and effective for certain aspects of the immediate or tactical BI process but it is not the best way to understand an issue and to develop a new way forward. The problem is that the business intelligence cycle, like the intelligence cycle, is very useful from the director/manager's viewpoint but it often does not allow for aspects of the current situation's past to be discussed or allow to be proposed futures or forecasts that the leaders are unaware of or have not considered effectively. As with all attempts to understand the current reality or possible future, unpredicted aspects probably should be considered and sometimes taken into account. Before developing this aspect of the possible futures for this field of intelligence it is important to review the traditional and historical uses of BI and its effects.

History of Business Intelligence

From time immemorial the purpose and intention of business has been to gain new customers and to profitably retain and grow the service and/or product

---

[2] *IBM Journal*, Vol 2, No 4, pp. 314–19.

supplied to established customers. This of course has been undertaken in different ways by different organizations around the world, even businesses and companies that work within the law and others partially or entirely outside the law. Nevertheless, a BI strategy is useful for any type of operation and one of the central ways of understanding and improving this process is through better understanding and use of the markets, competition, customer feedback and internal customer knowledge, and internet working processes. The aim is to have an accurate, continuously updating picture of the market reality with underlying information that your competition is unaware of. This should offer information on and knowledge of the preferences of customers, their buying habits, and their own internal regulations, customs, and 'beliefs'. The need to understand your customer and the marketplace you are working within is crucial and is often taken as read by many business owners and senior management. Yet ignorance, both in this area, and of the general marketplace, are surprisingly widespread since the desires of the customer change more frequently than most businesses believe.

Some business analysts have used Sun Tzu's *Art of War* as a point from which to start to clarify their business's purpose, intentions, understanding of customers, and potential going forward. Sun Tzu was of course referring to the enemy when he talked about understanding the strengths and weaknesses of the opposition but he also stressed the need to understand your own strengths and weaknesses and these two fundamentals remain the core behind most business success and why many businesses fail. Understanding your strengths and weaknesses and really engaging with the preferences and purposes of your customers is vital. To achieve this end you must collect, analyse, and use primarily three types of data: knowledge of your own business, knowledge of customers and potential customers, and third, different perspectives and understandings of the marketplace and the other players, and what can improve and affect their actions.

A Business Intelligence Model

The BI model begins with a vision statement; moves to strategic planning; and then different parts of the business create a linear BI strategy based on the company's overall strategy. From this process a strategic outcomes model is created to understand where the business perceives the strategy to be going and how this will happen. Next, within each part of the business there should be an applications research model, which will attempt to give very focused views on different, departmental aspects of the business. Finally, as the process of business continues at different times and for different reasons, aspects of the business will need to be analysed to understand why certain parts are working, either positively or negatively, outside the strategy or forecasts. Here Key Performance Indicators (KPI) and the strengths, weaknesses, opportunities, and threats (SWOT) of particular products or services are analysed in depth. To begin the process after the strategy is created, different versions of the BI model process should also be undertaken.

This can develop from the same vision statement but take different perspectives on the business plans and new projects. This should be undertaken within the same timescale as the strategic planning process and should be done by the different divisions or departments within the business. It should include different employees and outsiders with specialties to add to the mix. This can be described as the linear BI strategy (LBIS).

Linear Business Intelligence Strategy

A linear business plans and projects strategy should be developed by each division and department within the business. All departments or divisional business areas should review the overall strategy for the business and then, starting with their own objectives, review the people, processes, technologies, and required results. They should report to the board with their initial considerations for discussion and analytical arguments. A review of different strategic processes should then be undertaken at the completion of this process and should not be seen as 'soonest done, soonest forgotten'. This should be an infrequent but continuous process that includes different parts of the business and different outside researchers, clients, and service providers. Adequate time must be allowed for the process to take place, especially when there are significant changes to the markets, competition, and internal changes. It is then that a greater amount of review time should be allocated for the next strategic planning process to be undertaken.

In many businesses the review and analysis process is flawed, rarely used, or even generationally non-existent, and only when some businesses get into real difficulty do they feel the problems through cash flow (problems with payment, salaries, wages, etc) and have to go to the bank for an overdraft or overdraft extension. Often a consultant is then called in and some form of review takes place. Conversely, some more analytically motivated operations regularly employ different methods to give some valid perspective.

Strategic Outcome Model

Business analysis techniques have grown significantly over the last 50 years as business schools and consultancies have increased, electronic information and tagging techniques for monitoring the information have improved, and businesses have generally broadened their range and outlook. BI models and techniques range from the business intelligence model, LBIS, and strategic outcome models, via applications research models and KPI, to SWOT analysis, and this list is not exhaustive. However a review of those highlighted will give a good background to what is being done to analyse the different areas of business using business intelligence.

Howard Dresner of the Gartner Group, a leading IT research and advisory company, used BI as a concept that brought together and focused 'concepts and methods to improve business decision-making by using fact-based support systems'. These ideas can be made into a five-step process that is set to drive the performance, goals, and values of a business. This is a strategic outcome model and the first part ('measurement') helps to build a pyramid or hierarchy of performance goals that measures actions and outcomes by first collecting data and focusing its analysis. The second step is 'analytics', deep analysis of unfocused business data to create predictive analysis by modelling past and current business processes. The third stage ('reporting') is done by building strategic and operational feedback that creates systems for reporting, and encourages discussion with senior management of the business. The fourth, 'collaboration', has the objective of connecting different parts of the business with others outside the business (such as suppliers) to coordinate and share data, understanding, and their current and future interests in their aspects of the business. And finally the fifth step is to build a knowledge management program that coordinates the first four steps and then creates a system that can lead to deeper understanding, review, training, and learning within the organization about the process and its effectiveness. This should be directly connected to and reviewed against regulatory and compliance laws and what are considered best practices.

Having produced a strategic plan each area of the business should analyse its own objectives and how these relate to the overall business strategy. The divisional business plans and new projects should be reviewed using the LBIS. Then for different parts of the business a series of applications research models should be reviewed and built. Supervisors and middle managers should be taught how to do this so they and their colleagues begin to really understand the process and its applications. And to really get into the review and to focus the process, these groups should be encouraged to understand and discuss the strategy and their aspects of the business.

Applications Research Model

This process should receive assistance from the centre's analysts. Relevant data should be collected and analysed for different parts of the operation and then turned into information about a particular subject, product, or service. As this process continues focused knowledge will be begin to be created that should be recorded and used to identify what elements of the overall picture now need more data, information, and detail to produce real BI when applied to the relevant product process, sales perspective, or service. Doing this will help to produce a relevant system application that will improve the efficiency and/or profitability of that part of the business.

Each of the five elements of the process should be recorded—data collection, data analysis, distillation as information, gap analysis, final business intelligence. A distillation should be created as a report and a visual presentation that should be given to the participants. Then, once a review has taken place a new presentation should be given to the senior management team at which questions and debate should again take place, with a number of the divisional/departmental employees being present.

Key Performance Indicators (KPI)

This is another area of review that has had a lot of use for analysing very specific areas of the business, often the more positive or particularly negative parts, to understand the current state of business. But formulating correct and not-over-complicated KPI is a task that should be undertaken reasonably often, by insiders and by outsiders who have an understanding of the current operation. It should be reviewed reasonably frequently to ensure product and service effectiveness. The ability to add customers and achieve growth and effective profitability and savings is what is important. Broader BI tools can include analysis software and data collection and modelling systems, but the operational purpose for a particular part of a business is to grow the size of the business effectively, by improving its relationship with existing and prospective customers. To develop KPI you need to understand the workings of your own business, how it achieves strong customer relationships, and to analyse and review the current and potential new markets for your products and services.

SWOT Analysis

Finally in this chapter we will review the technique of SWOT analysis (Figure 10.2), which aims to identify the *s*trengths, *w*eaknesses, *o*pportunities for, and threats to a whole business, parts of an operation, and/or specific sectors or products. It is a useful tool for looking at different futures or (more realistically) potential outcomes. It should be used as a way of linking different internal aspects of the business with outside interests such as suppliers, customers, and specialists, in conversation and debate. It should be recognized as a way of being analytical, forward-looking, and inclusive. To make it work well as a process, like a number of other models that have been discussed, presenters should be allocated (visual and analytical recorders of the information), and there must be objective reviewers of the process (at least two or three) who are not directly connected with each other and who report independently. This is important, to get different perspectives and to reduce recording bias, which often occurs in any formalized process.

BI Model: Summary

From these different models the company should choose the ones that work for different aspects of the business and before active use is made of them. The process in each area should be tested a number of times before the process becomes fixed into the internal landscape. Nevertheless, businesses of all sizes have the potential, ability to use, and need for these more considered and sophisticated

	Positive Factors	Negative Factors
Internal Factors	Strengths	Weaknesses
External Factors	Opportunities	Threats

Figure 10.2 SWOT analysis

analysis tools. Web applications and cloud computing offer many examples of tools and focused usage but business knowledge and understanding is the first requirement and from this the competitive landscape and the broader markets should be kept at the forefront of the research and review process. These elements then must be gauged and evaluated against the review of the internal business, its current capabilities, and where and what type of change is needed to meet the goals and potential going forward.

In this chapter, we have concentrated on the broader definition, which is more to do with strategic analysis of the business than with BI as a sophisticated data collection and analysis tool. For the average commercial IT department little has changed since the invention of the relational database, which produced and almost fixed the IT purpose as a service-oriented, architectural structure. This was reinforced by the creation of Structured Query Language (SQL), which was developed by IBM in the 1970s and was designed to retrieve data from IBM computers. This idea of BI as an IT function still exists but is now beginning to change with the onset of 'BI 2.0'. The effects of this are similar in outline to the effects of Web 2.0 and parts of Web 3.0—using the semantics of a search more effectively to analyse and focus the research in deeper, more specific ways for particular users of the information and intelligence.

Traditional and more recent IT use of BI as a process was to gather, collect, and analyse vast quantities of data and to make business sense from the analysis based on what was being asked for by other departments. Some of the more sophisticated users of this type of BI came from the banks, which analyse credit cards and approve uses in real time, and (in similar ways) air traffic control. However, most of the users of this type of BI did not want to discuss the process of this type of IT analysis and the software companies that sold the applications maintained their knowledge and tried to gradually improve the process for the client without getting into the technical longer grass. Nonetheless, this also is gradually changing and, just as individuals expect more from their Web searches, so business analysts will expect far more sophistication from their IT analysis and not only will they expect to understand the IT processes and their broad analysis but they will want more personal business sophistication that fits more directly into their current and potential future business needs.

This process will gradually broaden and affect all areas of intelligence, not just commercial and business intelligence. Social media are altering the way people expect to locate and use information and this of course is affecting BI. Decisions can be made in the moment and data will be linked more directly with actions being taken, across very large amounts of global data. The divisions between the expert and the crowd, at least intellectually, are being reduced by the practice and concepts of social media. However, from a broader intelligence as well as a BI perspective, using and understanding these changes is vitally important as they are affecting not just the ways consumers act and think but also the way commercial, political, social, and criminal activities will take place and take advantage of the current environment, and how much of this will alter and change business in the near future. The capability and skill to analyse and identify new patterns within large amounts of data through new, creative, pattern recognition will become more common and this will not be done just by the IT experts but by a broader group of analysts and researchers. Data will be linked far more directly with actions to be taken, and in the next chapter we will focus on a particular area of government control (law enforcement) and review some of the radical changes that two senior participants consider very necessary.

11

A 'Paradigm Shift' in Police Intelligence

Sir David Phillips and Dr John Phillips

This chapter reviews the current and accepted political and public understanding of law enforcement in the UK, and offers a radical rethink of the organizational process.

It is written by Sir David Phillips, former Chief Constable of Kent, who helped create and introduce Intelligence-Led Policing in the UK, and Dr John Phillips, who is currently a Detective Inspector with Kent Police.

Currently no one from the research community, senior police leaders, the intelligence community, or even front-line police, has highlighted the need for a more effective intelligence process. The National Intelligence Model has been delivered and the intellectual drive is directed towards the usual political agenda of popularity. Discussion about effective intelligence once again lurks in the long grass.

The reason why this debate should be resurrected is ironically because public support for the police is more likely to rise if the police were more effective at dealing with those who adopt a criminal or terrorist/insurgent lifestyle. And the efficient use of intelligence is certainly one of the most effective ways of reducing crime and detecting terrorist activity. Pandering to an ill-informed populist agenda around local visibility of police on the street is expensive and wasteful if it does not produce this result, and there is little evidence that it has. The visibility argument rests upon two dubious presumptions: first that presence is reassuring; second that the presence of patrols will deter crime and bad behaviour.

There is an element of truth in both but no more than a sliver. Presence will not reassure if it is merely passing and cursory, and (given actual levels of availability) that is all it can ever be; and police presence on the streets patently does little to deter the drug dealer, the shoplifter, the fraudster, the careful burglar, the street robber (who chooses his moment), the drunken lout, the sex offender, etc. The case for intelligence is to have sufficient knowledge of crime to be able to neutralize it—and this can be done.

Visibility and Invisibility

The problem is that even to police management, intelligence activity is largely unnoticed. Operational problems are visible enough but prediction and indeed tactical solutions are not. What the police see is volume. They are well rehearsed in the vocabulary that is associated with crime and criminal neighbourhoods—the imbalance between resources and demands for service; the need for more cooperative activity between public services; and the hindrances of a bureaucratic system for dealing with criminal cases, largely imposed by the inflated role of the Crown Prosecution Service. But they are also able to quote in their defence statistical falls in volumes of crime that themselves are a function of poor analysis—quite simply, styles of crime have shifted from the definitions laid down in the 1950s and the categories we now count miss out large numbers of undetected crimes (shoplifting by addicts, identity theft, telecommunications fraud, cyber crime, dealing in illegal substances and black-marketeering, etc) whilst flatteringly including categories such as stealing cars, the incidence of which has fallen because low-value cars can be purchased for next to nothing.

Home Office classifications of crime no longer fit the profile of offending by lifestyle criminals. Thus, when there are statistical falls in crime they do not accord with public perception. But more significantly, because the police response to crime is geared almost exclusively to reports of crime from the public, criminality is still not seen in pre-emptive terms. If it were, the intelligence deficit would be immediately clear. It is quite different for terrorism, when we do think pre-emptively, and the first thought after an attack is always to question why the current intelligence did not allow us to forestall the event.

If the police do not observe the problem it is not surprising there is little open public disquiet. The simplistic public response to the problem of crime is to call for more 'men on the beat' and the simplistic police response is to try to organize something along those lines, for example 'neighbourhood policing', even though there is little evidence of defensive patrols arresting criminals about to commit crimes or driving them away. As has been implied, at best pre-emptive policing by patrol can only hope to deter in the immediate vicinity of the patrolling officer, and the level of presence (other than in critical locations) is bound by the equation between the vast acreages and mileages to be patrolled and the actual levels of policing—a reality that no amount of relief from paperwork will alter. Alternatively, pre-emptive policing can work if the intelligence effort is good enough to allow direct targeting of recidivist offenders or neutralizing their opportunities, but sadly such thinking does not fit the 'reassurance agenda'.

143

The public do have a vague expectation that the police have an intelligence capacity but neither they nor politicians interest themselves in its value. In fact, outside the corridors of police management, the only time that capacity gets an airing is in court proceedings when lawyers seek to invade intelligence dossiers to inhibit prosecutions of offenders serious enough to have become subjects of such records. And even here the scope of debate is largely settled. The law has stabilized and disclosure battles follow a tricky but uncontroversial route.

Intelligence and Policing

The literature on intelligence is almost entirely about national security. Most of the material is American and as 10 per cent of the American defence budget goes in this direction that is perhaps not surprising. Also, as intelligence gathering by the police in the United States is of doubtful legality unless there is 'probable cause' to suspect involvement in a crime, there is comparatively little police investment in intelligence gathering as an activity separate from investigation. Perhaps the greatest deficiencies in the literature as far as police intelligence systems are concerned are the emphasis on analysis and the strategic *locus*. Even in the national security world for most operational people better information collection is the heart of the matter. After all, if the source is reliable and the information verifiable, interpretation is a lot less speculative. This truth is why in most intelligence services specialist collectors have more influence than analysts, even though the supremacy of the 'all-source' analyst is an axiom in the theory of the intelligence world. In the literature intelligence collection is described (HUMINT, SIGINT, ELINT, IMINT, etc) but it is rarely seen as the heart of the dilemma, for all that questions are raised about the suitability of human-source intelligence programmes.

As far as the strategic emphasis is concerned such is the natural priority in the world of national security, but in policing most useful intelligence is actually tactical in nature. There may be patterns in crime but there are few criminal masterminds directing major campaigns of crime. Even criminal markets are in a sense disorganized, although there are discernible characteristics that are properly open to analysis. Perhaps it is unnecessary to determine whether the study of criminal networks and systems is tactical or strategic, but in general it is specific enough that it would hardly rank as strategic in military terms. But the distinction is important because strategic intelligence doctrine usually emphasizes its disinterest in operations whilst tactical intelligence has no value unless it can be turned to operational account. The literature, concentrated as it is on the strategic contribution intelligence can make, rarely considers the interface between operational user and intelligence producer, whereas it is probably this relationship that is at the heart of effective intelligence use in the police.

Thus, whilst the intelligence effort is largely tactical it is not closely integrated with routine operations, and arguably that is where the real potential for leveraging performance lies. The basis for an upgrade, then, is not to be found either in more effective prioritization by commanders or in the greater professionalism of intelligence staff, desirable though these may be, but in the universality of intelligence use. A defining change would be to make intelligence integral to the main business, not something important though marginal to the activity of most officers, as is presently the case.

There is something contemporary and almost inevitable about the prospect of information systems extending to front-line staff in the field. The very idea is inherent in the way people use information technology in the wake of the internet and hand-held mobile data devices in their ordinary lives. The real paradigm shift is probably in the way modern man views information—not as a function of memory and discussion but as an immediate electronic resource available at a touch. Thus the inspiration for change does not come from theories of intelligence, whether they be descriptive or critical, nor from contemporary theories of policing, which (as we have somewhat caustically observed) are motivated by political rather than operational assessments, but flows naturally from what may be termed the 'second enlightenment'—the so-called 'information age'. Put another way, technological push—inevitable in an age where near-universal private usage of digital technologies makes police systems appear antediluvian—must eventually seep through with great consequence for the basic tenets of intelligence thinking. For its part, the intelligence community has to be careful that its attachment to methods designed when obtaining and manipulating information required specialist skills does not become a barrier to development, by judging universal access as a threat to their craft. Indeed, as shall be suggested, the old paradigm—analyst-led intelligence targeting—still has a place and a better place more suited to their craft, focusing analytical effort on criminal associations that are difficult to fathom and providing intelligence profiles on the 'network' for universal users to exploit.

The new opportunity is much more immediate than the processes of the National Intelligence Model, achieving a change of context in which intelligence assets are central to most investigative activity and a frequent originator of operations. Such is the idea of 'network centricity'. It requires technological investment as an enabler but just as much it calls for a proper comprehension of the potential such a methodology might enable, and a management willingness to create the operational conditions in which it may flourish. In a word paradigm shift is about obtaining symmetry between intelligence capability and universal working practice.

If the standard intelligence model has problems associated with the proper comprehension of intelligence as an asset, there may be a countervailing influence on the new model. If and when officers on general patrol and routine investigative work get access to information products that seriously add value to their enquiries, and sometimes reveal opportunities to exploit situations that hitherto would have passed unremarked, the take-up will not need much direction. Technological push will unite with demand pull—from the bottom up. Thus, perversely, the 'new model' might actually not need the active direction of the command ranks for it to function, at least not if operating practice were to be sufficiently liberal to allow self-organization around operations.

Exactly how might such a system be arranged? First, it is the versatility in modern computing software that offers the prospect. In a sense we are looking at a parallel to the 'internet'. Its users do not go on courses, read instruction manuals, are not subject to audit of their transactions, are little restricted by operating rules, and yet most people become adept and uninhibited users of information. They learn to ask questions, follow intuitive pathways, they know where they find success, become familiar with operating systems, and carry out complex related transactions. Analogously, police users of a modern intelligence system should be afforded similar freedom. Rather than returning to the police station to search record management systems offering unrelated pages of limited information, the user should be able to follow any number of enquiries simultaneously, trace their origins, identify material from previous files, access images and maps, employ graphics packages to carry out simple analytical tasks, search vehicle recognition systems, receive and publish information on a live basis, and check the current status of persons, vehicles, warrants, etc. Provided the same relational database is the bedrock of all operational transactions, enquiring officers and analysts should be able to trace and link every transaction that any person, location, vehicle, or other 'entity' has had with policing. Investigation is about building pictures—sequences of events, biographies, associations, previous histories, access to criminal know-how and criminal supply lines, movements, *modus operandi*, predisposition, current intelligence—it is from these connections that we ascribe motive, identify suspects, and build evidence. It would be a quantum leap to make such functionality available to front-line operational officers in the field, yet surprisingly the technology is readily available.

It may not be too dramatic to describe such a proposal as representing a 'paradigm shift,' a term taken from Thomas Kuhn's grand thesis.[1] It may be a presumptuous sobriquet for changes in the relatively small domain of the intelligence world, but it does catch the meaning better than most expressions. It suggests not merely advancement but change in the way we think about things.

Thus, without claiming anything truly momentous but using the idea of 'paradigm shift' analogously, we might see some parallels. First, the existing model of intelligence for police is too cumbrous to make for effective front-line use. Necessity demands a different approach. Second, we might expect resistance from existing practitioners who see their specialism being invaded. The solution is about injecting information into current operations so that all the users on the network can make intelligence inferences simultaneously, including analysts working on existing problems. The intelligence pictures that emerge might then afford immediate operational 'strike opportunities' by self-organizing players on

---

[1] *The Structure of Scientific Revolutions* (University of Chicago Press, 1962), examining change in basic assumptions, or paradigms, within the ruling theory of science.

146

the network. Access to information, often leveraged by links to intelligence models (analysis), would enable a shift in the normal operational paradigm.

In a sense, in this mode, we are redefining intelligence from a 'product' to a method. And in this regard it is worth a digression into our understanding of the meaning of intelligence as a heuristic—an aid to comprehension. Indeed, given the capacity of modern technology to dazzle and confer the impression of certainty our thinking should be properly based. According to Drs Lambert and Scholz,[2] philosophers of knowledge have distinguished three phases: knowing what there is; knowing what is known and how it is known; and lastly comprehending the use of what is known. The final phase, associated with the impenetrable Wittgenstein, contemplates 'meaning as use' rather than meaning deriving simply from a classification of what there is (ontology) and an appropriate theory for handling the knowledge in question (epistemology). And following the idea of 'meaning' being defined by 'use', we might speculate whether the opportunity for uninterrupted usage in the manner of internet browsing amongst a privileged internet community (those on the intelligence network) might redefine intelligence—always presuming that doing so proves to be functional rather than dysfunctional. The change of use in a network-centred model is not in quality as such, but in the rapidity of supply and the potential for building up associations on a near-instant basis. In this way intelligence becomes part of the investigation, not an alternative to investigation. Inevitably, intelligence experts should always be searching for new methods of collection and analysis to lessen the uncertainties, that is evolution within the existing paradigm, but the 'paradigm shift' implied by the new model is about universal and instant use, not a change of theory, although this is implied by the change of use.

In the last decade or so, through the agency of the National Intelligence Model, policing has structured intelligence with products and disciplines and given some order to its formal employment by 'tasking and coordinating groups'; in other words, an operating doctrine has emerged. We have as yet to move on to a stage where the 'user community' makes its own adaptation to the potential for immediate information access, though.

'Centricity'

The question then is, without setting aside the formal and still valid early paradigm capability, can the 'user community' be enabled to operate beyond the formal disciplines and make intelligent usage of information tailored to their immediate requirements? The difference is between intelligence used mainly as a discipline to limit what is done so as to achieve focus, and intelligence as a

---

[2] Dale Lambert and Jason Scholz, 'A Dialectic for Network Centric Warfare', *Proceedings of the 10th International Command and Control Research and Technology Symposium* (ICCRTS) MacLean, VA, 13–16 June 2005.

universal means of problem solving guaranteed by immediate access to relevant information. Current writing about intelligence is peppered with references to centricity: information-centric, intelligence-centric, network-centric, and target-centric are prime examples. Thus the term 'network-centricity' in intelligence work does not of course refer specifically to the wonders of the digital (and often-invisible physical) network upon which it relies; rather, it represents the innovations that may flow from the availability of networked information channels and the remarkable means we now have to manipulate the data they carry in voluminous streams. Put another way, intelligence as an asset stands to be transformed by the availability of modern information networks and the computerized analytical tools that modern computing has to offer. The problem is that intelligence systems can and inevitably do benefit from the advantages of the information age but often without that transforming impact that is their potential. Common usage, even against greatly enhanced supplies of information, merely enhances the scope of the existing regime; it does not change how the business is conducted. At best it perhaps makes some decisions better informed. 'Network-centricity', on the other hand, envisages a great deal more than this; it forecasts a change in the very nature and use of intelligence, impacting massively upon the business it serves.

State enterprises, military bodies, police forces, and commercial organizations, as typical users of intelligence, are archetypically hierarchical bodies. In the standard paradigm, their intelligence systems collect information at the operational and tactical levels; analyse and process it within a confidential environment; and make its product available to commanders whose operational decisions then radiate downwards. The 'intelligence cycle' has its high point at the command level of the hierarchy and serves to reinforce the hierarchical model of control. Hierarchy, these days a negative term like bureaucracy, is actually the logical means of achieving coordination in otherwise large and unwieldy bodies. Warfare without hierarchy would devolve into innumerable individual skirmishes without tactics or strategy. The greater potency of the whole (as against the sum of the parts) entirely depends upon coordination. Hierarchy is not, as some sociologists would have it, simply a pathology associated with large organizations—it is essentially functional, albeit it carries with it the inherently dysfunctional characteristics of miscommunication and delay.

On the down side intelligence in the traditional and standard model too often tends to be wreathed in secrecy and an asset available to very few, constricted by the rules of hierarchy, sometimes difficult for front-line personnel to access, and subject to malfunction because of delays and communications blockages. Consequently, whatever the propaganda to the contrary, it is not pervasive as a methodology throughout an organization.

As a model it is easily critiqued. As Robert Clark,[3] a modern writer on analysis, has observed, the 'cycle' itself is a misnomer. Its organization is linear rather than

---

[3] Robert M Clark, *Intelligence Analysis, a Target-Centric Approach* (CQ Press, 2004).

cyclical and it is often made to work by short-circuiting its disciplines. New information is constantly interacting with the current intelligence picture; persistent users find ways to subvert the hierarchical discipline and take early advantage of situations where they can; its operation tends to be linear rather than cyclical with far less feedback than is appropriate; and lastly, the adoption of tight rules of operation and the 'need to know' principle create bottle-necks, inflexibility, and support misconception and delay.

Clark suggests a close and interactive working relationship between the analyst, responsible for creating the models, and the customer, but his conception of intelligence is very much around the skill set of the analyst and to some extent the specialist collector. But he is addressing problems with a level of complexity and seriousness (conflict at the level of national security and warfare) at which the expert evaluation of copious and unclear source material may be necessary. Nonetheless Clark's concept of 'target models' can be nicely linked with the network-centred theory. Target models reside on a network which different users can access different versions of for different purposes, sometimes, at a tactical level, interacting in real time, and sometimes for planning purposes.

The network-centred concept is located very much more at the tactical end of the business and it is the military who have been the most critical of the recondite and dilatory aspects of traditional intelligence systems. Modern technology has conferred on the military the ability to see where once there was obscurity; to strike with enormous velocity and sometimes precision; to move with celerity and agility; and to deploy firepower of frightening intensity. The sheer pace and three-dimensional character of modern military capability means there is simply no time for a cyclical and hierarchical process to work. Command and control, and the information critical to decision making, have of necessity to be decentralized or the weaponry they have at their disposal will not have utility.

Dr Scholtz,[4] a scientist working for the Australian military and proponent of the alternative, information-centric approach, explains how the new process entails shifting power to the margins and democratizing decision making, leading to the formation of rapidly constructed local alliances to achieve immediate and possibly fleeting objectives as network users view the available options. Unity of purpose, previously supplied by the hierarchy, is the outcome of logical decision making in the context of the extended awareness the network confers upon its users.

In this network-centred scenario operatives can pull information from the network and push it further around the network. Vast data streams can be merged, searched, and analysed quickly because of the sophisticated software tools available. Modern automated software enhances decision making—expertise can be downloaded and knowledge assimilated. Search engines can now go beyond syntactic searches of the data to semantic and cognitive searching. Anomalies

---

[4] Scholz & Lambert, 'A Dialectic for Network Centric Warfare'.

and links can be found across widely held intelligence and storylines suggested that match the information against possible meaning. Interactive programmes can act out scenarios; artificial intelligence can track and simulate different options and so on.

For police purposes the essence of the scheme is to provide a wide network of intelligence users who will have different levels of need and different levels of access. Nonetheless the minimum presumption is a general and immediate access to standard intelligence products and to the corporate history of dealings with that person, location, vehicle, or whatever entity is in question. Incidental checks on persons of intelligence interest might well provide opportunities for physical and information search and reveal opportunities to enquire into other criminal behaviour. Analysts providing synthetic models of criminality (network charts of criminals and their organizations illustrating key locations and roles, for example) will, so to speak, launch their products onto the system as live entities likely to be added to and updated as investigators and patrols interact with the subjects on the chart. Investigators dealing with cases will have access to all previous encounter information about any of the parties to the investigation and the relevant associations they discover will be added to the system. Supervisors and managers can monitor opportunist operations and intervene.

Getting There from Here

But network-centricity is not just a matter of information holdings increasing and being accessible to enhance investigative reasoning, but calls for commensurate operational flexibility to organize the same kind of short-term alliances that Dr Scholz anticipates for the military. The revelation of opportunity needs to be supported by organizational readiness, specifically the need to assemble small-scale, competent, strike-team capability. The object is to impose information dominance over the criminal community, negating their primary advantage, which is obscurity.

Unfortunately today, as we have observed, the new mantra of 'neighbourhood policing', effectively no more than a dubious return to a nostalgically conceived 1950s model of policing, has superseded intelligence-led activity. Yet mathematics and a little common sense should rebut any faith in the simplest assumption that police presence alone can keep criminality in its place—a ratio based on the available officers for patrol set against the street mileage to be patrolled is always in excess of 1:100 and the justice system has completely failed to do what it did in the 1950s and back up the police authority. Honourable as the reformist cause may be, criminality will not be much abated by benign patrols or by social initiatives. The sheer level of recidivism amongst lifestyle criminals and the serially dishonest surely indicates that they have to be personally confronted. Indeed, reform is only likely if there is a much greater certainty of detection. Increasing the level of guardianship through increased patrolling at a level likely to make a real impact is unrealistic given the cost and the institutions of justice show no inclination for a preventative level of sentencing. If the enforcement model of policing is then to be pursued with more effect it has got to be by better targeting and a greater return on the interventions that are made; both are only likely through the better handling of information. The case for the network-centred approach is that it offers the means for the entire operational capacity to benefit from access to the intelligence world, progressively and relentlessly exposing the dark recesses of criminality.

As far as terrorism is concerned staff operating in routine security roles have generally been seen as running, guarding, and checking businesses at the very end of the intelligence food chain. They have been reared on the assumption that their role is to provide snippets of information, often valueless in themselves, that are aggregated by unseen intelligence professionals, used to provide banal general guidance, and very occasionally produce some kind of commando raid against a real target. In the new scenario those in the front line would be active network users and possessed of commensurate awareness. Better informed and enabled by information access they might be able to act rapidly on their own initiative, even making operational strike decisions in alliance with those near at hand, likewise aware as network users.

The essence of current threats, particularly the threat from Islamic extremism, is difficult to isolate and tie down. The movement is largely bereft of traditional organization; it is diffuse, its leadership messianic, and its targeting oblique; its front-line personnel may be transitory and suicidal, operating as single-mission projectiles; it has wide access to support amongst strongly religious communities characterized by poverty and hatred of Western culture; it is not subject to rational discussion in the Western sense and responds to very different motivations. Traditional means of counter-intelligence, for example penetrating the terrorist hierarchy by clandestine means, have little utility in the absence of an organized and conspiratorial opponent.

Future intelligence services will have to risk far more access to their networks of information by those having operating and security responsibility in the front line, and encourage far greater input to the process. Management and security personnel, particularly those in the transport sector, will need to make a step-change in their thinking, prioritizing security as the greatest risk to their businesses, investing in access to the networked world of intelligence, and perhaps themselves employing more analysts rather than more checkers and guards. It may mean a rebalancing of effort from physical to electronic search and this means a good deal more than simply another piece of kit; it means thinking about how the vast and potentially available streams of data about people and goods in transit can be searched against profiles, and how verifiable and legitimate transit can be separated from questionable travellers. Everyone with security responsibilities is going to have to learn to react much more quickly, probably in real time.

151

Almost all terrorist attacks, when they have been investigated after the event, left enough clues between their inception and the event to have raised alarms had the right questions been asked. The ability to ask pertinent and lucid questions is partly an individual skill but it is also a function of the kind of learning culture that all security-minded organizations need to foster at risk of peril in an uncertain and volatile world.

The reason why the concept of paradigm shift has been selected to escort the idea of versatile networks of intelligence is that clarity of thinking is most challenged, not so much by individual intellectual narrowness, as by the intellectual context within which we all work. The difficulty and danger is that, when faced with international conflicts that seemingly call for some kind of strategic response, military and political imperatives override calculation and assessment. Policing provides a less compelling scenario but the logic is familiar. Assumed imperatives about the minimal use of force in the execution of the law enforcement mission, and a political enthusiasm for intervention to be followed by benign, reconstructive measures, undermine the creation of forces fit for purpose in the long haul against criminality and terrorism.

Criminal justice reflects the same contention. Distaste for custodial sentences, both because they offend liberal sentiments and for reasons of cost, coupled with an enthusiasm for alternative, reconstructive measures that they would like to work but manifestly do not, perpetuate recidivism. Thus police chiefs, judges, Lord Chancellors, and ministers of state design a system for the conflict they would like to face, not the one that criminals engage in.

The real importance of the paradigm shift in favor of intelligent assessment is, then, not about to usher in a new set of policies but it may start to influence policymakers if intelligence assessments are repeatedly accurate and demonstrate success where they are adhered to. There is no panacea. In conflict the tactical successes of today are all too often reversed tomorrow. Given the humanitarian remit there are few short-term solutions, only the long haul. The best we can hope for is to read the situation accurately and be inventive and adaptive in the face of changing situations. Yet we will almost certainly be more often right than wrong if we dispassionately assess the context in which we operate and are brave enough to be objective in assessing the effectiveness of what we do.

12

Strategic Intelligence for the Twenty-first Century

This chapter examines current and new information and intelligence analysis methods that are used to understand the present environment. It includes examples of where traditional versions have been altered to work more effectively in the new, electronically globalized environment. The chapter suggests how the news and analysis can be used to integrate and focus information daily and the way in which this data and intelligence can be circulated to policymakers, law enforcement, government, and intelligence officials.

Regular briefing and discussions would also be used to break sectional groupthink and to continually monitor and examine current events and new analysis. Linear, cyclical, scenario, and mosaic intelligence methods are reviewed and their effectiveness and use is discussed. This strategic grid of methods can also be used to put the intelligence process into a historic, current, and forward-looking understanding in order to give a more objective, less biased, and clearer perspective on the current and potential reality.

Traditional, Modern, and Post-modern Intelligence

Prediction is set deep in the human psyche. The need to predict and the belief in suggested outcomes have fuelled the planning and methods we use for hunting, agriculture, religion, mysticism, science, philosophy, and intelligence. And both our success at forecasting and our (often) failure are what enable a few gamblers to make a living and the majority (who provide revenue and profit for betting shops, casinos, all the way to stock and financial trading) to lose so much. Nevertheless, attempting to understand and predict future outcomes, the opposition's capabilities and intentions, and even its belief systems can be very useful for supporting and changing your own strategy. And therefore analysing the current and potential reality has also proved to be effective in supporting your, or your organization's actions and beliefs. This intelligence analysis process should change as new threats or improved technologies alter the macro-economics, the geopolitical perspective of your country, and the actions of the organizations that make it work. Often, as history has shown, these changes require alterations to an organization's structure after their information collection, systems, and analytical processes sometimes fall out of step with the times. Besides, to really understand the current reality it is crucial to review the internal bias, expectations, and understanding among your own clients, your policymakers, and the perspective of your particular analysis.

To begin the process a vision statement and a strategic plan stemming from the vision are needed. This should grasp the current situation and the plan for where the process is intended to take the organization in the next few years. Often this strategic process itself is too short-termist and driven by the policymaker's current expectations, and therefore there is a tendency for the intelligence cycle itself to form part of this short-term strategic viewpoint. Frequently, the majority of intelligence timings follow the 24-hour news cycle, which is what can drive the policymaker's focus. Whereas historically many policymakers drove the media process, now (because of continuous global and electronic news) the drive is often from the general media, blogs, social networks, and the internet. To counter this effect political leaders have turned to their own media gurus who run teams of ex- or quasi-journalists with the intention of continuously monitoring, adjusting by discussions with journalists, or (by adding 'news' to the media and the web) hoping to alter and possibly change what is seen as the relevant media stories. These counter-intelligence and information engagements are often deployed after the event in a changing environment. Another significant problem with the use of strategic planning is the tendency to predict positive future prospects and outcomes by shortening project time, understating costs and completion times, over-emphasising potential successes, and playing down the possible negatives. There is another tendency, which is to respect the strategic process but to ignore the results. Therefore often a strategic plan is constructed and a report written which is then filed away until next time; after that players rely on the short term and use variations of the intelligence cycle as a way to appear to fully engage with the current and the possible futures.

The known and well-used traditional information and intelligence methods stemming from the intelligence cycle are still often exploited by established commercial, law enforcement, government, and intelligence agencies and it is clear that most government organizations involved with intelligence processes have not made the changes that the new environment requires. They are still employing a variety of the older and more traditional intelligence methods, often based on out-of-date structural models. However, we should step back and review the current intelligence structure and begin to see why the current time frame too frequently drives policy and lacks a longer-term perspective. Now let us review some of the current processes and look to see how they might be improved and enhanced.

There are four major types of traditional intelligence-gathering and planning, and each has its positive and negative aspects. The first type offers the policymaker current intelligence news and analysis. In the USA there are three major intelligence products that fit this model: the *Presidential Daily Brief*, which every morning has the President and a few senior executives as its audience; then *The Worldwide Intelligence Review*, another CIA product, is delivered electronically to several hundred senior legislative policymakers every day; and the *Secretary's Morning Summary*, a State Department product, is prepared for the personal use of the Secretary of State and senior executives. These briefing documents are created during the previous day and night and then delivered to the small, inner group of policymakers and their advisers described above early in the morning. Follow-up questions can be asked and answers attempted or new research undertaken.

In order to make these information and intelligence products more effective the intelligence service created its own version of *Wikipedia* called *Intellipedia*, and the FBI created *Bureaupedia*. *Intellipedia* was developed in 2005 and launched in 2006, partly as a response to the apparent intelligence failures surrounding 9/11. The project was partly inspired by the Galileo Awards, which encourage US intelligence staff to submit new ideas to improve information sharing. The *Intellipedia* online system for data sharing is currently used by the 16 US intelligence agencies and some of the other national security organizations. It has three levels of security classification—top secret, secret, and sensitive but unclassified. In 2010 the system had over 1 million pages, 5,000 daily edits, and about 100,000 current users. The *Bureaupedia* is a wiki system that the FBI created to retain and engage with agents' knowledge, information, and intelligence and it links to *Intellipedia*. Ben Bain of *Federal Computer Weekly* considers both *Bureaupedia* and *Intellipedia* to be knowledge management systems, which view was aired in an article in September 2008.

The second type of traditional intelligence-gathering and planning, which we would call a linear intelligence approach, is often referred to as the intelligence cycle and contains at least six phases; Direction, Collection, Collation, Analysis, Review, and Dissemination. In this traditional, one-dimensional method, a military commander would generate the intelligence requirement or direction by asking for information and intelligence about a current or up-coming battle issue. The intelligence team then analyse the problem against a matrix of available collection sources and assets. Information is collected and analysed. A senior analyst reviews the report or presentation and then it is delivered. This method is reasonably effective for operational intelligence, which should be capable of immediately being actioned. It is less useful for wider, longer-term planning and forecasting.

The third type is known as scenario or forecast planning, or Red Teaming, and here a group of analysts generate forecasts for policymakers. The games combine known facts such as demographics, geography, military lists, and political information with subjective interpretations or potential situations. The scenarios usually include plausible but unexpected situations and problems. These scenarios use the idea of consistency and thoughtful focus. The chief value of scenarios is that they allow policymakers to learn from mistakes without risking real-life situations. The problem is that usually they only consider the 'official future', which tends to be a straight-line graph of current trends projected forward to a particular date. These scenarios are good for some situations in which only one or two known changes might occur, such as the commercial implications of a shift in the price of oil following given market developments, but they often fail to work so well where a series of time-sensitive social changes are taking place and the outcomes can be more complicated or radical. This is akin to what Clinton saw in '*The Coming Anarchy*' and in the USA traditionally materializes as *National Intelligence Estimates,* which are created by National Intelligence Council with input from the rest of the intelligence community and offer an insight into issues of critical national security. Nevertheless, as a way of at least discussing, challenging, and perhaps offering a better understanding of some of the options and potential outcomes scenario-forecasting techniques do trespass outside the boundaries of accepted consideration and help the group to actively break aspects of groupthink.

During the Presidency of Gerald Ford in 1976, the then-Director of Central Intelligence, George H.W. Bush, commissioned an *Experiment in Competitive Analysis.* The aim was to review the strategic assumptions of American foreign policy towards Soviet Russia and to receive a second or third opinion about the current policy strategy. The Experiment was to review the current *détente* process. Critics of the process were engaged to analyse the data and classified information, including *National Intelligence Estimates* about the Soviet Union. The conclusions of this experimental initiative were subsequently called 'Team B'. This produced a review that differed sharply from the views of 'Team A' (the Ford Administration and the strategy coming from the intelligence community). This was to a degree a right-of-centre approach to the prevailing political understanding and later it was believed to have been regarded favourably by President Ronald Reagan who put the concept of *détente* under political and partially public review.

The fourth method is strategic intelligence (STRATINT), which gives a broader perspective at the national and international levels of the intended way forward and the issues, information, and intelligence that affect its intentions and actions. The aim of this planning is to give the policymakers foresight and the ability to create a clearer perspective of trends, opportunities, and threats.

The Mosaic Network Method

There have been a number of uses of the term 'mosaic' in the area of intelligence theory, which have suggested different methods of intelligence gathering. The US Department of the Navy defines 'mosaic' as a way of collecting apparently harmless data and information that, when pieced together, can show a new intelligence perspective. The process has been criticized in the USA because it can suggest monitoring American citizens before a crime has been committed, which breaks a US citizen's Constitutional right to freedom from government intrusion. However, the mosaic network method is a way of using traditional, modern, and post-modern collection and analysis techniques to give a broader and more focused picture of the current perspective from other players' viewpoints, as well as different internal views of the broader strategic scope. The mosaic network method looks at a current problem and analyses it from historic, political, economic, and cultural perspectives, from each side, and extrapolates trends or indicators as to why the current position has come about. It then overlays these trends on a different geographic, cultural, and social grouping to suggest possible new futures for that new situation. This analysis is not of the straight-line type and has the real advantage of stimulating imaginative planning processes and breaking different types of groupthink.

If this method, together with the four examined in the preceding section of this chapter, are 'mandatory' then new analysis and different types of thinking will begin to build new models and new trends for future planning and the old cycle of narrow, 'conservative' intelligence will gradually be broken. The whole process offers a more collective approach in which more structured information collection and post-modern analysis would work closely together to construct five types of intelligence. This does have ramifications for the way an intelligence organization would be physically structured, with specialists and generalists grouped together so they could overhear and take part in discussions and meetings. It means much more sharing of information and it means a lot more reviewing of reasoning. These types of analysis, or types similar to them, should be standard parts of any serious information process no matter where it is used. This means it can become as much a corporate as a governmental or military intelligence process. And discussion about process and systems of communication should not be left to corporate strategy experts, the military, or the intelligence professionals: we all need to consider what makes truth for us.

However, as the environment changes and particularly when new media, information, and communications come into play, different structures and processes are required if the new environment is to be clearly put into operational perspective. Today, a networked organizational structure makes more efficient sense than the old pyramid structure of management, and a horizon-scanning set of circular processes approach and focus the new reality, rather than a single process attempting to fit all. This new approach will often be preferable and necessary if we are going to get closer to some form of continuously objective intelligence and to reduce intelligence failure.

One of the more recent intelligence failures was the failure to predict the Arab Spring. Failures of this type come about through focus on the immediate, and because of the way in which the intelligence services are organized. The problem is often a lack of broader outlook and context. A monitoring of the social networks, including of course the gossip and conversations on Facebook, Twitter, and the like, would have revealed a very much clearer set of intentions that were widespread across North Africa and the Middle East. People in many different parts of the world, if they had friends and or relatives in North Africa or the Middle East, were aware that there were far more conversations going on and suggestions circulating. This monitoring does not in itself predict an outcome but it does indicate trends more clearly and so help understandings of potential outcomes. Many governments are at a loss how to explain the apparent change in monitoring that is required to take place. This has significant effects on the constitutional protection of US citizens from government monitoring and the answer is not easy, but this must be discussed, given the new electronic environment in which the collectivity of individuals and groups has meant that the traditional views of government and the legal systems are now out of step with the globalized and networked world.

However, the structure of intelligence organizations often does not follow changes in the environment. As with old, more traditional journalism the intelligence agencies' analysts have quite specific roles and responsibilities. The Tunisian analyst would focus on that country and would not be looking to see whether what happened in Tunisia was affecting other countries. Egypt would be someone else's responsibility. The analysts would not see it as their task, where not specifically asked to do so, to look at what effects activities in one location might be having in another country. This process is extended to the use of local agents, advisers, and spies. In June 2011 a former intelligence officer said in *Prospect* (a UK magazine): 'We used to be assisted by the Egyptians and Libyan and North African and Tunisian (security services), and by proxies in Pakistan...Now all that (work) devolves back on to CIA...'[1] He also added that the CIA is still locked into a Cold War organization and belief structure.

Because recently demand for longer-term analysis has been lacking, a more strategic view of the landscape has not been required. Therefore the analyst will tend to focus on short-term, factual evidence and scenarios, leading potentially to a reduced understanding of the longer term. There are of course differences between agencies and some will take a slightly extended view but most are locked into the 24-hour news coverage-and-response process.

The new strategic, operational, and tactical methods should, I believe, include continuous news and reporting from an intelligence operations viewpoint. There should be a new intelligence cycle that recognizes and reviews the difficulties with the traditionally used models. There should be regular use and discussion surrounding scenario-forecasting models and a much broader, mosaic method that actively breaks with groupthink and cultural bias and presents to the policymaker a personally tailored view of the social competitive landscape that they are currently examining. On a frequent and ongoing basis the process should also

---

[1] Michael Scheuer, former head of the CIA's Osama bin Laden unit, quoted in Browen Maddox, 'What should we expect from our spies?', *Prospect Magazine*, 26 May 2011.

include meetings that bring together the analysts, intelligence and/or law enforcement officers, and the policymaker's team, and regular meetings, discussions with, and briefings of policymakers themselves.

We will review and analyse each of the new intelligence models and methods, and how they interrelate with one another. However, there are some overarching changes to the organizational structure and work process that should first be recognized and included in our analysis. The first is the effect of the Information Revolution and the technology and software that are being introduced, and the second is the growing global networks and the impact that they are having on work practices and on the commercial organizational structures within which many people operate. All of these influences are beginning to radically change the way people work and operate more generally. There is an increase of work on the move and less working in a particular place (or even office environment). Work is more what one does rather than a place one goes to. Traditionally, the working environment defined your job by reference to the production line process, and time in and out of the office were often what was seen as the structure that defines major elements of a job.

Now, increasingly, the office environment will change and erode. Work will be done anywhere and at any time. Home, travel-time, and work environments will merge. The workplace as a social community will increasingly become history, an old paradigm. Work will be measured less by time and more by what an individual achieves and how effective the work that has been done is, measured against the current objectives and actions sought. Globalized information networks allow more work to be done on the move and closer to a client's needs and aspirations. People can work together without being required to physically meet as often as they previously did. The ridiculous practice of people sitting in the same office—even next to each other—and sending emails to their neighbour was an error-driven precursor to this new independent process. However, as with most of the office environment it did not achieve real measurement of work done and goals achieved.

Collaboration across distance between specialists, clients, management, and analysts will increase and software analysis tools will be used to measure the results and credible effects. If it is monitored and improved correctly, the efficiency of the process will gradually improve. There will be some blurring of the boundaries between working and the individual's personal and social life. This will potentially increase effectiveness and efficiency but will also increase isolation and many will regard this as a negative development in the more individual working experience.

The effects of these changes will gradually be felt in the intelligence agencies. The concept of an old-fashioned, physically separate office environment like Langley or MI5's Thames House headquarters, already seems in need of a paradigm shift. The new analyst should be networked into the policymaker's environment and should regularly be out and about, visiting areas that need analysis to gain understanding. They should be visiting and discussing with specialists as

159

well as continuously meeting their analytical intelligence requirements. This new organizational structure and process really begins to question how much fixed and separate office space is actually required and how effective the workplace environment has become. Analysis work that does not require a continuously highly classified, closed network can be done on the road and even at home. Increasingly the requirement to use a fixed office environment will only materialize once or twice a week (or month) depending on the type of work being carried out.

The bulk of the traditional intelligence process has been concerned with delivering the policymaker's requests by following, as sequentially as possible given the requirements, an established sequence. The intelligence cycle may well get broken in the process. Most intelligence agencies, law enforcement bodies, and corporate planning departments use the intelligence cycle process, in one form or another. In government bodies the particular methods of this established and traditional process go back many decades, sometimes to the time when a particular organization was first created. However, new methods have been used and created and one in particular should be cited as successful.

Reviews of Intelligence Processes

The intelligence process and the organizations employed need to review changes in technology and academic thought as new intelligence opportunities, and reflect them, reasonably frequently, using current information. Policymakers and their assistants, like the police on the ground, should receive data, imagery, and intelligence that are focused and relevant to their current requirements. To make this happen effectively organizations need to respond to the new challenges and every year they should review and test their organizations for operational and current technological purpose. This may mean reviews of the organization's effectiveness and weaknesses, then dismantling the organization and remaking it in line with the current intelligence requirements and the most effective and efficient methods.

One current method that should be employed to keep policymakers, strategists, and law enforcement critically focused is to deliver news, analysis, and intelligence that can generate immediate action. This should arrive on the user's hand-held in such a form that they should be able to go deeper and cross-reference the data to suit their purpose, and also to question and ask for more detail. The rigid, formalized structures of traditional, government-based organizations reflect their history, the reasons or excuses for their existence, and the often-high costs of establishing them. They often remain structurally similar to their original form because there is often little wish or willingness to change. It is different for commercial organizations in which, while internally there is often little willingness to change, the marketplace determines that the organization must change or else cease to exist. There is often a 'hard-wired' or 'brick-built' tradition that secures the hierarchy of the incumbent operational model and its high cost of maintenance. The internal and secret problems of intelligence creation are not the only aspects of the difficulties of creation. They also include changes to technology and society which, again, alter the requirements and methodologies that should be employed to make the changes needed. As many sociologists and historians will tell you, society frequently goes through radical transformations. Every decade someone will explain how locally effective and globally dramatic is the latest paradigm shift.

On a more popular level Alvin Toffler, a sociologist and futurist, described what he saw as the future in an article he wrote for *Horizon Magazine* in the summer of 1965. Features of his ideas were also published in *Redbook* and *Playboy* before being published as a book entitled *Future Shock*, followed by a film documentary based on the book, directed by Alex Grasshoff and presented by Orson Wells. These ideas describe what Toffler sees as the world changing too quickly for most people to be able to satisfactorily adapt: 'Western society for the past 300 years has been caught up in a firestorm of change ... Change sweeps through the highly industrialized countries with waves of ever accelerating speed and unprecedented impact.'[2] Someone wishing to give preference to their own beliefs and feelings will try to focus their audience on a current change, explaining that something radical is now taking place. However, these gears shift all the time in different parts of the globe and in different societies. Some of the changes are of course more schismatic, more radical, and widespread. Currently in the West we are going through one of these more radical shifts in the economic and information environments and it is affecting many other aspects of society.

If we look back at historic examples of just one current macro-economic issue it offers suggestions as to why historical analysis is important. Financial crises have happened regularly over the decades with one of the earliest (recorded by Dionysius) being the crisis of inflation in the 4th century BC at Syracuse. The Hundred Years War with France led England to a financial default in 1340; the Tulip Crisis of 1637 in the Netherlands, and the South Seas and Mississippi Bubbles of 1720 in England and France are other well-known examples. Every seven or eight years throughout the nineteenth century there were failures, recessions, and financial collapses in the USA and Europe. In 1893 Australia had its own banking crisis. In the twentieth century crises were recorded in both East and West: the Shanghai rubber market crisis of 1910; and of course the Wall Street Crash of 1929 followed by the Great Depression, which is still considered the largest financial crisis experienced by the developed world. Information and intelligence about, and prediction of these crises before they happen, is still a major problem for governments which rarely see them coming. Often the issues that cause the crisis are difficult to identify but of course buried in the data there is a clear story to be explained and countered if sufficient time and understanding were available to the makers of analysis and policy.

---

[2] *Future Shock* (New York: Bantham Books, 1971) p. 9.

Similarly, for the traditional intelligence world the collapse of the Soviet Union at the end of 1991 and the 9/11 attacks were not predicted in ways that made Western policymakers' desks. In a broader context significant changes in technology have dramatically altered the landscape of military intelligence. In the American Civil War the machine gun changed the methods of military attack and yet the machine gun and the role of deep trenches, a military technique the Romans used to their advantage, had not been fully integrated into intelligence strategy, planning, and tactics even by the first Battle of the Somme. Learning from previous consequences and picturing possible future actions has not been something we have really adapted into our thinking.

The changes to information delivery systems have not occurred in a vacuum, affecting 'only' the general public and most aspects of government: this revolution has also dramatically altered the traditional media, who surely should have known what was coming as this was part of their daily lives. This is a pertinent story for if commercially focused media moguls did not see the future coming and adapt to it why on earth should anyone else? Some of the answers to this question lie in the way in which a traditional industry is constructed and the way in which it sees and apparently understands its place in the culture. The traditional newspaper, magazine, and book publishing industries were an integrated part of a production-line process, which has similarities to the intelligence cycle. Instead of the client directly asking for particular information the publisher and the editorial staff believed they knew what was required and what would be of particular interest to those sections of the culture that traditionally bought this newspaper, or subscribed to that magazine, or should be expected to buy a particular book. The information was collected from press releases, pictures, reports, other media, journalists (by phone and face-to-face), photographers, interviews, and advertising data. Some publications quite strictly separated advertising from editorial and others did not. Stories were written and presented to various kinds of editor and through discussion, choice, and managerial decision, argument and bias constructed the text/pages. Once complete these would be checked and headlines/sidebars/jacket blurb constructed; lead stories/plot elements/points of argument might change position or even be dropped for another item. The finished article would be delivered to the print manager who then began the process of constructing type settings. Trial pages were then pressed or printed and again checked with editorial until all agreed to go and the presses started the printing, then binding or folding processes. From the end of the print line came the deliverable product, the publication that was then bound into packs and loaded into vehicles and delivered to retailers, shops, and street vendors and finally sold to the general public or sent to subscribers.

Then along came computers and the first to feel the pinch were the traditional, expensive reference books. Personal computer manufacturers decided that they could market their product if an encyclopedia came as part of the machine you were buying. The guilt that parents had felt when they considered buying the *Children's Britannica* was transferred to the PC once Microsoft loaded

Encarta onto it. Now, so parents believed, buying a PC would give their children a technological advantage, with the intellectual benefit of *Encarta* added and the combination often appeased parental guilt. From *Encyclopedia Britannica*'s point of view the competition had come from outer space. It was not traditional publishing competition and their business model, which gave their sales teams a relatively large bonus for selling books, turned this to disaster. The business model was very difficult to change. Printing, production costs, and sales commissions were high when set against the costs of producing a new Encarta database. But more fundamentally the business model, the reason why parents spent so much on the books in the first place, had been replaced. For the other aspects of traditional publishing the electronic insurgency had just begun. As the electronic options became clearer, traditional publishing models became gradually more irrelevant to the audience that had once connected to them. Just as radio had altered the newspaper, and television changed radio, so the PC altered the traditional media. The internet changed not only publishing, radio, film, and television but also the PC and telephone markets, which became more mobile and transitory.

Now we are seeing a different but similar process happening to the world of strategic information, tactical knowledge, and intelligence and, just as the traditional organization structures of publishing had trouble adapting and many did not, so the Information Revolution will disrupt and overturn traditional information and intelligence organizations and often this will happen in ways that take the traditional organizations by surprise. As has been said, we are in the midst of a cultural revolution that will take at least a decade to play out and the speed of the change has overwhelmed many commercial sectors (like publishing), as well as governments and their civil and military organizations. However, and this is a very important 'however', there are real benefits to be gleaned from these radical changes. As the philosopher and Jesuit thinker Pierre Teilhard de Chardin wrote in *The Phenomenon of Man* (his 1930s book posthumously published in 1955), sometimes disaster brings with it an acceleration of knowledge, enterprise, and understanding. Knowledge, according to Teilhard de Chardin, builds and is communicated with increasing layers of density and this improves our concentration and thinking methods. Layers of consciousness are focused into our minds allowing us to simultaneously be a part of and be present in all parts of the globe. In his terms humans have become cosmopolitan, with a sensitive skin stretching over the entire world. He called this the noosphere;[3] and it has been likened to the internet, which of course did not exist when he wrote his book. Jennifer Cobb Kreisberg suggests that Teilhard de Chardin 'saw the net coming more than half a century before it arrived'.[4]

---

[3] A term derived from Greek meaning 'the sphere of human thought' and interaction of human minds.

[4] In 'A Globe, Clothing Itself with a Brain', an article written for *Wired* magazine, Issue 3, June 1995.

From an intelligence standpoint what are the lessons that might be learnt? It is fair to say that data does exist about most crises of almost any kind but the concept of joining the dots (as was claimed to be needed before 9/11) is an easy idea that suggests to the public that a picture only needed to be drawn and such an event would have been stopped. Given the quantity of data involved that is of course far too simplistic. No amount of 'the information was within the data' can really get to the major issues involved in trying to identify the dots, let alone join and then act upon them. This is certainly not a simple process and yet there are ways that should be used to make the chances of seeing and joining the dots more likely. The list of US intelligence failures includes the Cuban Missile Crisis, the collapse of the Soviet Union, India's nuclear testing, and of course is quite long, as it is for any organization that is tasked with helping to predict the future. The CIA's new annual report to Congress describes the accidental bombing of the Chinese embassy in Belgrade in May 1999, during the Kosovo war, as 'a painful wake-up call'. The CIA Director at the time, George Tenet, had sounded the alarm a full two months before the bombing in a secret document issued in March 1999 outlining the weaknesses of American intelligence and setting a course for improvement. One of his top concerns was getting intelligence databases in shape for day-to-day military use, rather than updating them when a major crisis hit. 'To support these operations on a more-or-less continuous basis, the intelligence community must develop accurate and current databases—not just post-warning surge,' he stated in his *Strategic Intent for the United States Intelligence Community.*

A number of reviews took place in the US Defense Department after the bombing of the Chinese Embassy. The database used by the aircraft to identify the targets had contained out-of-date information about who occupied the building. A B-2 bomber dropped two 2,000 lb guided bombs into the building at midnight on 7 May 1999, killing three staff. 'The accidental bombing of the Chinese Embassy in Belgrade . . . reminded us of the critical importance of keeping our data bases current,' Tenet stated in his 1999 Annual Report to Congress. 'We were reminded this year that we must maintain our vigilance in areas that are considered routine or can fall into neglect.' In November 1999, a senior intelligence official spoke to reporters about the errors that had led to the bombing. 'The bottom line is: these (data bases) that were used to do verifications of the targeting were not up to date, and we need to find out why.'

It is of course very easy to say after the event that it should have been predicted since sufficient data was held beforehand to make a good prediction, or that the database was just out of date. And as one area of recent mathematical practice points out, predictions in complex systems are not just difficult but often impossible. An aspect of complexity theory suggests that complex processes cannot be predicted, since they are too complex. This is sometimes referred to as the butterfly effect. A butterfly flying in the Amazon jungle upsets the wind and pressure systems to an infinitesimally tiny degree, which finally sets off a thunderstorm in Northern Europe. Computer simulations of complex systems have also shown that there is no steady state from which predictions can be made and often a series of states is possible. A particular group of data at a particular time will give one prediction but the data could easily change, suggesting another outcome. Collecting and analysing data is of course necessary but making scenario judgements is also critical. Therefore, although not perfect, the four-tier scenario intelligence system is superior to simply employing the traditional intelligence cycle.

The world of policymaker expectation has significantly changed and the issues of controlling and analysing a complex system of information and data deluge are difficult and often unpredictable at the outset. The intelligence process has similarities to other complex systems and the effects of system comprehension and upheaval affect many parts of industry and government. Strategic management theory, which was progressively defined and redefined in the second half of the twentieth century, grew out of intelligence theory. In 1985 Ellen-Earle Chaffee outlined what she saw as the main elements of the theory as it then stood. It meant reformulating a business to the markets and competitive areas that it was operating and would operate within. The environment is complex and requires considered actions and responses by the whole operation that do not fit within traditional formulae. The whole process is partly planned and partly unplanned, should take place as a process throughout the organization, and requires planning as well as tactical response. This is not that far from Clausewitz's views on responses to war by a military organization and its command. Again, during the 1980s some business consultants realized the potential appeal of military strategy for the business community and took books by Sun Tzu, Clausewitz, and Mao Zedong and turned them into business strategy books. These books offered the business community a sense of the thrill of the military along with the hard-line strategies offered by the original writers. From Sun Tzu the tactical nature of business was suggested. From Clausewitz was drawn the fog of the marketplace and competition in an environment in which many aspects appear to be undetermined and difficult to predict, in which business intelligence can at times be misleading and wrong, and where an understanding of analysts and their bias and motives is vital for the business leader. And from Mao they leant the operational engagement of guerrilla warfare.

Different Intelligence Perspectives

However, as Professor Christopher Andrew at Cambridge University explains, we need to put these current changes of intelligence review and analysis into a historic perspective as well. He particularly wants review of the scenario and future trend analysis; he says those who practise these disciplines tend to collect in two camps. There are those who look at the present and say we have seen this before and it fits with the past, and then there are others who take little or nothing from the past and explain that a new perspective has to begin from the beginning. Most current analysts are of the second opinion: little is relevant from the past and history is largely irrelevant when predicting future outcomes. Short-termism has become the mainstay of our analytical models and processes and there is a culture of ignoring the past since the current assessment is far more relevant that any history lessons.

> For the first time in recorded history, there is nowadays a widespread conviction that the experience of all previous generations save our own is irrelevant to present and future policy and intelligence analysis. Our political culture is dominated by an unprecedented malady: Historical Attention Span Deficit Disorder...[5]

Christopher Andrew's analysis is, I think, very relevant and I would agree and argue that there is a need for a different structure to intelligence. I am offering a process with eight different aspects and processes.

The New Intelligence Model

The aspects of this layered model come from my publishing, academic, and open-source intelligence experience and, at least in part, have been used by some of the organizations I have been involved with over the years. I will begin by explaining the tactical and planning, and then the more strategic aspects of the process, but before any of this starts there must be a vision or mission statement that explains the objectives and purpose; this will form the central part of the diagrammatical model. Vision and mission objectives and statements usually come from the policymaker and are the overarching intention of the whole process. Mission or vision statements are often used as the essence of what the business, organization, or government intentions are to be. However, the mission and the vision can be seen as doing two different tasks. The vision communicates the values and the direction and is offered to the outside world. It is a marketing message. The mission statement defines the objectives and measures of success. This message is for an internal audience. For a business, it aims at the stakeholders and shareholders, but primarily (usually) aimed at the senior management team. Defining the vision and the mission is incredibly important as this gives considered purpose to the actions of the organization. In the military this is often seen as defining the enemy and the way in which they will be engaged. In government this might be the national growth strategy or a statement like 'changing the environment for a new tomorrow'. Coca Cola's mission in 2012 was 'to refresh the world...to inspire moments of optimism and happiness...[and] to create value and make a difference'. Another vision statement came from Tony Blair prior to being elected Prime Minister of Great Britain in 1997 when he adopted 'New Labour' and the 'Third Way' as vision headlines.

---

[5] Christopher Andrew, 'Intelligence Analysis needs to look backwards before looking forwards', *History and Policy*, June 2004.

Strategic Intelligence – post-modern method

1. **Mission and Vision** – created by policy makers

2. **Daily briefing and discussion** by analysts and policymakers

3. **News and analysis** – continuously updates mobile data, information, and intelligence

4. **Intelligence Cycle** – intelligence request by policymaker

5. **Strategic planning** – longer term view of the planned future

6. **Scenario planning** – potential future outcomes

7. **Mosaic Method** – historic, current, future, and strategic perspective of the different views of the different players

8. **Planning meeting** – discussion every four to six weeks of the results, problems, and processes

Figure 12.1   Strategic intelligence—post-modern method

Once the vision and mission are in place the underlying process drives how information and intelligence are collected and analysed, and intelligence created, although, as can been seen from comparing Figures 12.1 and 12.2, there is no set way in which the process must be followed. It is important that the elements of this process are covered but the linear process will change and is not set in stone. Within different organizations the sequence will alter along with time and capability constraints.

Therefore the daily work process can begin with a series of meetings, probably at the beginning of each shift or working cycle. These will discuss current issues and actions and how they are being addressed. These meetings would involve the managers and people/officers/analyst on the ground, and be the precursor to a meeting with the policymaker. Because of the paradigm changes to the working structures these shift meetings can largely take place in a connected electronic network environment and, like what takes place in many corporate operations, over very large distances and in different time zones. There are, however, advantages in doing some of this face to face where possible, because face-to-face communication remains more direct, sensitive, and conducive to mutual understanding than even the new communications technology.

These meetings should be preparatory to regular, daily, 20- to 30-minute, face-to-face meetings with policymakers, allowing the latter to explain how they see an issue they require data/intelligence about and the analyst to discuss data and intelligence recently provided, and data/intelligence that is soon to be provided.

Third, current news, analysis, and intelligence should be extracted from focused monitoring and analysis of current events and news analysis. This information/intelligence would be sent electronically to the policymakers and a similar process would be used to keep others engaged and aware of changing information and intelligence: for instance, law enforcement officers could be kept aware of actions on the ground. The current news and analysis would be transferred to the analyst, specialist, law enforcement officer on the ground, or policymaker via wearable, mobile, or location-based computer systems. As a process this will improve relationships and communications. Interplay and question-and-answer sessions will increase and recipients will feel more in touch and able to gain relevant information and intelligence quickly. They will be able to add relevant data back to the database and discussion mix. By its nature, this process of engagement would change the nature of the organization's structure and methods. Information collection, analysis, policing, current business, and the relationship with policymakers, who would also use this current information/intelligence service, would change the nature of use, engagement, and questioning.

Fourth is a linear/cyclical intelligence process, similar to the analysis that has been used for centuries to assess and analyse a problem, and this would still form part of intelligence gathering. This would allow policymakers to ask for and receive intelligence on subjects that they define. Medium-term intelligence outlooks, questions, discussions, and outcomes will form this part of the process. The intelligence cycle would occasionally be an addition to the current news and analysis process since, as they used the focused information and intelligence from the new briefing process (second stage), questions and queries would occur to policymakers along with suggestions and information/intelligence that they would want to put back into the process.

Fifth is a strategic planning process that should take place formally, at reasonably frequent intervals (every 6 to 12 months), and should involve non-biased outsiders in the process of review and strategic outlook. Although crystallizing at intervals, the strategic process should be continuous and information necessary to it should be updated at least weekly. The strategy should look forward between one and five years and will alter with the environment and changes to the outlook. Traditionally, these types of plan have often, in many organizations, been a rule-following exercise that gets completed as a file of papers that are put on a shelf until next time. There really is no point to such an exercise. Strategic planning must be real and generate an understanding of the real environment that the organization is working within, the real structure (the positives and the negatives) that makes the organization function well or not well as it is, and what changes are needed to improve its functioning. In government or commercial operations planners should ask clients, other parts of government, or outside organizations they work with or for, to present a view of what they appreciate and what they would change about the organization and its products and services.

The sixth aspect is scenario planning for future possibilities and possible outcomes. This is used to challenge and understand the possible outcomes from current actions and strategies. The scenarios can be visualized, analysed, and played out in discussions and presentations (both face to face and electronically) every few weeks. This would work as follows. Initially, list the key players who should be involved in the process and identify a key question. Set time limits and a scope for the scenario framework. Identify the major players and lay out the processes and trends that will drive the future scenarios and from these identify the known unknowns, the uncertainties, and the possibilities and extremes. Go on to define the scenarios and then discuss and adjust them. Establish where more information would be useful and how this might be obtained and in what time frame. Assess the good and bad outcomes of the scenarios, what needs to change within the organization, and what might alter out in the geopolitical or commercial space. This whole process should actively challenge group thinking and social agreements about situations and events.

The seventh element is the mosaic network method. This is used to put the intelligence process in a historic perspective and to give analyst(s) and their clients a clearer understanding of the current reality, as perceived by different players through the medium of each one's cultural understanding and bias. The mosaic would use semantically analysable databases, web, and visualization technology to give background perspective to a current scenario or real situation. This would have been of great use historically, to understand the tensions and beliefs underlying the conflicts in Northern Ireland, Vietnam, Iraq, Afghanistan, or the Arab Spring. It would also be of real use when analysing a current government or any organization. The mosaic would analyse the different personalities or organizational elements and put them into a connected, semantically analysable database. This would allow analysts and policymakers to develop pertinent, brief, psychological and organizational preferences about current and future areas of focus. For instance, a mosaic analysis of a current government or organization structure would collect consistent data about the different individuals and groups, the players and their advisers. It would monitor and register preferences and connections between the different players. It would record when events occur, how the individuals connected to the particular events, and would be able to indicate future preferences. Fundamentally, the mosaic method would review different current events and prospects from the opposition's view and understanding, and where this differs from our own perspective and why. The process is continuous and would be held on a database for analysts and policymakers to add to, question, and review.

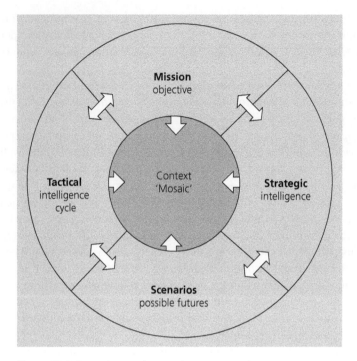

Figure 12.2 A continuous, interactive, connected process

My method in writing this book is to outline the mosaic network method (Chapters Four and Eleven are particular examples) and include views from other involved parties.

Finally, eighth, there should be monthly discussions of how relevant and useful was the data/intelligence recently sent to and used by the policymaker, where the successes were and why, and similarly why other data, information, and intelligence did not work because of perspective, factual error, poor timing, or other reasons.

There are some elements underlying the process that need to be considered, which relate to the way it operates and the basis of the practice. Objectivity and a sincere aim for the truth are crucial. Do not follow the real or apparent wishes of policymakers and their assistants. The purpose of intelligence is to get at the facts and to tell them in as truthful manner as is possible in the time frame within which you and the policymaker are operating. One of the current and often cited problems is the currency of the information and intelligence. In the traditional intelligence cycle model the commander in battle often needed the intelligence within hours. Today, the globalized world acts and feels similarly fast to the policymakers and the situations within which they have to operate.

The intelligence must be relevant and to the point. Here brevity plays an important part as all policymakers and commanders will tell you they have little time in which to operate effectively and therefore they expect pertinence and purpose. All the intelligence processes we have discussed must be to the point, with analysis, some scenarios, and background mosaic all presented in succinct reports and verbal communication.

Index